WOODEN TOYS, PUZZLES & GAMES

WOODEN TOYS, PUZZLES & GAMES

Ralph and Mary Dorazio

CREATIVE HOMEOWNER PRESS®

To:

Carol and Diane
Nicholas, Justin, and David
Bethany and Eliot

Manufactured in United States of America

Current printing (last digit)
10 9 8 7 6 5 4

Produced by ROUNDTABLE PRESS, INC.

Editorial: Arthur Hale, Judson Mead
Editorial Production: Marguerite Ross
Illustrations: Norman Nuding
Photography: David Arky
Design: Jeff Fitschen
Jacket Design: Jerry Demoney
Stuffed toys courtesy of: Child Craft Centers, Inc.
                           155 East 23 Street
                           New York, NY 10010

LC: 85-3839
ISBN: 0-932944-77-9 (paper)
       0-932944-78-7 (hardcover)

CREATIVE HOMEOWNER PRESS®
BOOK SERIES

A DIVISION OF FEDERAL
MARKETING CORPORATION
24 PARK WAY
UPPER SADDLE RIVER, NJ 07458

KEY TO SYMBOLS

The projects in this book are rated
by the length of time you can expect them to take and by the relative level of difficulty involved.
These ratings are indicated by
symbols at the beginning of each
project. In addition, when it is required that you protect your eyes,
you'll find a small pair of safety
goggles as a reminder.

Afternoon

Overnight

More than one day

Easy

Moderate

Difficult

Safety goggles

Introduction

Whenever children came to visit my studio, the first thing they wanted to do was to make something out of the ever-present supply of wood. Over the years, with a little help, they produced a variety of cars, trucks, boats, and other objects, of which they were justly proud. If you enjoy working with your hands and making wood toys, this book offers many different projects to satisfy you and delight the youngsters who receive them.

Some of the projects in the book are easy to make, and some require more advanced woodworking techniques. The approximate degree of difficulty and time required for making each toy are given. If your woodworking experience is limited, start with the easier objects and work up to the more complex. Read the opening chapters on materials, tools, and techniques.

Check the Materials List for each project to make sure you have all the materials needed on hand, whether from the lumberyard or your scrap box. Get in the habit of saving all scraps from other jobs—they will prove a valuable supply source for toy making. The Materials List is not rigid as far as the type of wood is concerned. Feel free to make substitutions according to your own taste, as long as you adhere to the dimensions given.

After you have familiarized yourself with the Materials List, read the step-by-step instructions carefully, and then read them again. Get a good picture of the entire project in your mind before you start cutting the individual parts for that project. The actual cutting and assembling of a toy will not always proceed in an orderly fashion because of such factors as the time needed for glue and paint to dry. A certain amount of juggling is necessary, so that while the glue is drying on one element, you can work on another. With experience, you will find it possible to take advantage of these unavoidable interruptions by working on two or more projects simultaneously.

The wood toys in this book were designed to be made with a combination of hand and power tools. Some operations can be performed with a number of different tools. A list of such tools is given with each project. What you use will be determined by your experience, preference, and the availability of the tools.

When you have totally mastered the three basic elements of woodworking—materials, tools, and procedures—you are ready to transform those plain pieces of wood into something that will be admired, enjoyed, and used from one generation to the next.

Contents

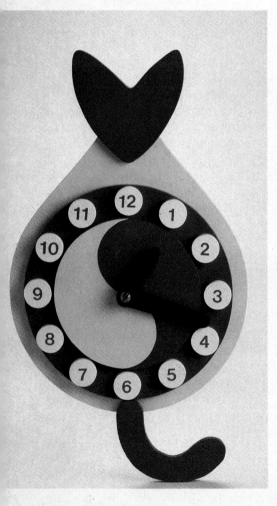

Materials

All the projects in this book call for hardwood, softwood, plywood, or, in some cases, combinations of these woods. *Hardwood* and *softwood* are botanical terms and do not refer to the relative hardness or softness of the wood in terms of its workability. Hardwoods come from deciduous, or leaf-bearing, trees; softwoods come from conifers, or cone-bearing trees. In general, hardwoods are more attractive than softwoods and are used where projects are to be finished with a clear finish to show their beauty. However, a piece of Clear sugar pine finished naturally can have a handsome appearance. Plywood is a manufactured wood made up of plies, or layers, for strength and uniformity.

WOOD DIMENSIONS

Solid wood is sold by its nominal, or rough, size—that is, the size of the wood before it is dressed or planed down at the lumber mill. In buying softwood, when you order a 1- × 4-inch board, what you actually get will measure ³/₄ × 3¹/₂ inches. However, with hardwood, the thickness of a nominal 1-inch board may measure ¹³/₁₆ inch, depending on the source. There are also variations in the sizes of plywood. These variations in thickness, both in solid wood and plywood, will not interfere seriously with your work as long as you are aware of what you are using.

HARDWOOD AND SOFTWOOD

Lumber is sold in different grades and with different surface treatments. The best grade is Clear, which is free of knots or blemishes. The next grade is Select, or Common, which is subdivided into three groups: Nos. 1, 2, and 3. No. 1 has a few blemishes, and each of the others, respectively, has more and will cost less. As far as hardwood is concerned, most lumberyards stock

Among the easy-to-find woods for toymaking are (clockwise from the far left): birch plywood, walnut, oak, mahogany, white pine, poplar, maple, sugar maple.

only Clear hardwood, which is either surfaced on two sides with the edges rough or surfaced on all four sides. It is sold in different widths, the narrower ones being less expensive. Depending on your needs, you can select just the pieces you want. Softwoods are usually available in different grades. Again, depending on your needs, you may be able to use the less expensive grades of softwood, cutting away the knots and blemishes. Softwoods usually come surfaced on all four sides.

Different woods, both hard and soft, present different degrees of difficulty in working them with hand and power tools.

The cost of wood, of course, varies in different locations. There was a time when softwoods were less expensive than hardwoods, but this is no longer the case. In some areas, Clear sugar pine is more expensive than hardwoods such as poplar, basswood, and mahogany.

PLYWOOD

Plywood comes in a variety of grades and face veneers. It is made in two basic ways: the face veneers are glued over a veneer or wood-chip core, or they are glued over a lumber core. The edges of wood-chip- or veneer-core plywood are harder to finish than the edges of lumber-core plywood. Plywood is faced with softwood or hardwood in different grades. The better grades can be used when the project is to be finished naturally, while the lower grades can be used when it is to be painted. A good grade of hardwood-faced lumber-core plywood is best for natural finishing.

MISCELLANEOUS MATERIALS

A variety of hardwood dowels are called for in the projects. These are usually maple or birch and are readily available. If you prefer dowels of other hardwoods, you can order them from specialty supply houses. Some projects call for ¹/₄-inch solid stock. For these you can use lattice strips, which come in different widths and are available at most lumberyards. Thin solid stock, in thicknesses such as ¹/₈, ³/₁₆, and ¹/₄ inch, is sold by stores and mail-order houses that supply wood for dollhouses. Some projects require wheels. If you want them ready-made, toy-supply houses are a good source.

WORKING QUALITIES OF WOODS

Hardwoods

Easy	Less easy	Least easy
Poplar	Birch	Ash
Basswood	Mahogany	Cherry
Butternut	Walnut	Elm
Whitewood	Cottonwood	Maple
	Sweet gum	Oak

Softwoods

Easy	Less easy	Least easy
Pine	Fir	Douglas
Sugar	Spruce	fir
Ponderosa	Eastern	Larch
White	red	Yellow
	cedar	pine
	Redwood	
	Cypress	
Cedar		
(White,		
Red,		
Western		
red)		

Tools

With some exceptions (to be discussed later), all the projects in the book can be made with different tools to achieve the same result. In all cases the tools should be kept sharp and clean. Nothing discourages a woodworker or spoils a project faster than a dull tool. When working with power tools, be sure you fully understand the operation of those tools and the safety precautions connected with their use.

HANDSAWS

There are two types of the basic carpenter's handsaw: the crosscut for cutting across the grain of the wood, and the ripsaw for cutting with the grain. The crosscut has more teeth per inch (expressed as point size), ranging from 8 to 12 points. Ripsaws are usually 5½ or 6 points. The lower point sizes cut faster and easier, while saws with the higher point sizes cut finer and smoother.

The backsaw, or miter box saw, has a rectangular blade with fine teeth ranging from 11 to 14 points. This is employed for making mitered or angled cuts, and the blade is held parallel to the work. It can be used freehand or with a miter box. The dovetail saw is a smaller, finer-bladed backsaw with 15 to 16 points for fine joint work. The smallest of the back-saws are the razor saws, which may have blades of 20 or more points for cutting thin stock and for delicate work.

For making curved cuts, especially those with a small radius, a coping saw is ideal. To make internal cuts with a coping saw, drill a hole in the work, pass the unfastened blade through the hole, and then refasten it to the frame. The blade in a coping saw can be turned to cut in any direction. For larger curved cuts and with thick stock, you can use a compass saw or a keyhole saw. The keyhole saw is narrower than the compass, and so it can cut to a smaller radius.

POWER SAWS

Some of the projects in the book call for saw cuts that are best made with a power saw. Long bevels, rabbets, off angles (22½°, for instance), and repetitive cuts can be made quickly and accurately on a power saw.

The table saw and the radial arm saw are the workhorses of the woodworking shop. Both will make all the basic cuts—crosscut, rip, miter, bevel—and, with the proper accessories, cut dadoes, make moldings, and sand workpieces. On a table saw, the table remains horizontal and the blade can be tilted to make angle cuts. The work is brought to the blade with the miter gage. Compound angles can be cut by tilting the blade and adjusting the miter gage. On a radial arm saw, the work remains stationary and the blade is

A table saw makes quick work of large cuts and small. When you cut small pieces, use a pusher stick for safety.

brought to it along the arm. The arm can be rotated for angle cuts. Our shop is equipped with a 10-inch table saw, and references to it are made in the text. However, anything that is done on the table saw can also be done on the radial arm saw.

BAND SAW AND JIGSAW

The band saw and the jigsaw are two power saws used primarily for cutting curves. The band saw has a continuous flexible steel blade that runs over two large pulleys. The capacity of the saw is determined by the distance between the blade and the frame. This can be 10, 12, or 14

Different cuts require different saws. The three sizes of razor saw here are used for increasingly fine cuts; the keyhole saw in the middle is used for interior cuts.

inches for most home workshop saws. The band saw is used for cutting external curves only because of the continuous blade. The jigsaw has a short blade, usually about 5 inches long, that is fastened top and bottom and moves up and down. Internal cuts can be made on the jigsaw by removing the blade, inserting it into a hole drilled into the work, and then refastening it to the saw. The fine blade of the jigsaw will allow

Cutting curves is a job most easily done on the band saw. The work can be steered through the thin blade at any angle.

quite intricate work. Both saws have tilting tables to allow angle cutting.

DRILL AND DRILL PRESS
The portable electric drill and drill press are very important tools in any shop and for the projects in this book. There are many holes to be drilled and dowel joints to be made in most of the projects. The portable drill will handle some of these. For precision drilling, angled holes, or repetitive drilling of holes to a specified depth, the drill press is the best choice. There are drill stands available that, combined with your portable drill, can serve as a drill press.

Used with care, they do a creditable job. The best bits to use in your drill are the spur-pointed wood bits. They are much more accurate than high-speed drill bits used for metal and wood.

PORTABLE POWER TOOLS
There are several portable power tools that can be useful in making the projects. The most important of these is the saber saw, which acts as

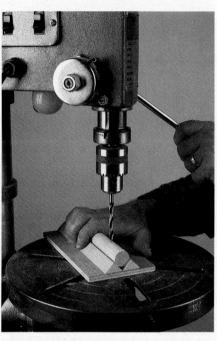

After the table saw, the drill press is probably the most generally useful power tool in any home workshop.

a portable jigsaw. The blade is fastened at one end to a shaft that moves up and down through the workpiece. The saw is extremely good for cutting curves. Varied blades for different types and thicknesses of wood are made for the saber saw, including very fine blades capable of accomplishing quite intricate cuts.

The portable circular saw has limited use in toy making; however, it is useful in cutting large plywood panels and long boards down to sizes that can be easily handled with other saws and tools.

The router also has limitations in toy making, being better suited to

furniture work. The router, however, will cut grooves, rabbets, and dadoes; in the hands of an experienced user, it can prove serviceable.

OTHER HAND TOOLS
For certain operations, several small hand tools are needed. A variety of wood rasps for shaping, rounding edges and corners, and smoothing rough edges will make your job easier. A small block plane and a smooth plane are necessary for cutting chamfers and for fitting operations. Two or three small-size carpenter's wood chisels, an awl for marking and making small holes, and a nailset will all aid you in putting the finishing touches on your projects.

USING TOOLS
The first rule for using tools, either hand or power, is to let the tool do the work. Do not force the tool or grip it too tightly. You are there to supply motive power and guidance. If you use a regular, uninterrrupted movement, neither too fast nor too slow, the tool will do the work for which it was designed. Whether you are sawing a piece of wood, by either hand or

Shaping tools—here, flat and round rasps and files—are used for shaping, smoothing edges, and removing small amounts of wood.

power saw, or using a drill press or a hammer, the same rules apply. If the whites of your knuckles show when you are gripping a tool, you are holding it too tightly. The most likely result will be trouble. Take your time, and enjoy the work as well as the finished project.

Fastening

Fastening the various parts of a toy together is one of the most important operations to be performed in making the projects in this book. Almost all of the parts in these projects are held together with glue joints or a combination of glue and dowel joints. From the standpoint of strength and appearance, and for a successful result in general, proper gluing technique must be observed and a glue formulated especially for wood should be used. We have found the aliphatic resin glue (commonly known as yellow wood glue) such as Elmer's Carpenter's Wood Glue to be excellent and have used it for all the projects. Always read the label on the glue you use; these instructions are designed to show how to get the best results from the product.

The first step in making a successful glue joint is fitting the parts. They must fit together snugly with no gaps. Do not expect the glue to make up for a loose-fitting joint. It is wood against wood with the glue that makes a good joint, not the glue alone. If you try to break a properly glued joint, the wood on either side of the joint will probably fracture before the glue joint does. The surfaces to be glued should be clean and dry, but preferably unfinished. Glue works best on bare wood. When you have a number of parts to be glued together, a trial assembly without glue to test the fit is a good idea.

The amount of glue you use and where you put it are the next considerations. Too much glue is as bad as too little. We have found that using a brush to spread the glue is far superior to applying it directly from a plastic squeeze bottle. One invariably squeezes out too much glue. Spread a thin, even coat of glue on each surface to be joined, keeping it away from the edges of the wood. This way, when the parts are pressed together, little or no glue will seep out. If any glue is squeezed out, do not wipe it off. This will only drive the glue into the pores of the wood and

1. To glue a curved shape from beveled slats (see pages 34–36), tape the unbeveled edges of the slats together as shown.

2. Turn over the taped slats and paint glue along the beveled edges. Using a brush controls the amount of glue.

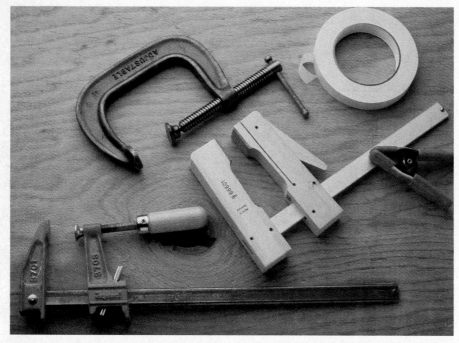

Glued parts must be held fast with clamps or tape while glue sets. Shown here are masking tape (see steps at right), C-clamp, slide clamp, spring clamp, and bar clamp.

3. Lift up the ends of the taped slats and tape tightly across the edges as shown. When the glue has set, strip off all the tape.

interfere with the finish, especially if you are using a natural finish on the project. Let the glue dry and scrape it off with a chisel, knife, or scraper. If you have a lot of gluing to do, keep a few glue brushes of different sizes handy in a jar of water. This will save you the trouble of washing out the glue brushes each time you use them. Be sure to dry the brushes before dipping them in the glue bottle.

CLAMPING

The instructions on the Elmer's Glue bottle (other glues may have different directions) call for a clamping time of thirty minutes and overnight drying for maximum strength. You do not have to leave the clamps on all night, but it will not harm the joint if you do. Depending on the size and shape of the joint, several devices can be used for clamping—C-clamps, spring clamps, bar clamps (both wood and metal), and masking tape. The clamps do not have to be overly tight; a firm, snug hold will do. Masking tape makes an excellent "clamp," especially when gluing small parts or irregular surfaces. When using tape, hold one end of the tape against one side of the joint with the thumb of one hand and pull across the joint with the other hand, using a little pressure, and press the tape firmly against the wood.

When you have more than two parts to be glued together, you can usually do them one after the other by employing the following procedure, and with the following provisos. Glue the first two parts together and clamp them. When the clamping time has elapsed (we use an hour for clamping time to be on the safe side), remove the clamps and glue the first two parts to a third part, providing—and this is important—there is no stress on the first joint in so doing. If there are more parts to be glued, proceed in the same manner. When the sequence is complete, set the whole assembly aside to dry overnight. It is important to observe the clamping and drying times for a good, secure joint. Gluing, like sanding and finishing, is time-consuming. Most of your

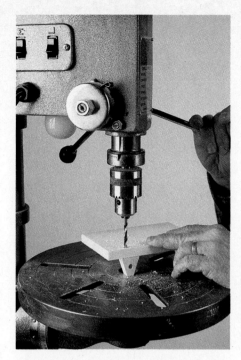

1. To make a dowel joint, glue the pieces together, then drill a hole the size of the dowel through one into the other.

2. Cut a dowel slightly longer than the depth of the hole. Tap it into place, cut off the excess, and sand smooth with the surface.

time will probably be spent with these operations. Plan your work so you can do things while waiting.

DOWEL JOINTS

The decision on when to use a dowel joint and when not to depends on the type of joint, the grain of the wood, and the stress the joint may be under when in use. There are three types of joints used in these projects: the butt joint, the miter joint, and the rabbet joint. The rabbet joints need no dowels because they brace themselves. There are two styles of miter joints. One runs with the grain, and the other presents end-grain surface to end-grain surface. The miter joints that run with the grain need no dowels or other additions such as spines. Some people feel that such joints, as well as edge-to-edge gluing (in making up a large panel of solid wood), need dowels or spines. However, based on our own experience of thousands of such joints without dowels, and on the research of the Forest Products Laboratory of the U.S. Department of Agriculture, no extra benefit is gained from the use of dowels or spines. One joint is as

good as the other, except that ours takes less time, effort, and materials. Those miter joints that present end grain to end grain, as in some frames, should have dowels, if they are large enough, or brads, finishing nails, or screws. Butt joints with end grain to end grain or with end grain to side grain should be doweled. Finally, joints that will be subject to stress in use should be doweled. An example would be the small axle holders on cars, trucks, and trains.

OTHER FASTENERS

Although most projects in this book call for glue joints, a few specify other fasteners in addition to glue. These fasteners include brads, finishing nails, and screws.

Brads are small, lightweight nails with practically no heads at all. They are used for light finishing work, especially where a finishing nail would be too large. Finishing nails are the same as common nails except that their heads are much smaller for setting beneath the surface with a nail set. All brads and finishing nails should be set below the surface and covered with wood putty.

Measuring and Patterns

Measure twice, cut once. This adage of old-time carpenters is as good advice now as it was then. Nothing is more annoying than to cut a piece of wood and have it miss the mark by a fraction of an inch. Make your measurements carefully, and mark the wood with a sharp pencil and a steel straightedge. Always make your cut just to the outside, or waste side, of the mark so as not to reduce the dimension of the work.

MEASURING TOOLS

The six-foot-extension folding rule can be considered your basic measuring tool. It can be used for all measurements, including, with the extension, inside measurements.

The try square has a metal blade set at a right angle to a fixed handle. It is used for marking 90° cuts and checking the ends of workpieces for squareness.

The combination square has a steel blade, usually 12 inches long, and a sliding handle with an angle of 90° on one side and a 45° angle on the other. This is a versatile tool. It can be used as a try square, miter gage, marking gauge, depth gauge, level, and straightedge. Two attachments are available for the combination square that make it even more useful. They are the protractor head

for marking and measuring any angle and the centering head for finding the center of round stock.

The 16- × 24-inch carpenter's square is useful for marking and checking the square of large panels.

For marking circles for wheels and other circular parts, supply yourself with a sturdy compass, preferably one with a center wheel for fine adjustment.

The sliding table jig for the table saw (see page 16) can also be used as a kind of measuring tool. When a number of pieces must be cut to the same length, set the sliding stop to that length by carefully measuring the distance between the saw blade and the stop. Lock the stop into that position and try a cut with scrap wood to test for accuracy. Once the accuracy has been determined, mark the stop and the rear brace so the stop can be returned to that position. Other lengths can be marked off along the rear brace. Always check for accuracy before marking the setting.

PATTERNS

Since it is impossible to show some of the designs in this book full size, they are presented on grids of reduced size with the actual grid size indicated. You can enlarge the pat-

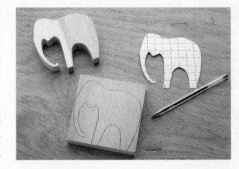

Transfer a pattern from a grid in this book to stiff paper, cut out the shape, and use this template to trace the outline for sawing.

tern to its proper size by drawing a grid of the right size (1-inch or 1/2-inch squares, as the case may be) on squared or other paper and transferring the pattern to it. Start by numbering the horizontal and vertical lines on the grid in the book. Put these same numbers on the corresponding lines you have drawn on the full-size grid. Select a starting point on the grid in the book where the outline of the pattern crosses one of the grid lines. Locate this point by means of the numbers on the lines, horizontally and vertically. Transfer this point to its corresponding location on the full-size grid, using the same numbers. Continue in the same manner until you have a point plotted for each intersection where the outline crosses a grid line. Next, connect all the points freehand or with a straightedge, flexible curve, or draftsman's french curve, as necessary. The aim is to achieve a smooth, continuous line. Make as many adjustments as you need to realize a good drawing.

The pattern can be transferred to the wood with carbon paper, or you can glue the pattern to stiff paper (about the weight of a 3- × 5-inch file card) and cut it out with a sharp scissors or mat knife. This will give you a durable template that you can mark around with a ballpoint pen over and over.

Accurate measurements are essential. Shown here: a versatile combination square with three handles for different jobs, a try square for checking right angles, and a folding rule.

Sanding and Finishing

Sanding your projects has two purposes: (1) to remove sharp edges and corners, and to complete the shaping necessary on some projects; and (2) to give the pieces a smooth surface for handling and to prepare them for finishing, whether with paint or a clear finish. Proper sanding techniques are easy to learn, but sanding does require time and patience. It is an important part of the work and should be done carefully.

SANDPAPER

Sandpaper—or, as it is more properly called today, abrasive paper—is made of several different materials and weights. The old flint papers are rarely used anymore, since they neither cut well nor last long. The newer papers are coated with garnet or aluminum oxide. Both work well on wood; which you use is a matter of preference. There are several weights of paper backing. We would suggest a D weight 80 (medium grit) sandpaper for first sanding and shaping. For second sanding we use a C weight 120 (fine grit) sandpaper, and for final sanding an A weight 220 (very fine grit) sandpaper. The heavier papers work well with power sanders and sanding blocks. The lighter-weight papers are easier to use in tight places. All papers are made with a closed grain or an open grain. The closed-grain papers are densely coated and fast-working, but those with an open grain are less likely to clog. After some practice with different papers, you can decide which ones suit you.

Sanding, of course, creates a lot of dust, all of which must be removed before you can finish the piece. Start with a brush to eliminate the worst of the dust, followed by a tack cloth. A tack cloth is a sticky cloth, which you can either buy or make by moistening a cloth with a mixture of one part turpentine and three parts varnish. It will pick up and hold dust particles.

SANDING AIDS

There are several sanding aids you can make yourself to help with the sanding and shaping jobs. To make a series of sanding sticks, cut several strips of wood ¼ inch thick and 9 inches long, and with widths varying from ¼ inch to 1 inch. A sheet of sandpaper is 9 inches wide. From sheets of 80 and 120 sandpaper, cut several strips to fit the widths of your wood strips. Glue a strip of 80 sandpaper on one side of each wood strip, and a strip of 120 on the other side. These strips will come in handy for small areas and for shaping. A sanding block is made from a 5½-inch length of 1- × 2-inch pine. Glue a piece of felt on the bottom and two sides of the block. This will give you a resilient surface with which to sand. A quarter sheet of sandpaper will just fit this block. Curved shapes can be handled with lengths of dowels from ¼ to ¾ inch thick. Glue felt to the dowels for backing.

Power sanding aids include drum sanders and sanding disks to be used in your electric drill for shaping and sanding curved surfaces. The flat surface of a finish sander will help with the final sanding of the projects. A belt sander may be serviceable in some cases, but it should be used with caution because of the ease with which it removes large amounts of stock. With any power sander, let the sander do the work. Do not put undue pressure on the tool.

With hand sanding, as in power sanding, always sand with the grain. Cross-grain scratches are difficult to remove. Keep an even pressure to avoid tapering the work.

FINISHING

The projects can be finished with paint or clear finish, depending on your choice and the woods you use. Hardwoods will look handsome with a clear finish, as will some softwoods. Others may need paint

There are a great variety of sanding devices: flat sandpaper, sandpaper glued to flat or round sticks, sanding disks, and drum sanding attachments for a portable drill.

Two simple jigs to make painting neater: nails driven through a board (points up), and a board drill for dowels to hold wheels.

Jig for Table Saw

and bright colors. In either case, the finish should be nontoxic. To aid in the finishing, painting jigs can be set up. Wheels or any parts with holes in them can be put on dowels that are inserted in pieces of scrap wood. In this way, you can paint the entire piece at once. Nails can be driven through pieces of scrap wood to provide platforms for painting other pieces. When you are painting parts that are to be glued to other parts at a later time, avoid getting paint on any surface that will be glued. Make sure the surface to be finished is clean and dry before you start. If the first or second coat picks up any dust while drying, you may want to touch it up with very fine sandpaper before applying the last coat.

PLYWOOD EDGES

Finishing plywood edges presents a special problem, admitting of at least three solutions. The edges can be covered with matching veneer tapes using contact cement. A second possibility is to cover them with thin strips of hardwood, either matching or contrasting, using wood glue or contact cement. A third solution is to finish them as you would any other piece of wood. If, after sanding, you decide the lines of the plies add anything to the project and they are not too badly scarred (as they might be with wood-chip or veneer-core plywood), finish them like the rest of the project. The lines of plies in lumber-core plywood can sometimes be pleasing and add to the design. If the project is to be painted, don't worry about the edges.

JIG FOR TABLE SAW

To make the angle and repetitive cuts called for in many of these projects, we found it useful to make this cutting jig. You may have to adjust the dimensions given in the plan above to your own saw. This jig, with its sliding stop and other accessories, will allow you to make cuts quickly and accurately. Other jigs will speed other kinds of work—they can be elaborate or as simple as the V-groove holding a dowel for drilling, shown on page 11.

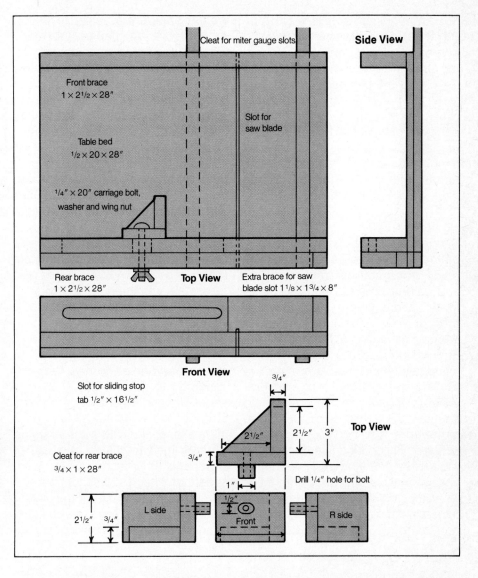

The adjustable stop on the cutting jig makes repetitive cuts of the same width a breeze. The whole jig rides in guides on the saw.

A wood template cut to the angle you want holds the work for an angle cut that doesn't require any other set up.

Color Tower

MATERIALS LIST
Top (1), 2″ × 2″ × 2″, pine or hardwood
Disks (19), (see plans for sizes), hardwood or plywood
Base (1), ³/₄″ × 6″ × 6″, hardwood or plywood
Upright (1), 11³/₄″ × ³/₄″ dowel, hardwood
Yellow wood glue
Nontoxic paint

Tools
Table saw
Band saw
Drill or drill press
Sandpaper, 80, 120, and 220

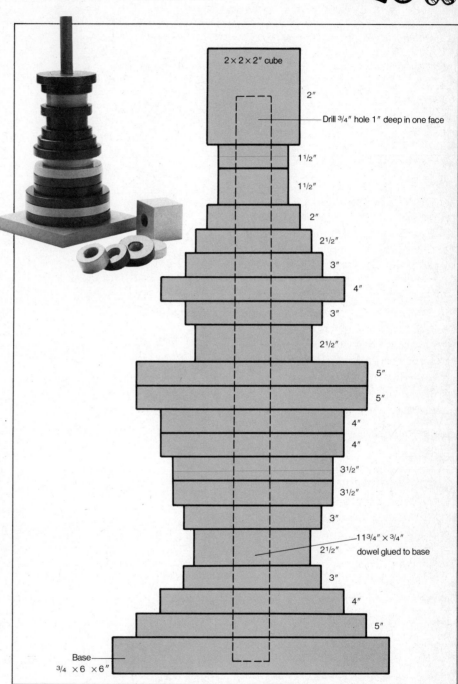

Making this tower of different shapes of wood painted in different colors should be a pleasant and easy project for you. After you've completed your part in building it, youngsters will have fun taking apart and then reconstructing the tower.

STEP 1
MAKING THE BASE, UPRIGHT, AND TOP

Cut a square 6×6 inches from ³/₄-inch stock for the base. Drill a ³/₄-inch hole in the center of one face of the base ¹/₂ inch deep. Cut an 11³/₄-inch length of ³/₄-inch hardwood dowel and glue it into the hole in the base, making sure the upright is perpendicular to the base. The 2-×2-×2-inch top can be made up of pine or hardwood scraps glued together. Drill a ³/₄-inch hole 1 inch deep in one face of the cube. Slightly enlarge this hole with sandpaper to allow the top to be slipped on and off the upright easily.

STEP 2
CUTTING THE DISKS

Sixteen of the disks are cut from ¹/₂-inch stock, and three of them are cut from ³/₄-inch stock. Lay out the circles on the appropriate stock with a compass to the diameters specified in the plan. Before cutting out the smaller disks on the band saw, it is a good idea to drill the ³/₄-inch hole required for each disk, for easier hand-ling. Cut and drill all disks. Slightly enlarge all holes with sandpaper so the disks will slide on and off the upright easily.

STEP 3
FINISHING

Sand all pieces carefully, using 80, 120, and 220 sandpaper as necessary, and be sure to remove all dust. Paint with brightly colored nontoxic enamels. Do not paint the upright dowel. If any paint gets into the disk holes, remove it with sandpaper wrapped around a piece of ¹/₂-inch dowel. We used three different colors for the disks; you may want to use more.

Pencil and Crayon Holder

MATERIALS LIST
1 1/2" or 1 3/4" stock 4 1/2" × 7", pine or
   hardwood
Nontoxic paint or clear finish
*(Dimensions larger than those shown in
drawings allow for saw, angle, or bevel cuts.)*

Tools
Band saw
Electric drill or drill press
Sandpaper, 80, 120, and 220

This sturdy bear will hold a lot of materials. With some modifications, it can be made to hold other materials such as paint brushes and nontoxic felt-tipped pens. Some children may need more than one holder for all their gear. They are easy to make, and you can turn out several in an afternoon. The stock can be laminated to make up the thickness needed to hold a fair number of pencils and crayons.

STEP 1
CUTTING THE HOLDER
Enlarge and transfer the bear pattern to the block. Make sure the grain runs from top to bottom, and then cut to shape on a band saw. Remember to cut outside the line so you have room to sand.

STEP 2
COMPLETION
Bore a series of 3/8-inch holes, 1 3/4 to 2 inches deep, in the pattern shown or in any pattern you wish. These holes will handle most pencils and crayons. You can adjust to larger holes if necessary.

STEP 3
FINISHING
Now you are ready to sand all surfaces thoroughly. Use a medium and then a fine grade of sandpaper to give the piece a smooth finish. Paint with a bright color or leave natural, if you prefer. Facial features may be added with nontoxic paint or a felt-tipped pen.

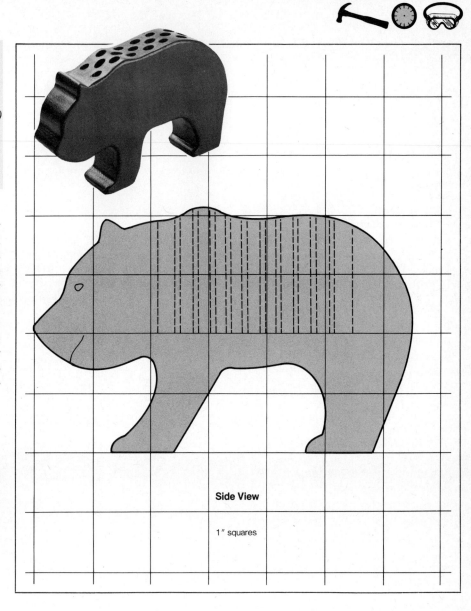

Side View

1" squares

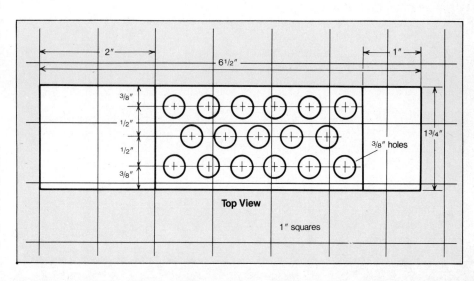

2"

6 1/2"

1"

3/8"

1/2"

1/2"

3/8"

1 3/4"

3/8" holes

Top View

1" squares

Animal Puzzles

MATERIALS LIST
1/2″, 3/4″, 11/4″, or 11/2″ stock, large enough to suit patterns, pine or hardwood
Nontoxic paint or clear finish

Tools
Band saw
Sandpaper, 80, 120, and 220

Being puzzled, and then fitting pieces together into a satisfying shape, not only delights small children but also gives them a feeling of accomplishment. Since these puzzles were designed to stand upright, kids can also have fun placing the completed form in a vertical position. For stand-up puzzles, use thicker wood, but be very careful to make the cuts straight so the parts do not fall when the puzzle is put upright. If you decide to stick to your own design of flat table puzzles, use 1/2-inch or 3/4-inch stock. They can be finished in any way you wish, with bright colors and facial features, or with a clear finish to show the beauty of the wood.

STEP 1
CUTTING OUT THE PUZZLE
Enlarge and transfer each animal pattern to a wood block with the grain running from top to bottom. Cut out the whole shape on a band saw. Before cutting the various pieces, sand the shape thoroughly and round the outer edges slightly with sandpaper. Then cut the individual pieces.

STEP 2
FINISHING THE PUZZLE
Complete any necessary sanding on the puzzle pieces. Paint the pieces with bright color or finish the wood naturally with a clear finish. Features may be added with nontoxic paint or a felt-tipped pen.

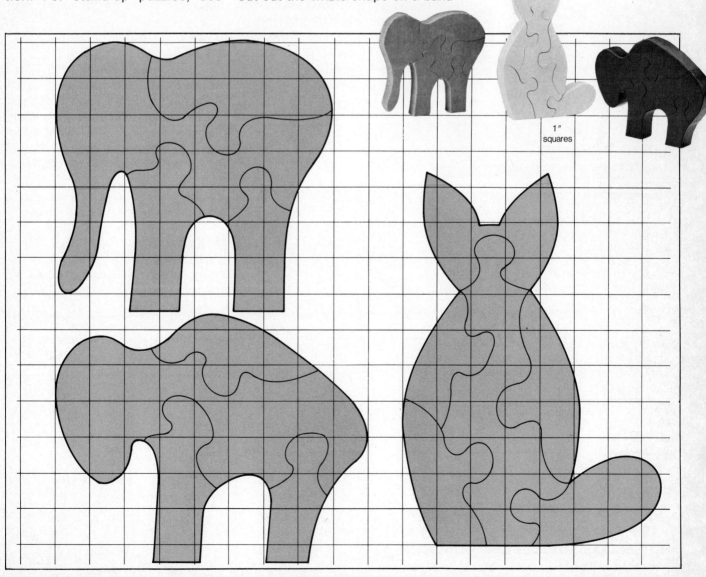

1″ squares

People Game

MATERIALS LIST
Play panel (1), 1/2″ × 12″ diameter, hardwood plywood
Support panel (1), 1/2″ × 14 1/4″ × 16 1/4″, hardwood plywood
Frame, 3/8″ × 1″ × 64″, hardwood
Pieces (17), 3/4″ × 1″ × 3″, pine or hardwood
Support dowels (17), 3/4″ × 1/4″ dowel, hardwood
Brads, 1″
Yellow wood glue
Nontoxic clear finish
Paint

Tools
Table saw
Band saw
Drill or drill press
C-clamps
Bar clamps
Masking tape
Sandpaper, 80, 120, and 220

Each player removes from the play panel one, two, or three "people." When there is only one of the people left, the player whose turn it is loses.

STEP 1
CUTTING AND DRILLING
Cut the rectangular support panel and the circular play panel to the sizes indicated. Drill a series of eight 1/4-inch holes through each of the two short sides of the support panel, 1 inch from the edge of the panel and spaced 1 1/2 inches apart. These holes are for pieces after they have been removed from the play panel during the game. Seventeen 1/4-inch holes are to be drilled through the circular play panel. The first is drilled in the center of the panel. The other sixteen holes are drilled on three concentric circles 1 3/4 inches apart,

starting at the center of the panel. Drill four holes in the first circle, 90° apart. Drill six holes in the second circle, 60° apart, and six holes in the outer circle, 60° apart. Enlarge all holes slightly with sandpaper.

STEP 2
ASSEMBLING
Glue the circular play panel to the center of the support panel, using C-clamps to hold it in place. When the glue is dry, miter the four corners of the frame strip and glue to the base, using masking tape to hold in place. You can also use light brads or bar clamps to attach the frame.

STEP 3
MAKING THE PEOPLE
Cut seventeen blocks 3/4 × 1 × 3 inches from pine or hardwood. Drill a 1/4-inch hole 1/4 inch deep in one end of each block. The people are made from two designs. Transfer the designs to the blocks and use a band saw to cut out eight pieces of one design and nine of the other. Glue one of the 1/4-inch support dowels to each figure, in the hole provided.

STEP 4
FINISHING
Sand all parts carefully, using 80, 120, and 220 sandpaper as necessary, and remove all dust. Finish the board with two coats of nontoxic clear finish. Paint the people with brightly colored nontoxic enamel.

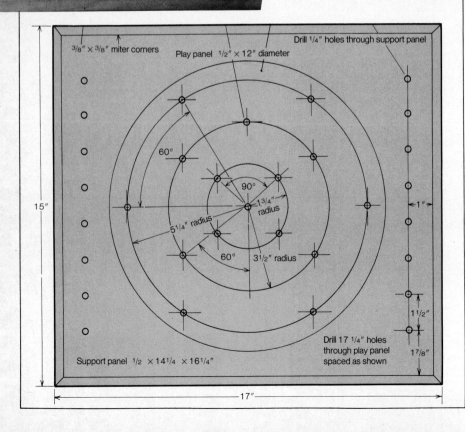

3/8″ × 3/8″ miter corners
Play panel 1/2″ × 12″ diameter
Drill 1/4″ holes through support panel
60°
90°
1 3/4″ radius
5 1/4″ radius
60°
3 1/2″ radius
15″
1″
1 1/2″
1 7/8″
Support panel 1/2 × 14 1/4 × 16 1/4″
Drill 17 1/4″ holes through play panel spaced as shown
17″

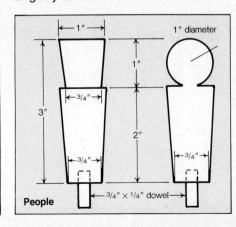

1″
1″ diameter
1″
3″
2″
3/4″
3/4″
3/4″
3/4″ × 1/4″ dowel
People

Giant Checkerboard

MATERIALS LIST

Checker squares (64), 1/4″ × 2³/4″ × 2³/4″, hardwood, 32 one color, 32 contrasting color
Square dividers (56), 1/4″ × 1/4″ × 2³/4″, hardwood
Row dividers (8), 1/4″ × 1/4″ × 23³/4″, hardwood
Center divider (1), 1/4″ × 1/2″ × 23³/4″, hardwood
Edge strips (2), 1/4″ × 1/4″ × 24¹/2″, hardwood
Edge strips (2), 1/4″ × 1/4″ × 23³/4″, hardwood
Backing board, 1/4″ × 24¹/4″ × 24¹/2″, plywood
Frame, 1/2″ × 3/4″ × 120″, shoe molding
Checkers (30), 1/2″ × 2″ diameter, hardwood, 15 one color, 15 contrasting color
Yellow wood glue

Tools

Table saw
Band saw
Disk sander
Finish sander or sanding block
Large carpenter's square
Straightedge
Masking tape
Sandpaper, 80, 120, and 220

The game of checkers needs no introduction. Played on this handsome outsized board made of contrasting woods, it may acquire even more distinction. This is an easy project, but one cautionary note is in order: the squares require precise cutting—or your whole checkerboard will be off balance.

STEP 1
CUTTING THE PIECES

To get the required contrast, cut 1/4-inch hardwood with a table saw into thirty-two 2³/4- × 2³/4-inch squares of one color wood and thirty-two of a contrasting color. We used poplar and mahogany, but any two woods can be used. Next, cut the square dividers with the table saw. Check all pieces with a square as you cut them, to ensure a good fit. Before cutting the other pieces, make a trial dry assembly of a row of eight squares, with seven square dividers between them, with masking tape to check the measurement of a row. Even a small error in each square will add up. If the measurement checks out, you can go ahead. If it doesn't, you can make a small adjustment in the dimensions of the row dividers, center divider, edge strips, and backing board; then go on and cut out these pieces. Cut out the row dividers, edge strips, center divider, and back-

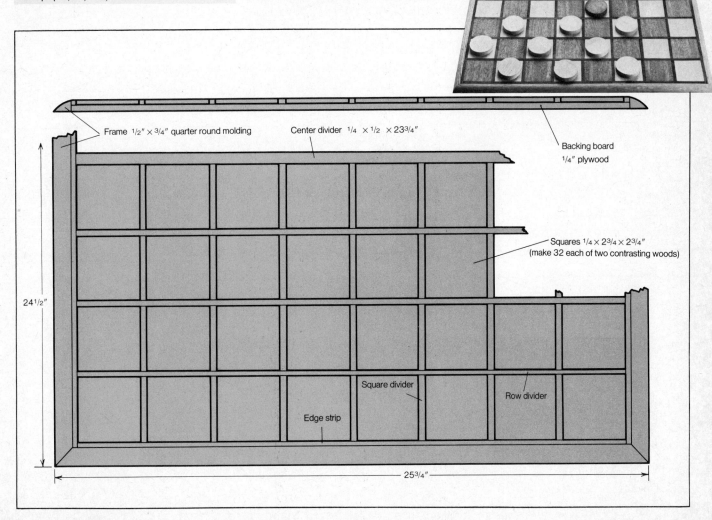

Frame 1/2″ × 3/4″ quarter round molding   Center divider 1/4 × 1/2 × 23³/4″

Backing board 1/4″ plywood

Squares 1/4 × 2³/4 × 2³/4″ (make 32 each of two contrasting woods)

Square divider

Row divider

Edge strip

24¹/2″

25³/4″

ing board. The dividers and strips can be of a third color of wood.

STEP 2
ASSEMBLING THE BOARD

Begin the assembly by gluing the squares and dividers together in rows as separate units. Line up a row of eight squares (four of each color) and seven square dividers against a straightedge, put a small amount of glue on each surface to be glued, and press together. Secure with masking tape, making sure the line is straight and square. Repeat until you have eight rows of eight squares each. The backing board is not an exact square (it is 24¼″ × 24½″) because

the center divider is ¼ inch wider than the row dividers. Glue one of the edge strips to one long (vertical) edge of the backing board and one of the row dividers to the adjacent shorter (horizontal) edge, making sure you have a right angle. You are now ready to glue in the pre-glued rows of squares. Glue one row at a time, with a row divider between each pair and the center divider in the middle, securing each row with masking tape as you go along. At the end, glue in the remaining edge strip and divider strip. Secure with masking tape and cover the entire board with a panel, or with boards, and a heavy weight. Leave it to dry over-

night. When dry, glue the shoe-molding frame to all four sides, with mitered joints.

STEP 3
CUTTING THE CHECKERS AND FINISHING

Cut out the thirty checkers (fifteen of one wood and fifteen of the contrasting wood) from ½-inch stock, 2 inches in diameter, on the band saw. Sand the pieces with a disk sander or by hand, finishing up with 220 sandpaper. Sand the board with a finish sander, or by hand with a sanding block. Remove all sanding dust and finish with two coats of nontoxic clear finish.

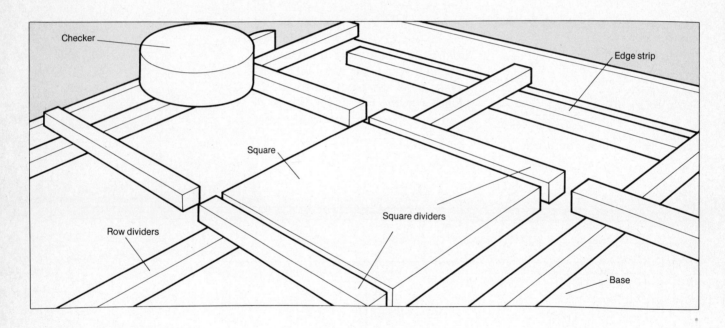

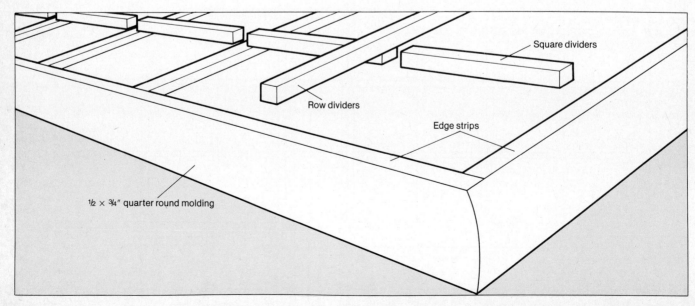

Photo Puzzle

MATERIALS LIST
Photograph, 8″ × 10″ or larger
Puzzle board, ¼″ plywood to fit photo
Paper glue

Tools
Band saw or jigsaw
Masking tape

It is easy to make your own jigsaw puzzles from your children's favorite pictures. If you follow our guide, you can easily design your own puzzle. Since the pieces are big, small youngsters will have no difficulty fitting them together and re-creating the picture.

STEP 1
PREPARING THE PUZZLE
Cut the plywood panel to the size of your photograph. Make sure the panel is smooth and dust free. Glue the photo to the panel with a good paper glue.

STEP 2
CUTTING THE PUZZLE
Enlarge the cutting diagram and transfer it to a sheet of white drawing paper. The diagram can be adjusted to fit the size of your photo. Place the diagram on top of the photo and secure it to the plywood with masking tape in several spots on all four sides. Cut out the puzzle along the cutting lines, using the jigsaw or band saw with a fine blade.

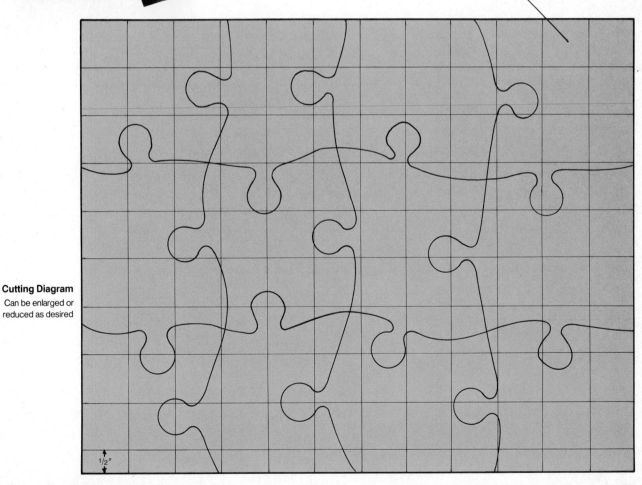

1″ squares

Cutting Diagram
Can be enlarged or reduced as desired

½″

Animal Pull Toys

MATERIALS LIST

Cat
3/4" stock for animal body, pine or hardwood
1/4" stock for body parts, pine or hardwood
Crossbars (2), 3/4" × 3/4" × 4", pine or hardwood
Wheels (4), 1/2" × 13/4" diameter, pine or hardwood

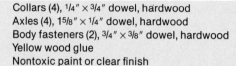

Collars (4), 1/4" × 3/4" dowel, hardwood
Axles (4), 15/8" × 1/4" dowel, hardwood
Body fasteners (2), 3/4" × 3/8" dowel, hardwood
Yellow wood glue
Nontoxic paint or clear finish

Hippo
3/4" stock for animal body, pine or hardwood
1/4" stock for body parts, pine or hardwood
Platform (1), 1/2" × 4" × 9", pine or hardwood
Wheels (4), 1/2" × 13/4" diameter, pine or hardwood
Collars (4), 1/4" × 3/4" dowel, hardwood
Axles (4), 15/8" × 1/4" dowel, hardwood
Body fasteners (2), 3/4" × 3/8" dowel, hardwood
Yellow wood glue
Nontoxic paint or clear finish

Dog
3/4" stock for animal body, pine or hardwood
1/4" stock for body parts, pine or hardwood
Platform (for dog) (1), 1/2" × 4" × 81/2", pine or hardwood
Wheels (4), 1/2" × 13/4" diameter, pine or hardwood
Collars (4), 1/4" × 3/4" dowel, hardwood
Axles (4), 15/8" × 1/4" dowel, hardwood
Body fasteners (2), 3/4" × 3/8" dowel, hardwood
Yellow wood glue
Nontoxic paint or clear finish

Tools
Backsaw
Table saw
Band saw
Electric drill or drill press
Sander or sandpaper, 80, 120, and 220

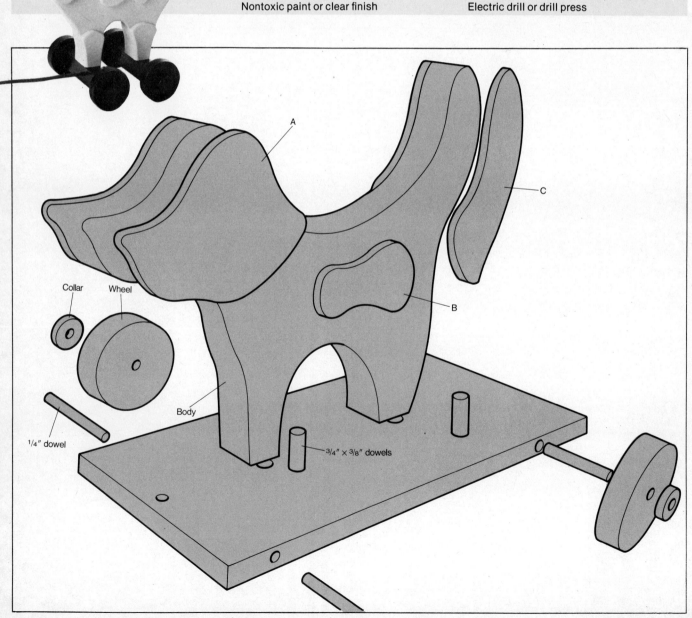

Collar
Wheel
A
C
B
Body
1/4" dowel
3/4" × 3/8" dowels

These substitute pets (which can't object to being hauled around) will provide lots of activity and fun for toddlers who love animals. When the youngsters graduate to live animals and other interests, these sturdy pull toys can be passed along to other children.

On these three pages you will find designs for dog, hippo, and cat pull toys, but almost any animal can be used on these wheeled platforms. Follow the designs, and the step-by-step instructions, and then use your imagination to design still more.

STEP 1
CUTTING THE PARTS

Enlarge and transfer the animal-body pattern to the ¾-inch stock and the patterns for the body parts to the ¼-inch stock. Cut out the parts on the band saw, being sure to cut outside the drawn line, leaving room to sand to the proper form. Next cut out the wheels on the band saw—or you might purchase them ready-made—and then cut out the crossbars (for the cat) or platform (for the dog or hippo) on the table saw.

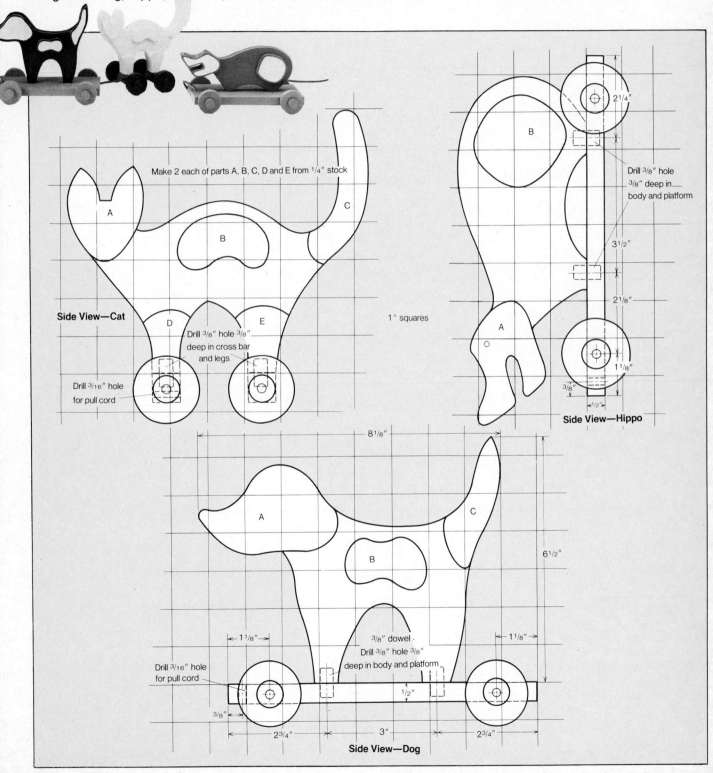

Make 2 each of parts A, B, C, D and E from ¼" stock

Side View—Cat

Drill ⅜" hole ⅜" deep in cross bar and legs

Drill 3/16" hole for pull cord

1" squares

Drill ⅜" hole ⅜" deep in body and platform

2¼"

3½"

2⅛"

1⅛"

⅜"

½"

Side View—Hippo

8⅛"

6½"

1⅛"

⅜" dowel
Drill ⅜" hole ⅜" deep in body and platform

1⅛"

Drill 3/16" hole for pull cord

½"

⅜"

2¾"

3"

2¾"

Side View—Dog

STEP 2
GLUING

Glue the body parts to the body, one on each side to make a thickness of 1 1/4 inches, as shown in the drawings. When the glue is dry, sand the piece thoroughly, blending the body parts with the main body, where necessary, and rounding all edges.

STEP 3
DRILLING FOR AXLES AND COLLARS

Drill a 5/16-inch hole in the center of each wheel. Drill all holes in bodies, crossbars, or platforms as indicated in the drawings. To form the collars, drill a 1/4-inch hole through the length of a short piece of 3/4-inch dowel and slice off four 1/4-inch lengths with a backsaw. Glue an axle collar to one end of each axle.

STEP 4
PAINTING

Sand all parts carefully and remove all dust with a tack cloth. Before assembling the toys, paint the various parts. The bodies can be painted all one color or the main body one color and the added parts another color. The platforms (dog and hippo), crossbars (cat), and wheels can be a contrasting color. Paint axle collars, but do not paint the axles. The toys can be finished naturally with a nontoxic clear finish.

STEP 5
ASSEMBLING THE PLATFORM

To attach the dog and hippo bodies to the platforms or the cat body to the crossbars, put a small amount of glue into each leg hole and into the corresponding hole in the platform or crossbar; insert one of the short lengths of 3/8-inch dowel and then press body and platform together. To attach the wheels, put a small amount of glue into the holes in the sides of the platforms or the ends of the crossbars; put an axle with collar through a wheel and press into the axle hole, but be careful not to glue the wheel to the axle.

A trial assembly without glue is advisable to make sure all parts fit together.

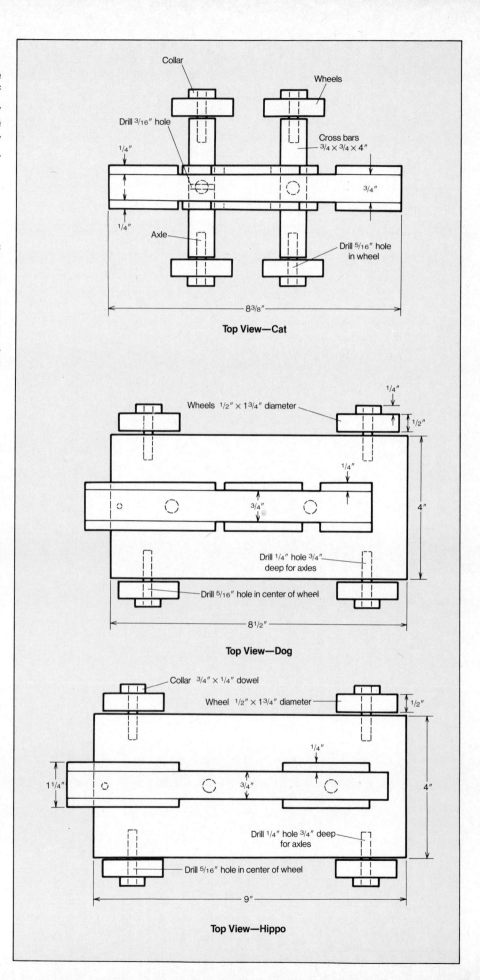

Top View—Cat

Top View—Dog

Top View—Hippo

Face Puzzle

MATERIALS LIST

Background panel (1), 1/2″ × 8″ × 10″, plywood
Lower puzzle pieces (1), 3/8″ × 8″ × 10″, plywood
Upper puzzle pieces (1), 1/4″ × 8″ × 10″, plywood
Long dowel pins (6), 1″ × 1/4″ dowel, hardwood
Short dowel pins (8), 5/8″ × 1/4″ dowel, hardwood
Brads, 1/2″ 18 or 19 gauge
Yellow wood glue
Nontoxic paint

Tools

Table saw
Band saw or jigsaw
Drill press
Hammer
Masking tape
Sandpaper, 80, 120, and 220

This puzzle provides a starting point for many variations in form and color. The parts fit into a basic series of holes. Ours is a clown face, but you can use your own.

STEP 1
CUTTING THE PIECES

Cut out the three 8- × 10-inch plywood panels. On the 1/4-inch panel, lay out the pattern of the oval shape of the puzzle, the location of the fourteen 1/4-inch holes, and the shapes of the various puzzle pieces. While the panels are still square, fasten all three panels together with light brads, with the 1/4-inch panel on top and the 1/2-inch panel on the bottom. Now drill all fourteen 1/4-inch holes through the 1/4-inch and 3/8-inch panels, but only halfway through the bottom 1/2-inch panel. Cut out the oval

shape from all three panels at once with the band saw or jigsaw, and sand all sides smooth. After the sanding, remove the bottom 1/2-inch panel. With the band saw or jigsaw, cut out the puzzle shapes from the other two panels together. Sand all edges. Cut the dowel pins to length.

STEP 2
ASSEMBLING AND FINISHING

Three of the puzzle pieces are made from both the 1/4-inch pieces and the 3/8-inch pieces—the hair, nose, and chin. Glue these together and glue in the longer dowel pins. The remaining parts are from the 3/8-inch panel; glue in the shorter dowel pins. You can vary this arrangement if you choose. Paint all pieces in whatever colors you want. Paint the 1/2-inch background panel a neutral color.

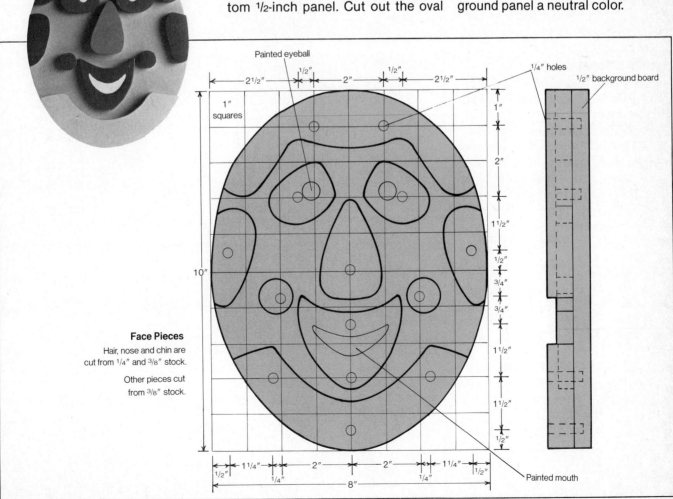

Face Pieces

Hair, nose and chin are cut from 1/4″ and 3/8″ stock.

Other pieces cut from 3/8″ stock.

Painted eyeball
1/4″ holes
1/2″ background board
1″ squares
Painted mouth

Loose-Jointed Doll

MATERIALS LIST
Body (1), $3/4'' \times 13/4'' \times 41/2''$, pine
Body front (1), $1/4'' \times 11/4'' \times 2''$, pine
Upper arms (2), $1/2'' \times 5/8'' \times 31/4''$, pine
Lower arms (2), $1/4'' \times 1/2'' \times 3''$, pine
Upper legs (2), $3/4'' \times 5/8'' \times 31/2''$, pine
Lower legs (2), $1/2'' \times 5/8'' \times 23/4''$, pine
Feet (2), $1/4'' \times 1/2'' \times 1''$, pine
Joints (6), $3/16''$ dowel, hardwood
Yellow wood glue
Nontoxic clear finish

This is not the usual sort of doll, but it comes from a long tradition of toy making and folk art. Children will find their own ways to play with it. The loose joint is used today in wood sculpture as well as in toys. This particular version of the doll is scaled for the Doll Seesaw and Doll Swing on pages 30 and 32, but it can be made in any size.

STEP 1
CUTTING THE PIECES
Cut all parts to overall sizes indicated. Do not cut the marked notches at this stage. Next drill all holes $3/16$ inch in diameter. The center of each hole is $1/4$ inch from the end of the piece, where required, and equidistant from each side of it. Now cut all notches and round off all ends where indicated. Be sure to see that the upper parts of the notches in the

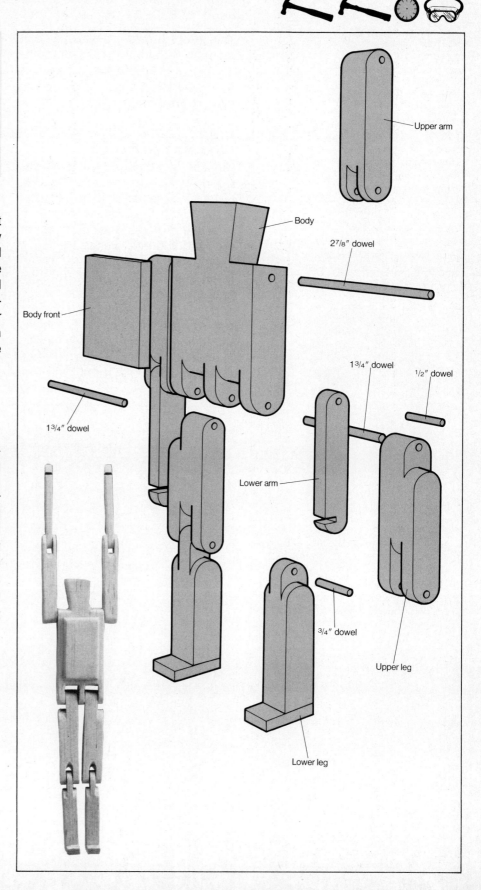

Upper arm

Body

$27/8''$ dowel

$13/4''$ dowel

$1/2''$ dowel

$13/4''$ dowel

Body front

Lower arm

Upper leg

$3/4''$ dowel

Lower leg

body, upper arms, and upper legs are rounded so as to allow free movement of the parts.

STEP 2
FITTING THE PIECES

When all parts have been cut to their proper dimensions, they will make a tight fit—too tight for free movement. Therefore, the following parts must be sanded to provide a loose fit: lower arms, upper legs, and lower legs. Next the holes in the upper body and lower arms, and the *upper holes* in the upper and lower legs, must be slightly enlarged with sandpaper or a thin round rasp—again, to provide free movement.

STEP 3
FINISHING THE PIECES

Before finishing the pieces, glue the feet to the lower legs. Then finish all pieces before assembly. Sand each piece carefully and remove all dust. Finish with two coats of a nontoxic clear finish.

STEP 4
ASSEMBLING THE DOLL

Start the assembly with the upper arms. Glue a 2⁷⁄₈-inch length of ³⁄₁₆-inch dowel into the top of one of the upper arms. Insert the dowel through the upper body and glue it in the hole at the top of the other upper arm. Be especially careful not to get any glue on the body so that the arms can swing freely. Next go on to the lower arms. Insert a ¹⁄₂-inch length of dowel through one side of the bottom end of the upper arm, through the corresponding hole in the lower arm, and only slightly into the hole in the other side of the upper arm. Then put a bit of glue into that hole and a bit of glue on the protruding end of the dowel on the other end, and push the dowel through until it is flush with both sides of the upper arm. If any of this glue is squeezed out, it can easily be wiped off the finished surface. The upper legs and the lower legs are attached in the same way as the arms. The main thing to remember is not to get any glue on the movable parts.

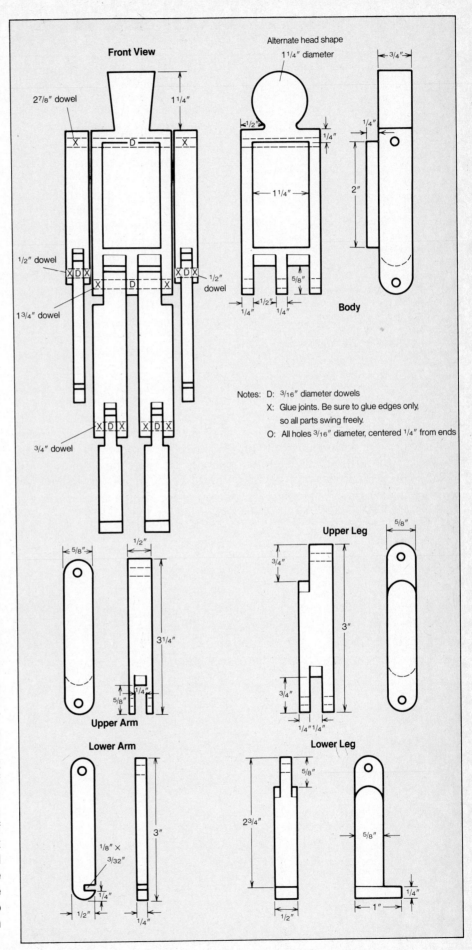

Notes: D: ³⁄₁₆″ diameter dowels
X: Glue joints. Be sure to glue edges only, so all parts swing freely.
O: All holes ³⁄₁₆″ diameter, centered ¹⁄₄″ from ends

Doll Seesaw

Up and down and round and round! Here's an opportunity to exercise your ingenuity and provide recreation for a child and two dolls. The Loose-Jointed Wood Doll (page 28) is scaled for this seesaw.

STEP 1
CUTTING AND ASSEMBLY

Start with the base. Glue up enough stock to make a laminated block measuring 4 inches high × $51/2$ inches square. While the glue is drying, cut out the main plank to size. Cut and drill the plank swing block. Glue this block to the center of the bottom of the main plank. Cut out the 3-inch pivot disk. Drill a $3/4$-inch hole centered in the bottom of the disk, $1/2$ inch deep. Cut and drill the two swing blocks. Glue these blocks to the pivot disk $1/2$ inch apart, centered on the side opposite the drilled hole. Use a scrap of $1/2$-inch stock as a spacer to test that the plank swing block will fit smoothly in between the two swing blocks. Make sure the $1/2$-inch holes match up. Then glue the $3/4$-inch pivot dowel to the pivot disk, but do not glue the $1/2$-inch swing dowel now. On the glued-up base block, draw a 3-inch circle in the center of the top (one of the $51/2$- × $51/2$-inch sides). Set the table or band saw

to 15° and cut out a flat-topped cone with a 3-inch diameter on the top and a 5-inch diameter on the bottom. Drill a $3/4$-inch hole in the center of the top, $21/2$ inches deep. Cut chair pieces and drill holes as shown. Sand all pieces, and assemble chairs with glue and masking tape. Then, when the glue is dry, glue a completed chair to each end of the main plank.

STEP 2
FINISHING

First make a trial assembly to make sure all parts work smoothly, inserting but not yet gluing the $1/2$-inch swing dowel. Then finish with two coats of clear nontoxic finish. Do *not* apply finish to the underside of the pivot assembly or the inside of the swing blocks because finishing will impede movement. These sections can be waxed. After reassembling, glue the swing dowel in the holes in the two swing blocks of the pivot assembly. Thread a piece of leather thong or cord through the arm holes.

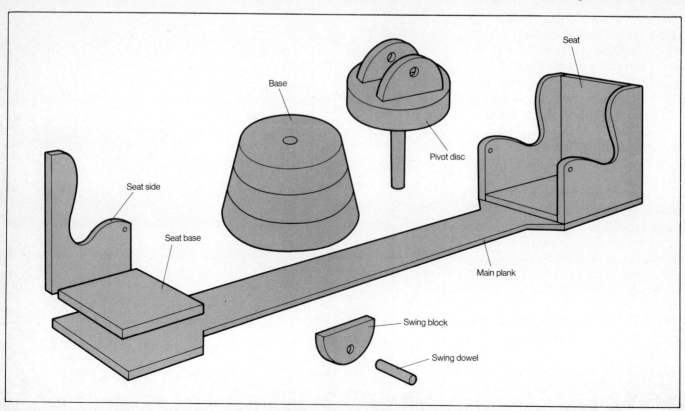

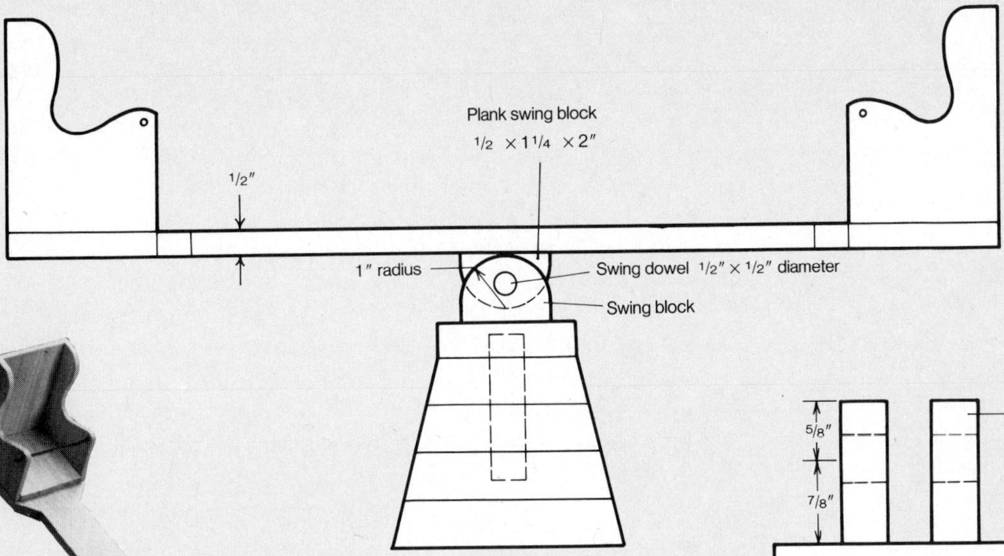

Plank swing block
$1/2 \times 1 1/4 \times 2"$

1/2"

1" radius — Swing dowel $1/2" \times 1/2"$ diameter

Swing block

Side View

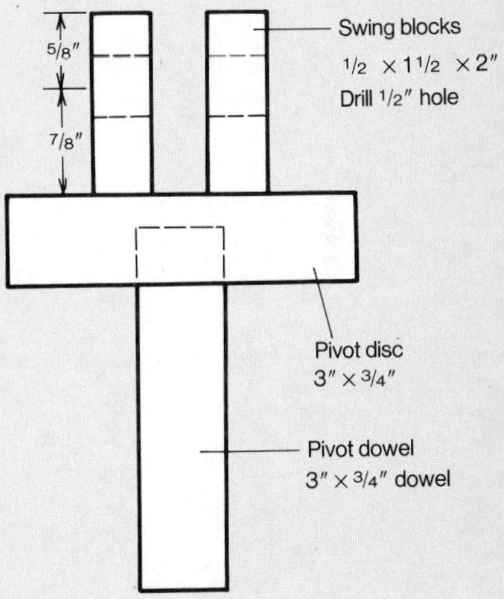

Swing blocks
$1/2 \times 1 1/2 \times 2"$
Drill $1/2"$ hole

5/8"

7/8"

Pivot disc
$3" \times 3/4"$

Pivot dowel
$3" \times 3/4"$ dowel

Pivot Disc—Swing Block Assembly

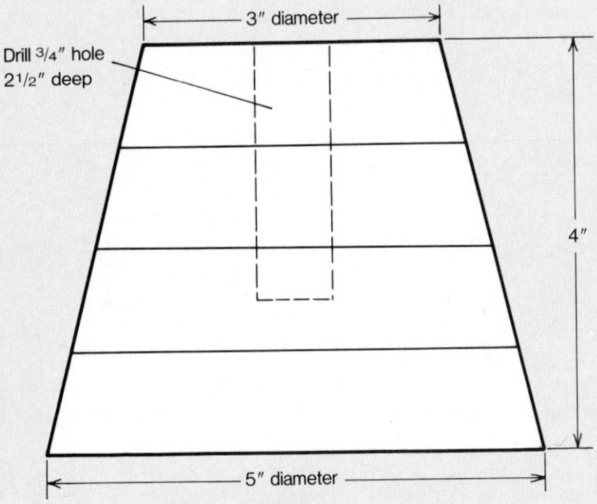

3" diameter

Drill $3/4"$ hole
$2 1/2"$ deep

4"

5" diameter

Base

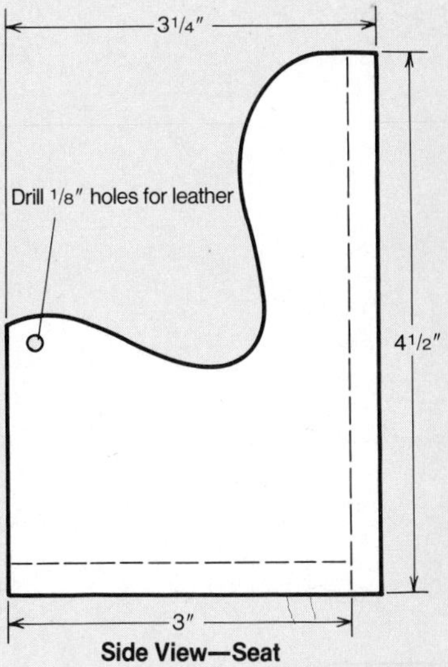

$3 1/4"$

Drill $1/8"$ holes for leather

$4 1/2"$

3"

Side View—Seat

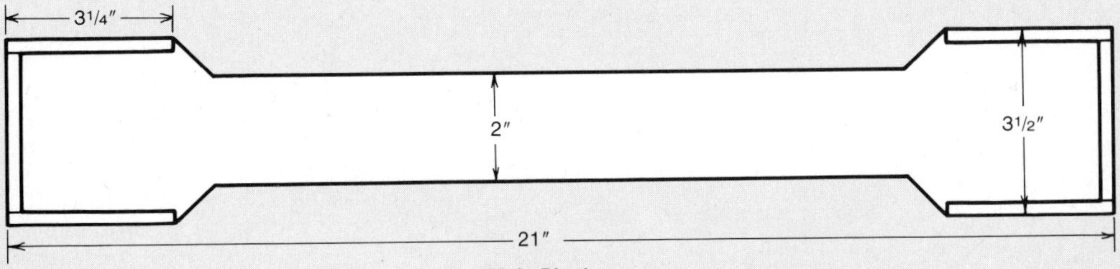

$3 1/4"$

2"

$3 1/2"$

21"

Main Plank

Doll Swing

MATERIALS LIST

Sides (4), 1/2″ × 3/4″ × 17 1/2″, hardwood stock
  throughout
Side braces (2), 1/2″ × 3/4″ × 10 3/4″
Cross braces (2), 1/2″ × 3/4″ × 11″
Top crossbar (1), 1/2″ × 3/4″ × 11″
Chair seat (1), 1/4″ × 3″ × 3″
Chair sides (2), 1/4″ × 3 1/4″ × 4 1/2″
Chair back (1), 1/4″ × 3″ × 4 1/2″
Glue dowels, 3/16″ dowel (as needed),
  hardwood
Yellow wood glue
Nontoxic clear finish or paint
Leather thongs (1/8 flat leather lacing),
  about 2 yards
*(Dimensions larger than those shown in
drawings allow for saw, angle, or
bevel cuts.)*

Tools

Table or handsaw
Band or scroll saw
Drill or drill press
Masking tape
Sandpaper, 80, 120, and 220

Children, like adults, love to have others share in what is important to them. What young child doesn't like long sessions on a swing and wouldn't like to give his or her dolls a taste of this? Youngsters can take their favorite dolls or the Loose-Jointed Doll (see page 28) for a ride without worrying about falls and bruises, since the chair seat will keep the doll safe. This is a variation of the familiar porch or playground swing.

STEP 1
CUTTING AND ASSEMBLING THE SWING

Cut all frame pieces to size, taking special care with the angle cuts. Drill holes in top crossbar as shown. Sand all frame pieces carefully and assemble with glue and dowels. Cut chair pieces with table saw or band saw. Drill all holes as shown. Knotted leather hanging thongs will be threaded through the 1/4-inch holes. Assemble the chair with glue, securing it with masking tape.

STEP 2
FINISHING

Sand all parts carefully, dust, and finish with two coats of clear nontoxic finish or paint. When frame and chairs are thoroughly dry, hang the chair with two leather thongs on each side. We used 1/8-inch flat leather lacing. Brightly colored cords can also be used. Hang the chair so it tilts backward. The weight of the doll will bring it level. Thread a piece of leather lace through the two 1/8-inch holes in the chair arms for the doll's arms to rest on.

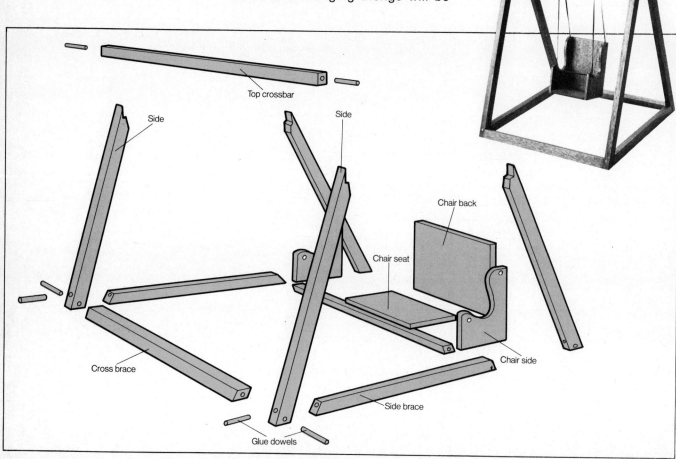

Top crossbar

Side

Side

Chair back

Chair seat

Chair side

Cross brace

Side brace

Glue dowels

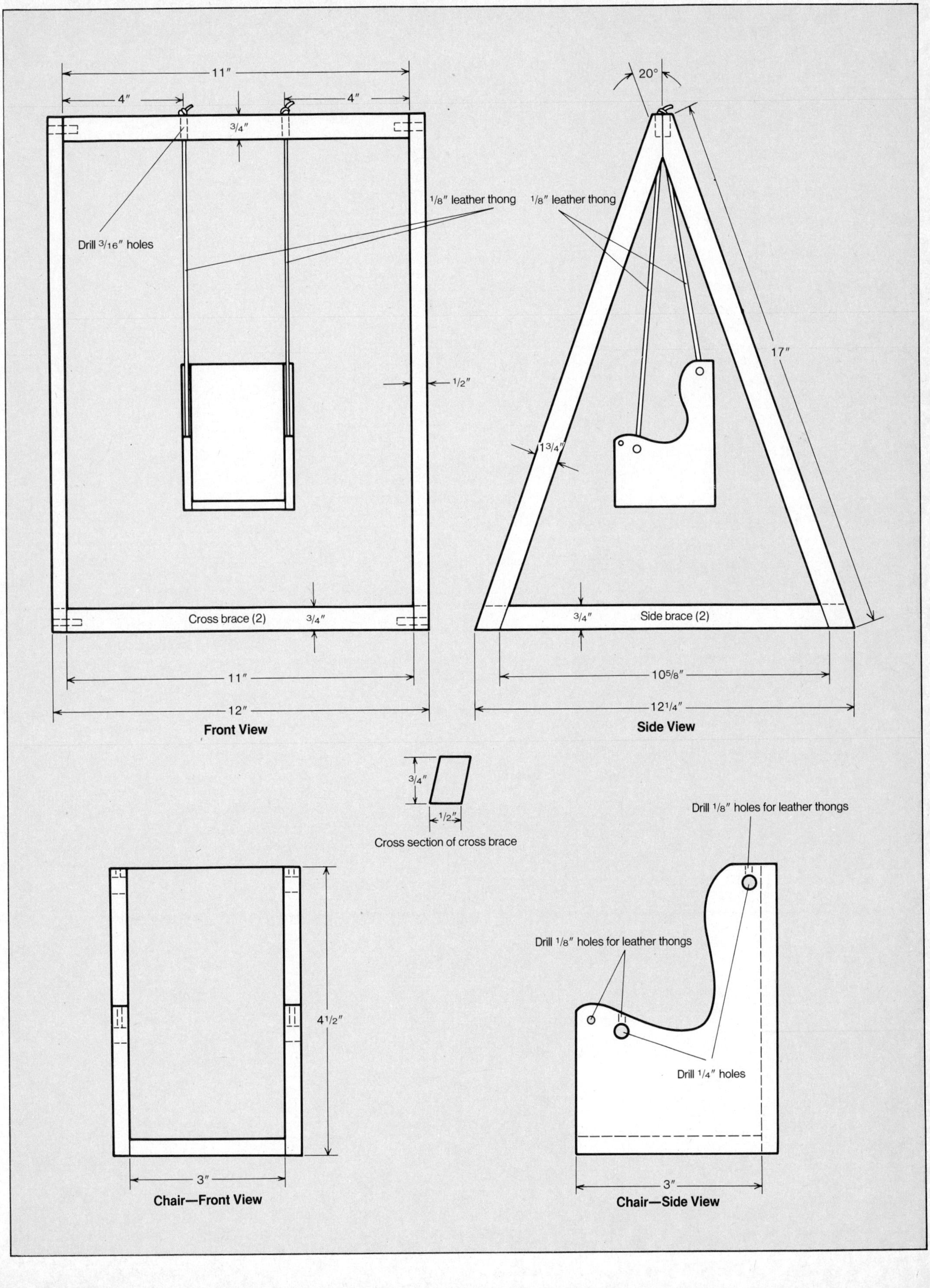

11"

4"

3/4"

4"

1/8" leather thong   1/8" leather thong

20°

Drill 3/16" holes

17"

1 3/4"

1/2"

Cross brace (2)   3/4"

3/4"   Side brace (2)

11"

10 5/8"

12"

12 1/4"

Front View

Side View

3/4"

1/2"

Cross section of cross brace

4 1/2"

3"

Chair—Front View

Drill 1/8" holes for leather thongs

Drill 1/8" holes for leather thongs

Drill 1/4" holes

3"

Chair—Side View

Doll Cradle

MATERIALS LIST

Body slats (9), $1/2'' \times 2'' \times 20''$, hardwood stock throughout
Hood slats (9), $1/2'' \times 2'' \times 6''$
Cradle foot (1), $1/2'' \times 7'' \times 10''$
Cradle headboard (1), $1/2'' \times 10'' \times 10''$
Uprights (2), $1/2'' \times 4'' \times 12''$
Base brace (1), $1/2'' \times 4'' \times 21 1/4''$
Cross braces (2), $1/2'' \times 2'' \times 12''$
Upright braces (2), $1/2'' \times 4'' \times 4''$
Pivot collars (4), $1/4'' \times 1 1/2''$ diameter, hardwood
Pivot pins (2), $1 5/8'' \times 1/2''$ dowel, hardwood
Glue dowels, $1/4''$ dowel (as needed), hardwood
Yellow wood glue
Nontoxic clear finish or paint
(Dimensions larger than those shown in drawings allow for saw, angle, or bevel cuts.)

Tools

Table saw
Band or saber saw
Drill or drill press
Belt or pad sander
Rasp or surform tool
Masking tape

Sandpaper, 80, 120, and 220

All dolls need rest, as children understand, and this modern cradle, with its gently rocking motion, supplies the perfect place for an afternoon nap. You can add a blanket or piece of foam rubber for a mattress, and material for bedclothes. Children will get absorbed in settling their dolls or teddy bears comfortably in the cradle and rocking them until it's time to do something else. This interesting project utilizes contemporary wood-sculpting techniques.

STEP 1
CUTTING AND ASSEMBLING

Begin by cutting the slats for the body and hood of the cradle. These slats are all cut exactly the same, except that the body slats are 20 inches long and the hood slats are 6 inches long. Cut a 10° bevel on both long sides of each slat. Once your table saw is set properly with the blade at 10°, you can cut as many identical slats as you need. The dimension across the wide, or upper, side of the slat is important because it controls the diameter of the finished cylindrical form. In this case, it should be $1 11/16$ inches. Lay out the nine 20-inch slats on a flat, level surface with the wide side up. They should be flat and straight, with no warp or twist. Line up the ends with a straightedge. All the long edges should be touching each other. Put strips of masking tape along all the edges where two slats meet. Then put a few strips across these for extra security. Next, turn the whole assembly upside down so that you are faced with a series of long V-shaped grooves. Put a small amount of glue all along the inside of these V-shaped grooves. Do not use too much glue, as it will be

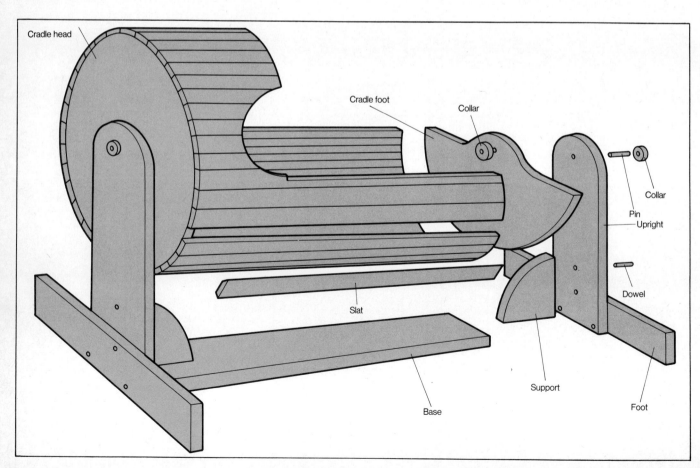

Cradle head

Cradle foot

Collar

Collar

Pin

Upright

Dowel

Slat

Base

Support

Foot

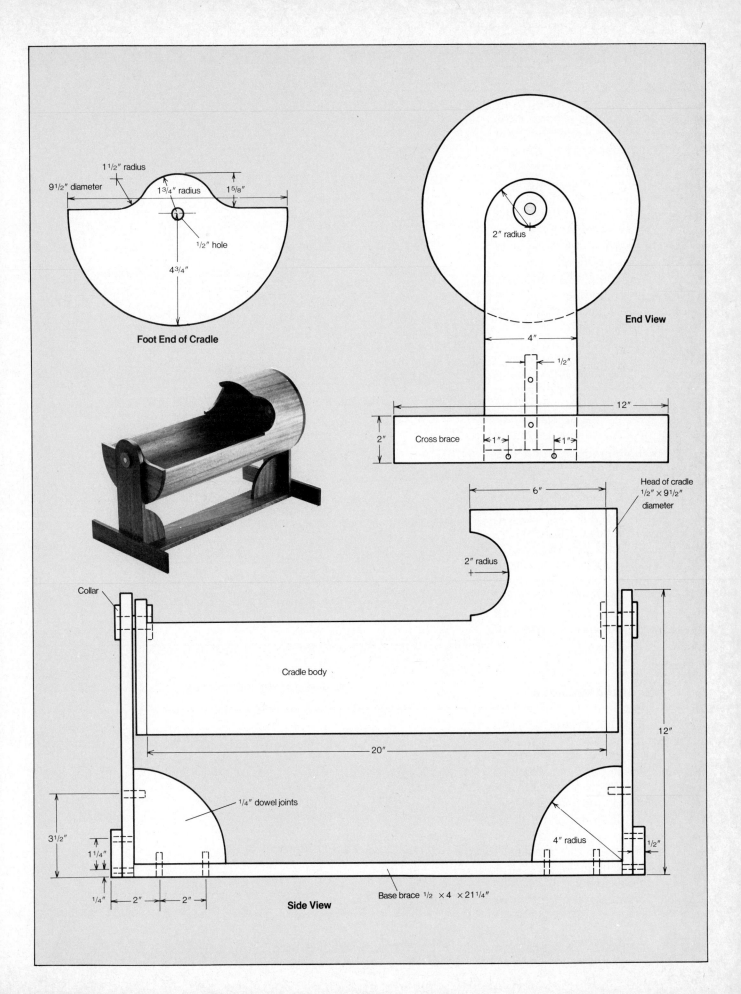

Foot End of Cradle

1 1/2" radius
9 1/2" diameter
1 3/4" radius
1 5/8"
1/2" hole
4 3/4"

End View

2" radius
4"
1/2"
12"
Cross brace
2"
1"
1"

Head of cradle
1/2" × 9 1/2" diameter

6"

2" radius

12"

Collar

Cradle body

20"

1/4" dowel joints

3 1/2"

1 1/4"

4" radius

1/2"

1/4"   2"   2"

Base brace 1/2 × 4 × 21 1/4"

Side View

squeezed out when you roll the slats together. Do not put glue on the two outside beveled edges. Roll the slats together (the tape will act as hinges), and you will have half of a long cylinder. Put strips of tape across the open side of the cylinder to hold it while the glue dries. When you turn the half-cylinder over, the two outside edges (the edges without glue) should be flat to a level surface.

Lay out the nine 6-inch slats for the hood in the same manner. Before gluing them, transfer to the taped slats the pattern for the hood shape as shown and cut it out on a band saw. Then glue them together as you did the other slats. While the glued slats are drying (let them stand overnight), cut all pieces for the supporting structure. Assemble with glue and dowels as shown. When the slats are completely dry, remove all masking tape and clean up the inside of the two half-cylinder shapes. Scrape off any glue that might have squeezed out, and sand thoroughly. Then glue the hood to one end of the body of the cradle. Hold it with masking tape. Next cut the headboard and footboard as shown and drill ½-inch pivot holes as indicated. Sand the inside smooth and glue the two in place. Now you are ready to shape the outside of the cradle. Take down the sharp edges where the slats meet, using a rasp, surform, or belt sander, until you have a smooth shape.

STEP 2
FINISHING AND ASSEMBLING THE CRADLE

Cut the four pivot collars and glue one collar to one end of each pivot pin. After a final sanding and cleanup, give all parts two coats of clear nontoxic finish. Make sure the two pivot holes in the head and footboards are clear, sanding them slightly oversize so the cradle will rock freely. Put the cradle in position between the two uprights and push a collar-and-pin assembly through the upright and cradle at each end. Glue this to the upright only. Then glue the other collar to the inside end of the pin, being careful not to glue it to the cradle. The cradle is ready to rock.

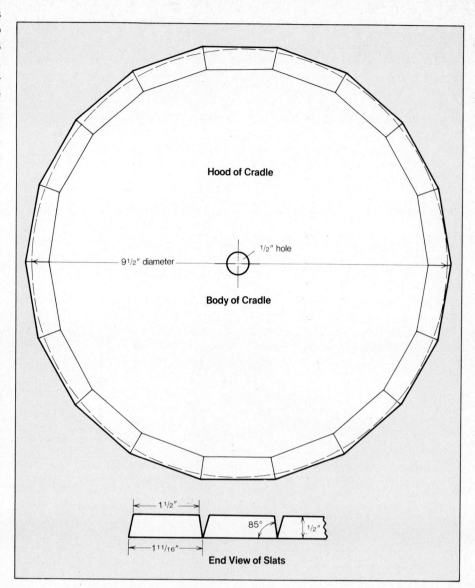

Hood of Cradle

9½″ diameter · ½″ hole

Body of Cradle

1½″ · 85° · ½″

1¹¹⁄₁₆″

End View of Slats

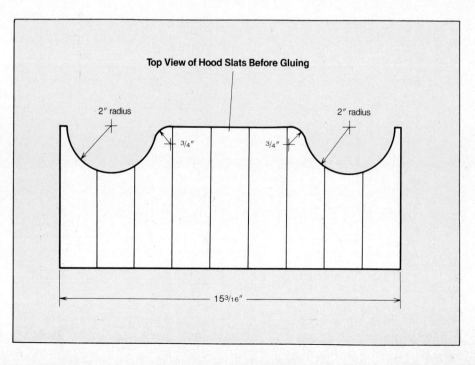

Top View of Hood Slats Before Gluing

2″ radius · 3/4″ · 3/4″ · 2″ radius

15³⁄₁₆″

Clown Doll

MATERIALS LIST

Hat crown (1), $1^{1}/_{2}'' \times 2^{1}/_{8}'' \times 2^{1}/_{4}''$, pine
Hat brim (1), $^{1}/_{4}'' \times 4''$ diameter, pine
Head (1), $2^{1}/_{4}'' \times 2^{3}/_{4}'' \times 2^{1}/_{2}''$, pine
Neck (1), $1^{1}/_{2}'' \times ^{3}/_{4}''$ dowel, hardwood
Collar (1), $^{1}/_{4}'' \times 3''$ diameter, pine
Body, outer parts (2), $^{3}/_{4}'' \times 4'' \times 5''$, pine
Body, center part (1), $^{3}/_{4}'' \times 4'' \times 5^{1}/_{4}''$, pine
Arms (2), $1^{1}/_{2}'' \times 1^{7}/_{8}'' \times 5^{1}/_{4}''$, pine
Legs (2), $1^{3}/_{4}'' \times 2'' \times 4^{1}/_{2}''$, pine
Hands (2), $^{3}/_{4}'' \times ^{7}/_{8}'' \times 1''$, pine
Feet (2), $^{3}/_{4}'' \times 1^{1}/_{2}'' \times 2^{3}/_{4}''$, pine
Base (1), $^{3}/_{4}'' \times 6''$ diameter, pine
Ears (2), $^{3}/_{4}'' \times 1'' \times 1^{1}/_{2}''$, pine
Nose (1), $^{3}/_{8}'' \times ^{1}/_{2}''$ dowel, hardwood
Joint dowels (as needed), $^{1}/_{4}''$, $^{3}/_{8}''$, and $^{1}/_{2}''$,
   hardwood
Yellow wood glue
Nontoxic paint
(Dimensions larger than those shown in drawings allow for saw, angle, or bevel cuts.)

Tools
Table saw
Band saw
Drill or drill press
Wood rasp
Sandpaper, 80, 120, and 220

Here's a doll that will bring a touch of the circus into your living room. Clowns, with their aura of the ridiculous and the uproariously funny, are always appealing. This clown doll has some movable parts—the legs and feet turn in and out and the arms can be raised or lowered—and gives your imagination a chance to contrive differently shaped parts and colors. Make one to the plans here, then make it for a friend with your own variations.

STEP 1
CUTTING AND DRILLING THE PIECES
Cut all pieces to sizes given in the Materials List, making sure the grain runs vertically in all pieces. While the pieces are still square, locate and drill all joint holes. Note that the body is made up of three sections: two outer parts with the center part sandwiched between them. The holes for the arms and legs are drilled into the

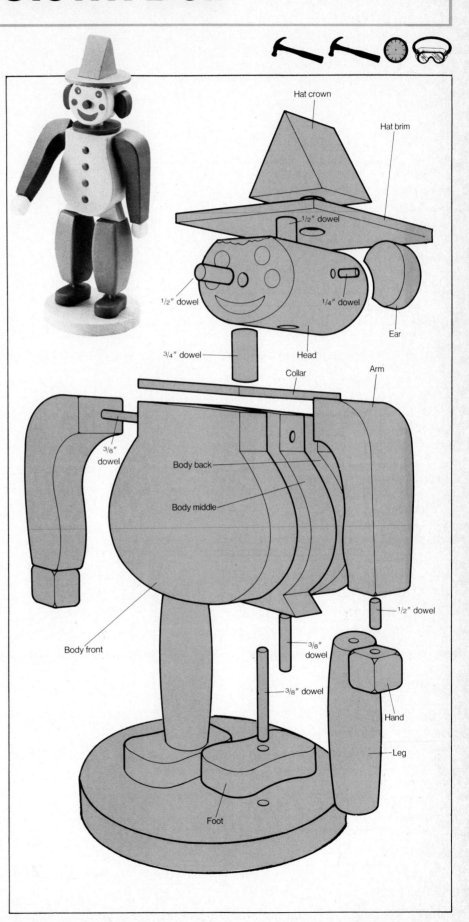

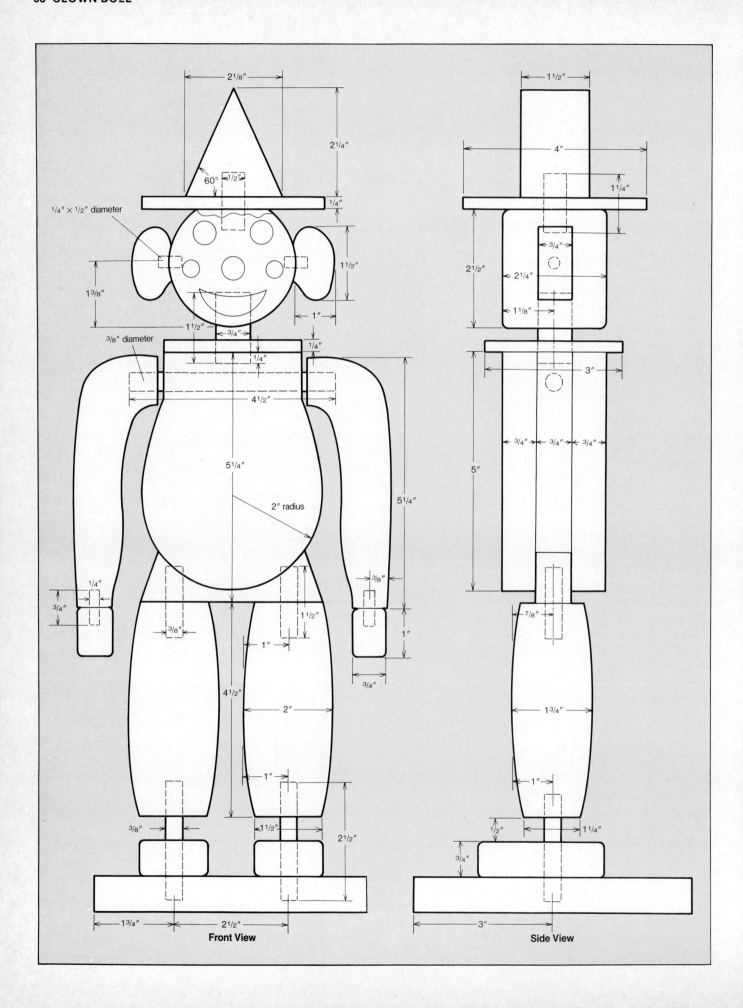

Front View

Side View

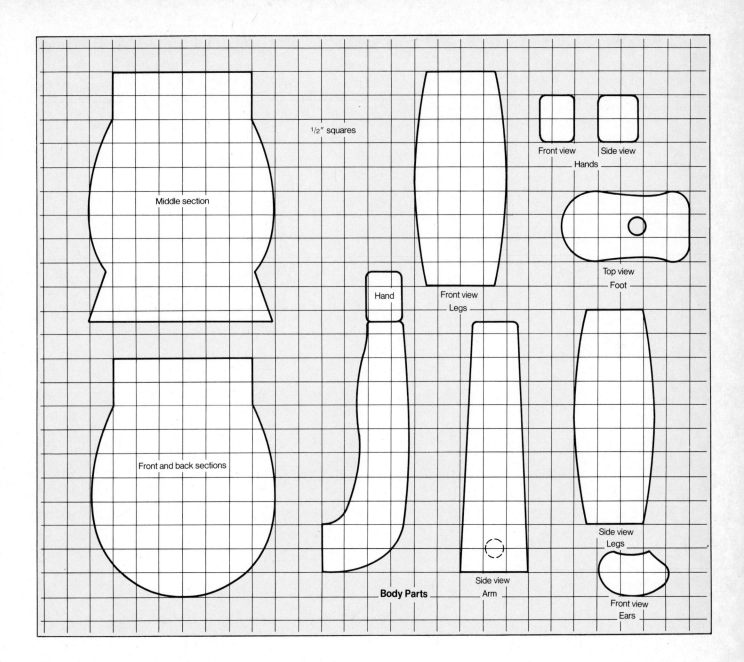

½" squares

Middle section

Front and back sections

Hand

Front view
Legs

Front view   Side view
Hands

Top view
Foot

Side view
Legs

Body Parts

Side view
Arm

Front view
Ears

center section only, before the three parts of the body are glued together. Lay out the patterns for the various pieces and cut them out on the band saw. The arms, legs, and hands have one pattern for the front and back and another pattern for the two sides. From the side, the arms have a taper from top to bottom. Cut this taper first, and then lay out and cut the pattern for the front and back. The two patterns for the legs and hands should be laid out and cut one at a time. Cut all joint dowels to length. Sand all pieces and round all edges slightly, except for the three sections of the body, which will be sanded after they are glued together.

STEP 2
ASSEMBLING THE PARTS
Glue the three sections of the body together. When the glue is dry, sand thoroughly and slightly round all edges. Next glue the hat crown to the brim and the hat dowel to the crown. Now glue the ear dowels to the ears, the leg dowels and the neck to the body, and the dowels to the hands.

STEP 3
PAINTING THE PARTS
All parts should be painted separately before final assembly. Paint the head white—a good background for the facial features. The nose dowel should be bright red. The re-

maining facial features should be painted as shown in the face plan. The other parts can be painted with bright colors of your choosing. Note that parts of the base dowel and neck dowel can be seen and should be painted. Optional decoration could be colored upholstery tacks for buttons.

STEP 4
ASSEMBLING THE DOLL
Most of the parts are not glued together so that the clown has some mobility. Glue the hands to the arms, the ears to the head, and the nose to the face. The other parts are put together without glue.

Pinocchio

MATERIALS LIST

Hat (1), $1^{3/4}'' \times 2'' \times 2''$, pine
Head (1), $2'' \times 2'' \times 2^{1/4}''$, pine
Collar (1), $1/4'' \times 2^{1/2}''$ diameter, pine
Neck (1), $1^{3/4}'' \times 3/4''$ dowel, hardwood
Body (1), $2^{1/2}'' \times 2^{1/2}'' \times 4^{1/2}''$, pine
Upper arms (2), $1'' \times 1'' \times 2''$, pine
Lower arms (2), $5/8'' \times 5/8'' \times 2^{5/8}''$, pine
Hands (2), $3/8'' \times 1/2'' \times 1''$, pine
Upper legs (2), $1^{1/8}'' \times 1'' \times 2''$, pine
Lower legs (2), $3/4'' \times 3/4'' \times 3''$, pine
Feet (2), $3/4'' \times 7/8'' \times 2''$, pine
Base (1), $3/4'' \times 5''$ diameter, pine
Small nose (1), $1'' \times 3/8''$ dowel, hardwood
Large nose (1), $2^{1/2}'' \times 3/8''$ dowel, hardwood
Buttons (4), $3/8'' \times 3/8''$ dowel, hardwood
Joint dowels (as needed), $3/16''$, $1/4''$, and $3/8''$, hardwood
Yellow wood glue
Nontoxic paint

Tools

Table saw or backsaw
Band saw or coping saw
Drill or drill press
Flat wood chisel
Wood rasp
Sandpaper, 80, 120, and 220

Whether they encountered him in Carlo Collodi's classic tale *Pinocchio: The Story of a Puppet,* or in the animated movie or a musical version, children seem to recognize Pinocchio as a familiar friend and neighbor. He is always young and always mischievous, and when he lies, his nose grows. This Pinocchio has interchangeable small and large noses, but if you have very small children around, you may want to glue one nose in place so it won't disappear or even be swallowed.

STEP 1
CUTTING AND DRILLING THE PIECES

Cut all parts to dimensions given in the Materials List, making sure the grain of the wood runs vertically for all pieces. While the blocks are still

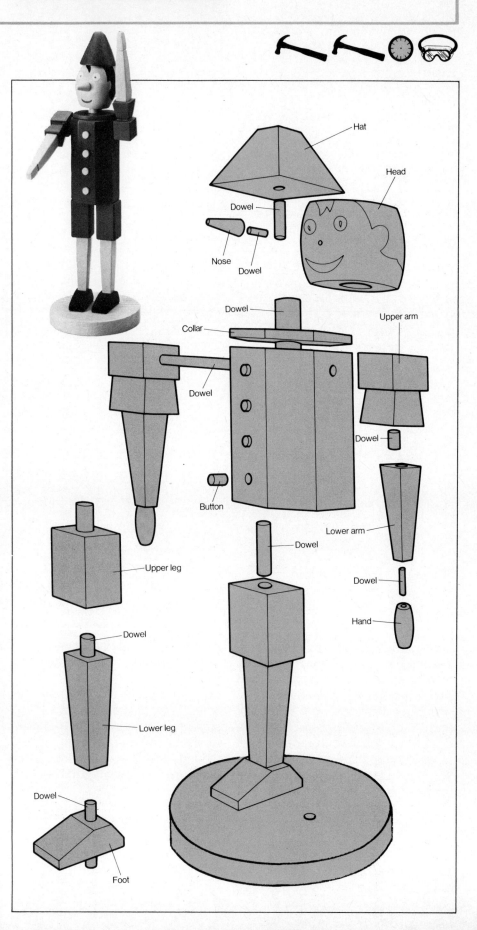

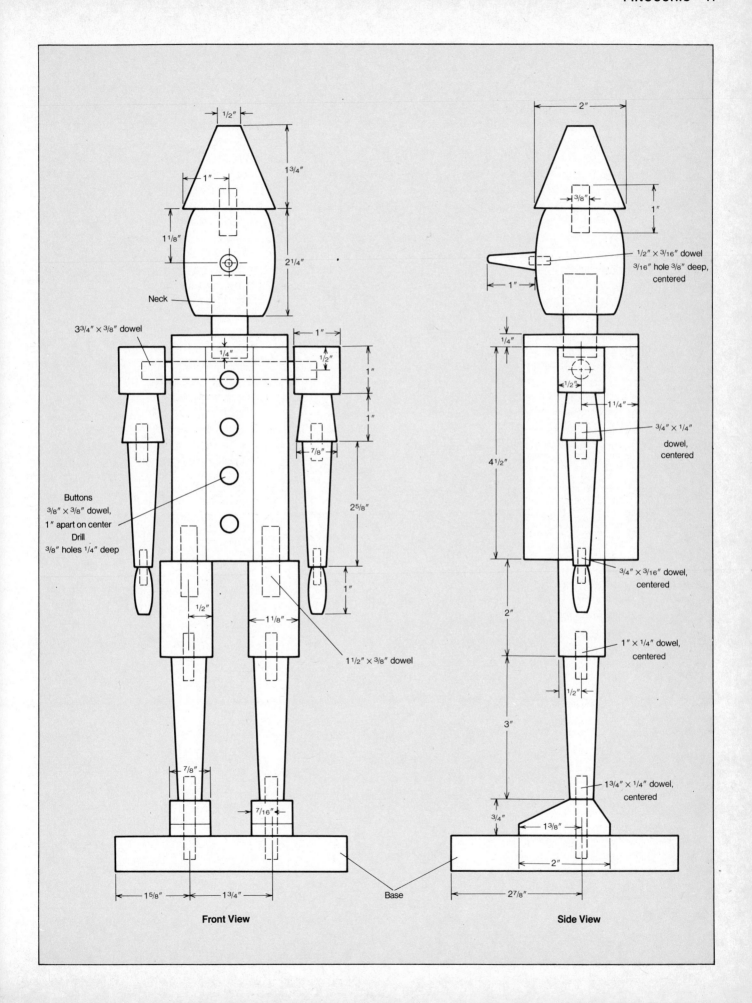

Front View

Side View

1/2"
13/4"
1"
11/8"
21/4"
Neck
33/4" × 3/8" dowel
1/4"
1/2"
1"
1"
1"
7/8"
Buttons
3/8" × 3/8" dowel,
1" apart on center
Drill
3/8" holes 1/4" deep
25/8"
1"
11/2" × 3/8" dowel
1/2"
11/8"
7/8"
7/16"
15/8"
13/4"
Base

2"
3/8"
1"
1/2" × 3/16" dowel
3/16" hole 3/8" deep,
centered
1"
1/4"
1/2"
11/4"
3/4" × 1/4"
dowel,
centered
41/2"
3/4" × 3/16" dowel,
centered
2"
1" × 1/4" dowel,
centered
1/2"
3"
13/4" × 1/4" dowel,
centered
3/4"
13/8"
2"
27/8"

square, locate and drill all joint holes, including the holes for the front buttons. Now the parts can be cut to shape. The tapered cuts on the arms, lower legs, and feet can be cut on the table saw, band saw, or with a backsaw. The upper legs are square, but edges are rounded with a rasp and sandpaper. Cut the hands with the band saw or coping saw. The body is octagon-shaped and can be cut on the table saw with the blade set at 45°. Round the top and bottom edges of the body with the rasp and sandpaper. Cut the head out on the band saw. It has the same profile from the front and sides. Round off the edges of the cuts with the rasp and sandpaper. The hat is cone-shaped, with a diameter of 1/2 inch on top and 2 inches on the bottom. This can be cut out on the band saw with the blade set at 22°. Alternatively, the hat can be cut out with several angled cuts, using a backsaw, and then finished with the wood rasp and sandpaper. Cut out the collar, base, and the neck dowel. The two noses are made from 3/8-inch dowels, tapered to a rounded end with the wood rasp and sandpaper. Cut all joint dowels to size.

STEP 2
PAINTING THE PIECES
Sand all parts carefully, rounding all sharp edges with 80 sandpaper and finishing with 120 and 220. Paint all parts with nontoxic enamels. The traditional colors for Pinocchio are red and green, but you may want to start your own tradition. The head should have a neutral background, with the features painted in as shown in the pattern. When painting the buttons, avoid getting paint on the undersides where they are glued onto the body.

STEP 3
ASSEMBLING THE DOLL
Begin by gluing the hat to the head, the neck to the body, and the collar to the body. Do not glue the head to the neck. Next glue the two parts of the arms together and the hands to the arms, with the dowels. The 3/8-inch upper-leg dowels are glued to the body. The two parts of the legs are glued together with their dowels, and the feet to the legs. Note that the 1/4-inch lower-leg dowels project 1/2 inch below the feet; they are to be inserted in the base. Glue the buttons onto the body. Glue the 3/16-inch nose dowels to the two noses. The final assembly is accomplished without further gluing so that the head, the arms, and the legs can be turned. Fit the head onto the neck. Insert the 3/8-inch arm dowel through the body and put the arms onto each end of it. Next push the legs onto the dowels that have been glued into the body. Now insert the doll into the base, using the dowels projecting from the feet. Finally, put one nose in place—or glue it on for safety if this toy is for a small child. Pinocchio is ready.

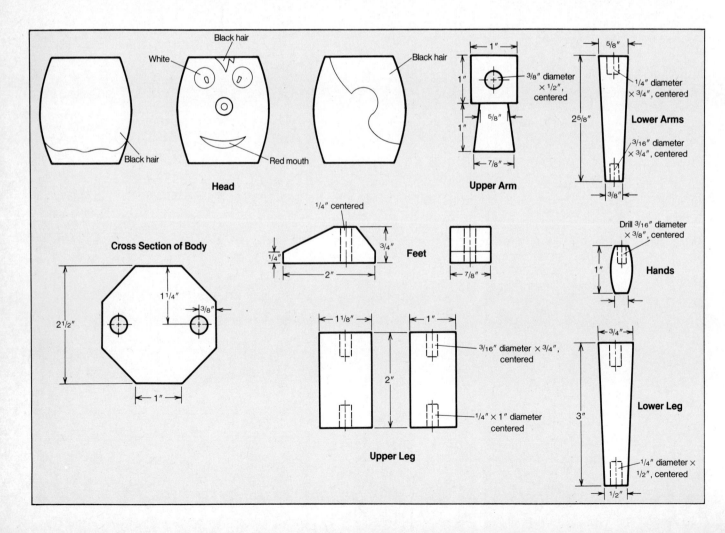

Tugboat

MATERIALS LIST

Hull (1), 1⅛″ × 4⅛″ × 13⅜″, pine
Rail and stern plate (1), ¼″ × 4″ × 13½″, pine
Deckhouse (1), ¾″ × 2″ × 6″, pine
Wheelhouse (1), 1⅛″ × 1¾″ × 1¾″, pine
Smokestack (1), ¾″ × 1⅛″ × 2⅛″, pine
Bollards, A and B (11), 1″ × ¼″ dowel,
    hardwood
Mast (1), 5″ × ¼″ dowel, hardwood
Security pegs, C,D, and E (4), ½″ × ¼″ dowel,
    hardwood
Yellow wood glue
Nontoxic paint or nontoxic varnish
(Dimensions larger than those shown in drawings allow for saw, angle, or bevel cuts.)

Tools

Table saw	Surform tool
Band saw	Double-faced tape
Drill or drill press	or small brads
Vise	Sandpaper, 80, 120,
Wood rasp	and 220

Tugboats go back many years; some of the tugboat companies in New York harbor are more than one hundred years old. Most tugs are rather drab because they were built for strength and not beauty. Our model is brightly colored, but you can choose your own color scheme. Since most children will want to put the boat in water, it might be a good idea to use a waterproof glue. Modern yellow wood glue is very strong, however, and a few coats of enamel (or spar varnish, if you decide on a natural finish), should be safe.

STEP 1
CUTTING THE PIECES

Cut the pieces for the hull and rail to size on the table saw. Fasten the two pieces together temporarily with double-faced tape or small brads, with the thinner piece on top. Enlarge and transfer the hull pattern to the two joined pieces and cut them to shape on the band saw. Before taking the two pieces apart, sand them thoroughly so that they both have the same outer contour. After sanding, separate the pieces, taking care to mark the bottom of the rail piece and the top of the hull piece for fitting together when you assemble the boat, and then transfer the rail pattern to the ¼-inch piece. To cut out the rail on the band saw, first cut off the stern plate and then cut out the rail. The stern plate can be glued back on afterward. Carefully sand the inside of the rail so that it is a uniform ¼-inch all around. Set the pieces aside and cut out the deckhouse, wheelhouse, and smokestack on the band saw. Round the back corners of the wheelhouse and all corners of the smokestack with a wood rasp or surform and sandpaper. Cut the bollards and mast to size. Round the tops of

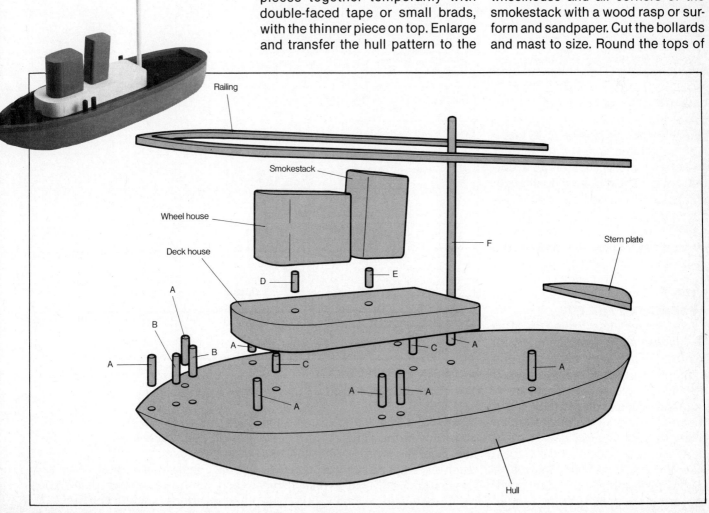

the bollards and the mast slightly with sandpaper.

STEP 2
SHAPING THE HULL

Transfer the hull-bottom pattern to the hull bottom. Using that line as a guide, and with the piece clamped in a vise, shape the stern and bow curves with a wood rasp or surform and sandpaper.

STEP 3
PREPARING FOR ASSEMBLY

Drill 1/4-inch holes 1/4 inch deep where indicated in the hull, deckhouse, wheelhouse, and smokestack. These are for the bollards and mast, and to secure the deckhouse, wheelhouse, and smokestack in the proper positions. You will need four pieces of 1/4-inch dowel about 1/2 inch long. Cut the dowels slightly undersize so that there is room for glue.

STEP 4
PAINTING

All parts should be painted before final assembly, but first make sure they are carefully sanded and all dust removed. The color scheme used in our model is blue for the hull, brown for the deck, white for the mast and deckhouse, blue for the wheelhouse and smokestack, black for the bollards, and red for the rail and stern plate. Do not paint the bottoms of the deckhouse, wheelhouse, smokestack, rail, and stern plate. An easy way to paint the bollards and mast is to drill a series of shallow 1/4-inch holes in a piece of scrap wood, insert the pieces, and paint.

STEP 5
ASSEMBLING THE TUG

Allow enough time for the paint to dry thoroughly. Before gluing, try all joints to make sure everything fits properly. In general, the glue should be used sparingly, keeping it away from the edges of pieces to be glued together. Since all the pieces are already painted, you will want to avoid getting glue on the painted surfaces. Have a damp cloth handy to wipe off any excess immediately. Start with the rail-stern piece. With a small

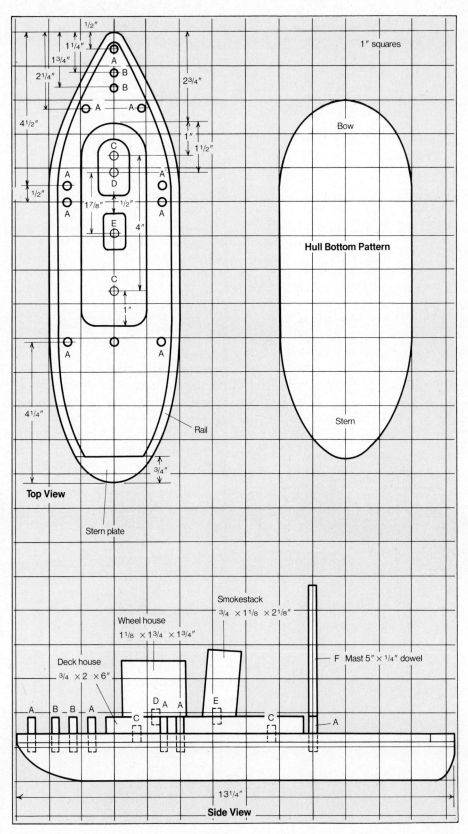

brush, put a thin coat of glue on the underside of the rail and stern plate and press it in place. You can use small pieces of masking tape to hold this in place while you go on with the gluing. Glue the white deckhouse next, using two of the small dowels. The wheelhouse and smokestack are then secured with one dowel each. Finally, put a drop of glue in each of the remaining deck holes and insert the bollards and mast.

Cat Play Clock

MATERIALS LIST

Back panel (1), $1/4'' \times 91/2'' \times 141/4''$
Head (1), $1/4'' \times 41/2'' \times 41/2''$
Face (1), $1/4'' \times 6''$ diameter
Sub-face (1), $1/4'' \times 8''$ diameter
Number disks (12), $1/4'' \times 1''$ diameter
Disk fasteners (12), $1/2'' \times 1/4''$ dowel
Hour hand (1), $1/4'' \times 3/4'' \times 25/8''$
Minute hand (1), $1/4'' \times 3/4'' \times 37/8''$
Tail (1), $1/4'' \times 31/4'' \times 41/2''$
Hanging disk (1), $1/4'' \times 2''$ diameter
Cover disk (1), $1/4'' \times 2''$ diameter
Brass or steel stove bolt, $1/4$—$20 \times 11/4''$
T nut (1), $1/4$—20
Thin brass washers (2), $1/4''$
Plastic stick-on numbers
Yellow wood glue
Nontoxic paint

Tools

Band saw or jigsaw	Masking tape
Drill press	Sandpaper, 80, 120,
Compass	and 220
Awl	C-clamps

Considering the pervasiveness of digital instruments, the traditional clock with circular face and moving hands may soon seem to many children as strange and intriguing a device for measuring the mysteries of time as the hourglass or the sundial. Children can move the hands, set their own time, learn the relation between the position of the hands and the numbers on the face, and discover those old favorites—quarter past, half past, and quarter to.

Hardwood plywood is used in making the clock, and since the edges of the plywood are exposed, we suggest you use lumber-core plywood, which has edges that can be sanded more easily and take paint better than veneer can.

STEP 1
CUTTING THE PIECES

Lay out the pattern for the back panel on the $1/4$-inch plywood and cut out on a jigsaw or band saw with a fine blade. The lower part of the back panel (the body of the cat) is a circle with a radius of $43/4$ inches. It is important for later assembly to mark the center of this circle clearly with an awl. The upper part of the back panel outlines the head and shoul-

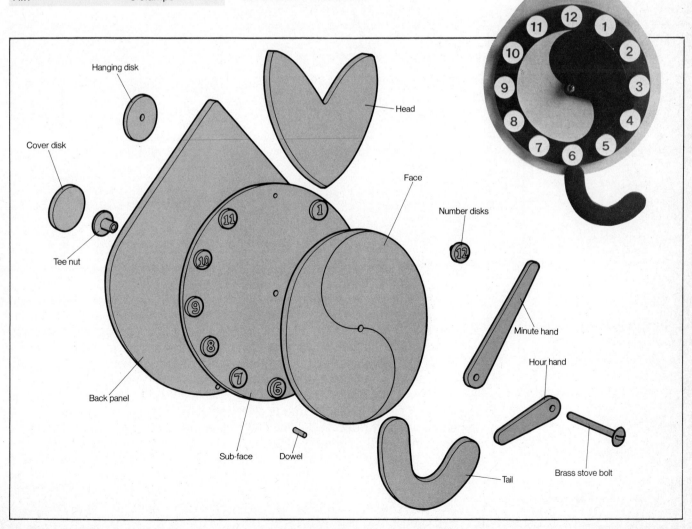

Hanging disk

Cover disk

Tee nut

Back panel

Sub-face

Dowel

Head

Face

Number disks

Minute hand

Hour hand

Tail

Brass stove bolt

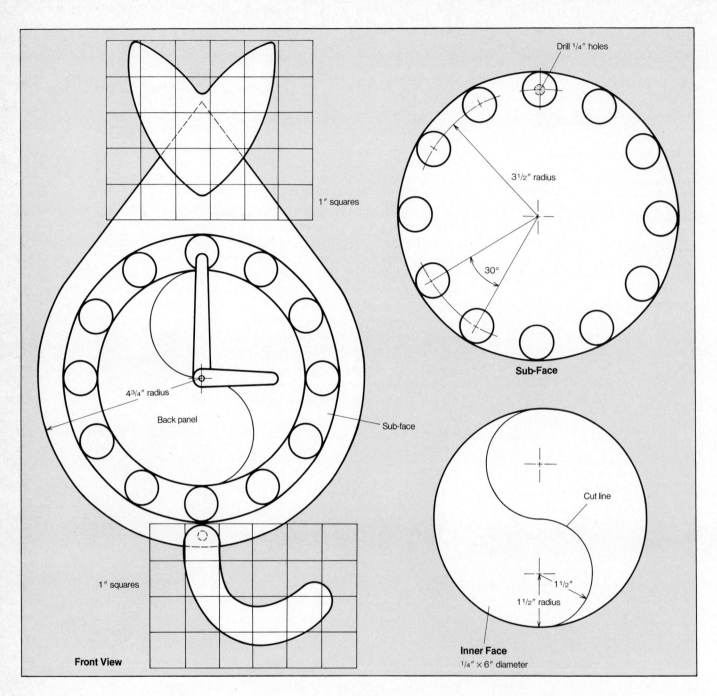

Drill ¼" holes

3½" radius

30°

Sub-Face

Cut line

1½"

1½" radius

Inner Face
¼" × 6" diameter

1" squares

4¾" radius

Back panel

Sub-face

1" squares

Front View

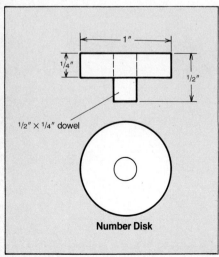

1"

¼"

½"

½" × ¼" dowel

Number Disk

ders of the cat. Next cut the head piece, which will be glued onto the back panel later. Then cut out the sub-face, which is an 8-inch circle. Again, mark the center of this circle. To locate the holes for the number disks, with a compass draw on the sub-face a circle with a radius of 3½ inches. Divide this circle into twelve equal parts by drawing six lines 30° apart through the center of the circle. The intersection of these lines with the circumference of the 7-inch circle will give you twelve centers. Drill a ¼-inch hole through each. For the number disks, lay out twelve 1-inch circles on ¼-inch plywood with a compass. Drill a ¼-inch hole in the center of each circle and cut out the disks on the jigsaw or band saw. Glue a ¼-inch dowel ½ inch long in each of the number disks.

For the face proper, cut out a 6-inch circle of ¼-inch plywood and cut it into two parts along an S-curve line formed with a 1½-inch radius as shown in the plans. Now lay out the patterns for the tail and hands, and cut them out. Then cut out the two ¼- × 2-inch disks for the back of the clock and drill a ¼-inch hole in one disk.

STEP 2
PREPARING FOR ASSEMBLY

Because of the thinness of the parts, we suggest that they be painted before assembly. Sand all parts carefully, especially the edges, and remove all dust. Paint all parts with contrasting colors, using any color scheme you like. Do not paint any edge or surface that is to be glued (see plans). The two halves of the face (the 6-inch circle) should have contrasting light and dark colors.

STEP 3
ASSEMBLING THE CLOCK

Since you will be gluing parts previously painted, care must be taken to protect the surfaces. Use the glue sparingly, keeping it away from edges. Protect the surfaces with wax paper and heavy cardboard when using clamps. Masking tape will not harm a thoroughly dry enameled surface. Only light clamping is necessary for this project.

When all paint is thoroughly dry, begin the assembly by gluing together the two halves of the face panel. Use masking tape to hold the parts while the glue is drying. Next glue the number disks to the subface. Glue the head to the back panel. Drill a 1/8-inch hole in the centers of the back panel, the sub-face, and the face. When gluing the three panels together, insert a 1/8-inch dowel through these holes. This will keep the three pieces properly aligned. Glue on the tail piece with a small 1/4-inch dowel. When the glue is dry, turn the clock around, remove the 1/8-inch dowel and, using the hole as a guide, drill a 3/4-inch hole in the back panel 1/16 inch deep, to accommodate the flange of the T nut. Inside this hole, drill a 5/16-inch hole 1/2 inch deep for the body of the T nut. Finally, drill a 1/4-inch hole through the face for the bolt. Now insert the T nut in the back of the clock and secure it with a light tap of the hammer. Glue the cover disk over the T nut and the hanging disk in the center of the back panel, just below the head. Attach the hands with the bolt and washers and attach the self-adhesive numbers to the number disks.

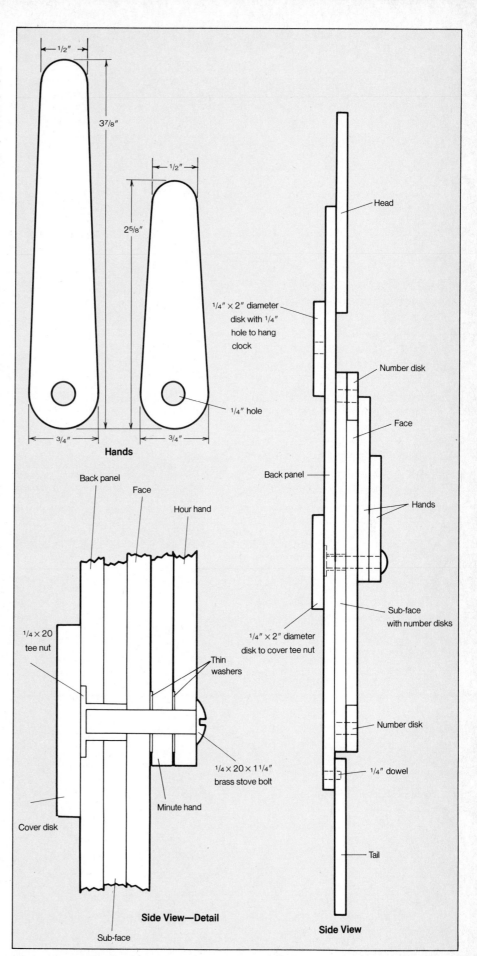

Giant Tic Tac Toe

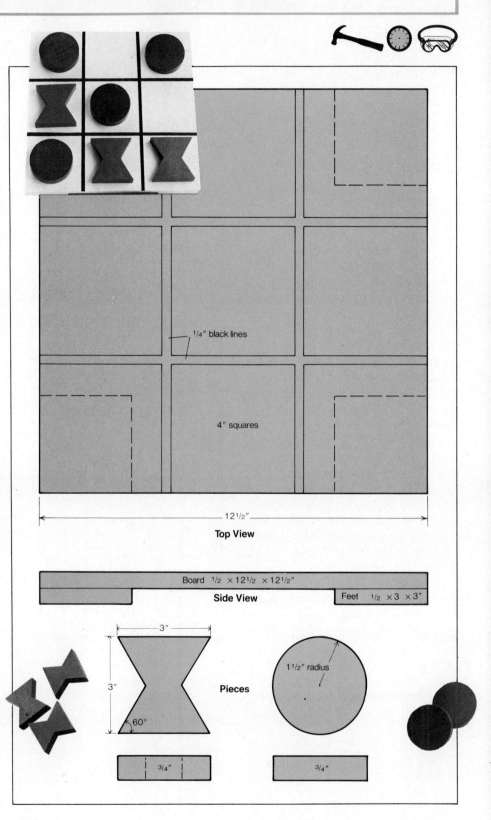

MATERIALS LIST

Game board (1), 1/2″ × 12 1/2″ × 12 1/2″, plywood or hardwood
Feet (4), 1/2″ × 3″ × 3″, plywood or hardwood
X and O pieces (6 of each), 3/4″ stock, plywood, pine, or hardwood
Yellow wood glue
Nontoxic paint

Tools

Table saw
Band saw
C-clamps or masking tape
Sandpaper, 80, 120, and 220

Here's a new twist for an old game. Instead of the usual pencil and paper, a playing board and X's and O's made of wood add excitement and immediacy to a perennial favorite. This is an ideal project for using scrap wood.

STEP 1
CUTTING THE PIECES

Enlarge the drawing for the game board on a piece of plywood or hardwood and then cut it to size. Do the same for the feet. For the circles (O's), cut six 3-inch-diameter disks from 3/4-inch stock. For the X's, first cut six 3-inch squares from 3/4-inch stock on the table saw. Then make four 30° angle cuts for each piece, using the band saw.

STEP 2
GLUING AND SANDING

Before you attach the feet to the game board, be sure to sand the edges of the feet thoroughly. Then put a ribbon of yellow wood glue on the face of each foot and on the four corners of the board. Let the glue stand for a few minutes before you press the feet to the board. You may want to place a heavy weight—a few books, perhaps—on each of the feet, or clamp the feet to the board. You can also use masking tape to secure the feet to the board after they have been glued. Let the glue dry well before you remove the weights or tape. Next, sand all the parts thoroughly. Use a medium and then a fine sandpaper for the job.

STEP 3
FINISHING

Paint the board white. Mark off the 4-inch squares with black paint or black self-adhesive paper, but make sure the white paint is completely dry before marking the squares. The six X's and six O's should be painted with contrasting colors, using any color combination you prefer.

1/4″ black lines

4″ squares

12 1/2″

Top View

Board 1/2 × 12 1/2 × 12 1/2″

Side View   Feet 1/2 × 3 × 3″

3″

3″

60°

Pieces

1 1/2″ radius

3/4″   3/4″

Shuffleboard

MATERIALS LIST

Playing panel (1), 1/2″ × 10 3/4″ × 39″, hardwood
  plywood
Support panel (1), 1/2″ × 15″ × 41″, hardwood
  plywood
Playing-panel trim, 1/8″ × 1/2″ × 100″,
  hardwood
Support-panel frame, 3/8″ × 11/2″ × 112″,
  hardwood
Score lines (4), 1/8″ × 1/4″ × 10 3/8″, hardwood of
  contrasting color
Target circle (1), 1/2″ × 2 1/2″ diameter,
  hardwood of contrasting color
Disks (6), 3/4″ × 2″ diameter, hardwood
Yellow wood glue
Nontoxic clear finish
Nontoxic paint

Tools

	Saber saw
Table saw	Router or dado head
Band saw	Masking tape
Hole saw	Sandpaper, 80, 120, and 220

Each player starts with three disks, and the aim is to slide the disk into the center of the 50-point target circle. The disk must be completely inside the target circle to get 50 points; otherwise, it scores only 10 points, with each of the other areas yielding the scores indicated. The disks can be knocked out by subsequent throws. If the disk is knocked off the playing surface, the player loses those points. If the disk is knocked into an area with lower points, that becomes the score.

STEP 1
CUTTING AND ASSEMBLING

Cut playing panel, support panel, trim, and frame pieces to size on the table saw. On the playing panel, cut four 1/4-inch grooves, spaced as shown, with a router or dado head on the table saw, to a depth of 1/8 inch. Glue the four 1/4-inch strips (of contrasting color) into the grooves to make the score lines. Cut out the 2 1/2-inch-diameter target circle, centered as shown, with a hole saw or saber saw. Then glue in a target circle (1/2 × 2 1/2-inch diameter) of contrasting wood. Cut the trim to size, miter the corners, and glue it to three sides of the playing panel, using masking tape to hold the trim in place until the glue dries. Glue the playing surface to the support panel with the untrimmed edge of the playing surface flush with one end of the support panel, using masking tape to hold it in place. Cut the disks on the band saw.

STEP 2
FINISHING

Sand all surfaces carefully, especially the playing panel and the tops of the playing circle and the score-line strips, to make a smooth sliding surface. Finish with two coats of clear nontoxic finish. Paint three disks in one color and the other three in a different color. More disks can, of course, be made for more players. Point numbers can be stick-on plastic numbers or painted on.

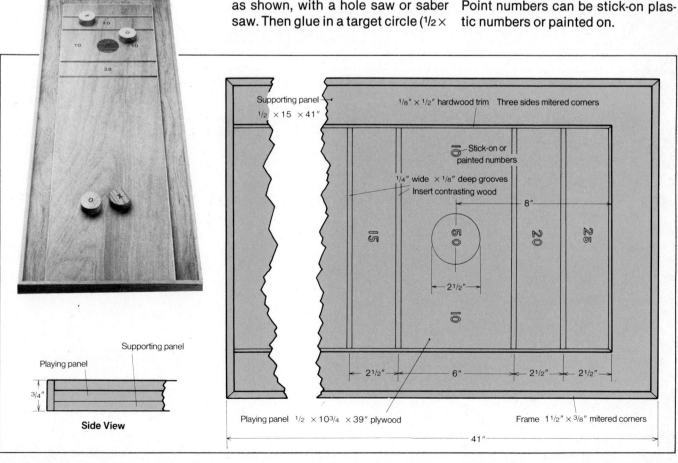

Side View

Supporting panel
1/2 × 15 × 41″

1/8″ × 1/2″ hardwood trim   Three sides mitered corners

Stick-on or painted numbers

1/4″ wide × 1/8″ deep grooves
Insert contrasting wood

8″

15   50   20   25

2 1/2″

10

2 1/2″   6″   2 1/2″   2 1/2″

Playing panel 1/2 × 10 3/4 × 39″ plywood

Frame 1 1/2″ × 3/8″ mitered corners

41″

Disk Bowling Game

MATERIALS LIST

Bowling panel (1), 1/2″ × 11 3/4″ × 40″, hardwood plywood

Support panel (1), 1/2″ × 16″ × 42″, hardwood plywood

Bowling-panel trim, 1/8″ × 1/2″ × 104″, hardwood

Frame pieces, 3/8″ × 1 1/2″ × 126″, hardwood

Pin-position markers (10), 1/4″ dowel, hardwood of contrasting color

Cat pins (10), 3/4″ × 2 1/2″ × 4 7/8″, hardwood

Bowling disks (2-4), 3/4″ × 2 1/2″ diameter, hardwood

Yellow wood glue

Nontoxic clear finish

Nontoxic paint

Tools

Table saw	Wood rasp
Band or scroll saw	Masking tape
Drill or drill press	Sandpaper, 80, 120, and 220

Each player gets two throws of a disk. Scoring can be based on the number of cat pins dropped, or points can be assigned to each cat pin to make a total score.

STEP 1
CUTTING AND ASSEMBLING THE PIECES

Cut bowling panel, support panel, trim, and frame pieces to size on the table saw. Glue trim to the bowling panel on three sides, using mitered corners as shown, and apply masking tape to hold in position until the glue dries. Mark positions of ten pin markers on bowling panel and drill 1/4-inch holes 1/8 inch deep. Fill these holes with short pieces of 1/4-inch dowel of contrasting color. Glue the bowling panel to the support panel with the untrimmed end of the bowling panel flush with one end of the

support panel, leaving a 2-inch "gutter" on each side. Next, glue the frame to the support panel, again using mitered corners, with masking tape to hold in position until glue dries. Now the bowling disks can be cut out on the band saw. Finally, trace the cat-pin pattern on 3/4-inch stock and cut out ten pins.

STEP 2
FINISHING THE BOARD AND PIECES

Round the edges of the cat pins with a rasp and sandpaper. Sand the bowling surface, support, and frame, paying particular attention to the bowling panel. It should be very smooth so that the disks slide easily. Finish with two coats of a clear nontoxic finish. The disks can be painted with different colors for different players. More disks can be made to accommodate more players.

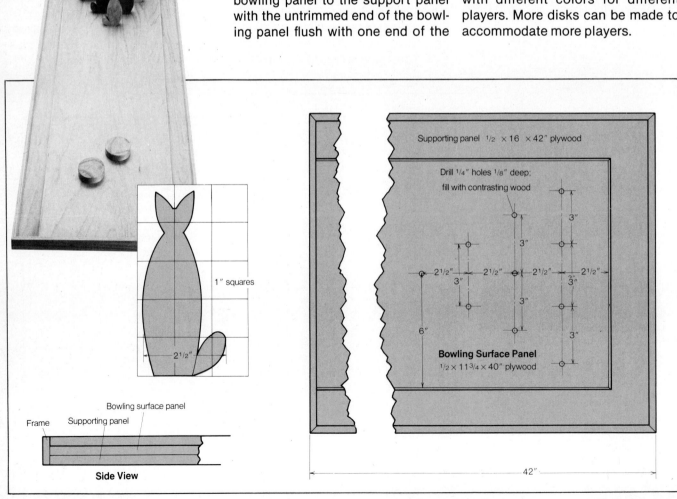

1″ squares

2 1/2″

Frame Supporting panel Bowling surface panel

Side View

Supporting panel 1/2 × 16 × 42″ plywood

Drill 1/4″ holes 1/8″ deep; fill with contrasting wood

3″ 3″ 3″

2 1/2″ 2 1/2″ 2 1/2″ 2 1/2″

3″ 3″

6″ 3″

Bowling Surface Panel
1/2 × 11 3/4 × 40″ plywood

42″

Toy Soldier

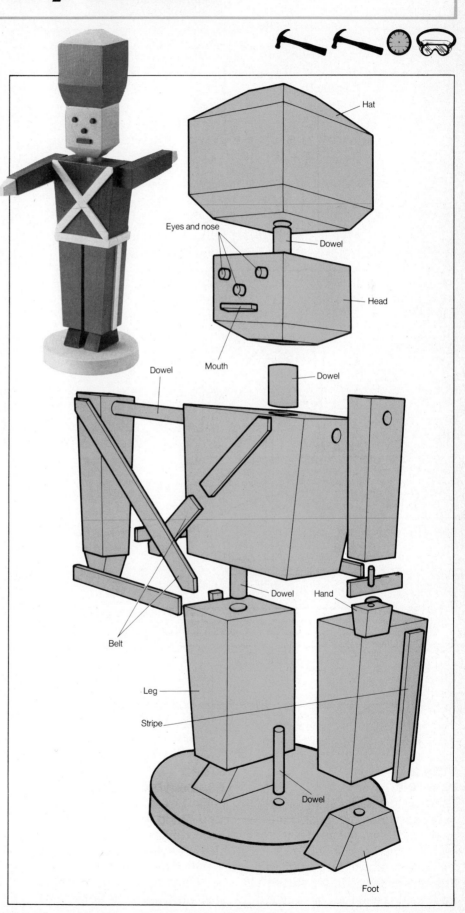

MATERIALS LIST

Helmet (1), $2^{1/2}'' \times 2^{3/4}'' \times 3^{1/2}''$, pine
Head (1), $2'' \times 2^{1/2}'' \times 2^{1/2}''$, pine
Neck (1), $1^{1/4}'' \times {}^{3/4}''$ dowel, hardwood
Body (1), $2'' \times 3^{1/2}'' \times 4''$, pine
Legs (2), $1^{3/8}'' \times 2'' \times 4^{1/2}''$, pine
Arms (2), ${}^{3/4}'' \times 1'' \times 4^{1/2}''$, pine
Hands (2), ${}^{1/2}'' \times {}^{5/8}'' \times {}^{7/8}''$, pine
Feet (2), ${}^{7/8}'' \times {}^{7/8}'' \times 2''$, pine
Base (1), ${}^{3/4}'' \times 5''$ diameter, pine
Joint dowels (as needed), ${}^{3/16}''$, ${}^{3/8}''$, and ${}^{1/2}''$,
   hardwood
Eyes (2) and nose (1), ${}^{3/8}'' \times {}^{1/4}''$ dowel,
   hardwood
Mouth (1), ${}^{1/8}'' \times {}^{3/16}'' \times {}^{3/4}''$, pine
Leg stripes (2), ${}^{1/8}'' \times {}^{3/8}'' \times 4^{3/4}''$, pine
Waist and body belts, ${}^{1/8}'' \times {}^{3/8}'' \times 32''$, pine
Yellow wood glue
Paint
*(Dimensions larger than those shown in
drawings allow for saw, angle, or bevel cuts.)*

Tools

Table saw
Drill or drill press
Fine-tooth backsaw
Razor saw
Light wood clamps
Masking tape
Sandpaper, 80, 120, and 220

Proud and correct, this soldier is always ready to stand guard and do his duty. His colorful uniform gives him a special attractiveness.

STEP 1
CUTTING AND DRILLING THE PIECES

First cut all pieces to sizes given in the Materials List. Before cutting the pieces to their final shape, locate and drill all joint holes. The helmet and head require several angle cuts. These can be made on the table saw or with a fine-tooth backsaw. The remaining pieces need slight taper cuts as shown. Cut all joint dowels to size, as well as the small dowels and mouth strip for the face. Cut the leg stripes, waist belt, and body belts. Note that the body belts require 45° cuts at the shoulders and waist.

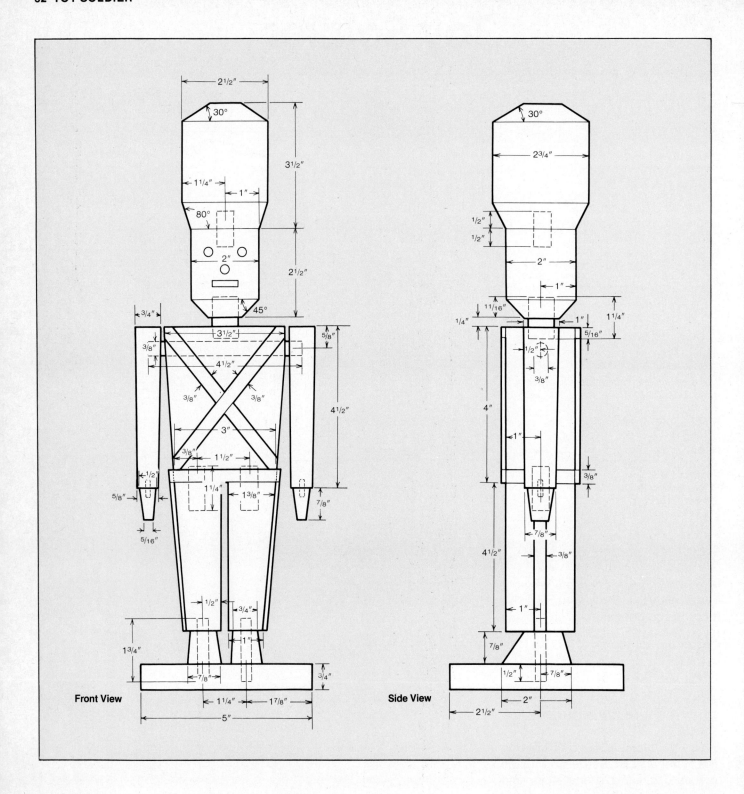

Front View

Side View

STEP 2
PAINTING

Sand all parts, finishing with 220 sandpaper. Remove dust. Paint all parts with bright colors of a nontoxic enamel. The head should be a neutral color—brown, tan, or off-white. The undersides of the leg stripes and body belting need not be painted.

STEP 3
ASSEMBLING THE SOLDIER

Begin assembly by gluing on the leg stripes and body belts, using light wood clamps or masking tape. Next glue the helmet to the head with the 1/2-inch dowel. Glue the neck to the body, but not to the head. The hands are then glued to the arms. Insert the arm dowel through the body and fit the arms on the dowel. Do not glue. Glue the leg dowels to the body. Insert these dowels into the legs, but do not glue them. Glue the base dowels to the legs. Insert these dowels through the feet and into the base, without gluing. Dowels that are not glued will permit some mobility.

Robot Puzzle

MATERIALS LIST

Body (1), 1¹/8" × 4" × 5", pine or hardwood
Head (1), 1" × 2" × 2", pine or hardwood
Arms (2), 3/4" × 3/4" × 5", pine or hardwood
Legs (2), 1" × 1" × 5¹/2", pine or hardwood
Feet (2), 1¹/8" × 1¹/2" × 2¹/2", pine or hardwood
Hands (2), 3/4" × 3/4" × 1", pine or hardwood
Eyes (2), 5/8" × 1/2" dowel, hardwood
Glue dowels (as needed; sizes shown in
   plan), hardwood
Accessories, 1/4" stock (as needed), pine or
   hardwood
Yellow wood glue
Nontoxic paint

Tools

Table saw or handsaw   Compass
Band saw or jigsaw   Sandpaper, 80, 120,
Drill or drill press   and 220

The possibility of constructing a mechanical imitation of a human being has tantalized man's imagination for centuries. This old-fashioned robot, which harks back to earlier prototypes so different from sophisticated contemporary, electronic models, should tug at the imagination of small human beings. It will especially intrigue those who like to handle things physically and put their constructional skills to work. The parts go together easily, and the robot toy has limited maneuverability.

STEP 1
CUTTING THE PIECES

Cut the main pieces, the head, body, arms, legs, hands, and feet to size as indicated. Drill all holes to sizes and depths shown. It is best to do this on the drill press so that you have depth control and the holes are true. The accessories are all cut from 1/4-inch stock. For the smaller ones, it is best to drill the holes first and then cut them out on the jigsaw or band saw. Cut the dowels to sizes and lengths indicated.

STEP 2
ASSEMBLING THE ROBOT

Glue the dowels into the joints in the head, arms, legs, hands, and feet. Glue dowels in the accessories. Glue

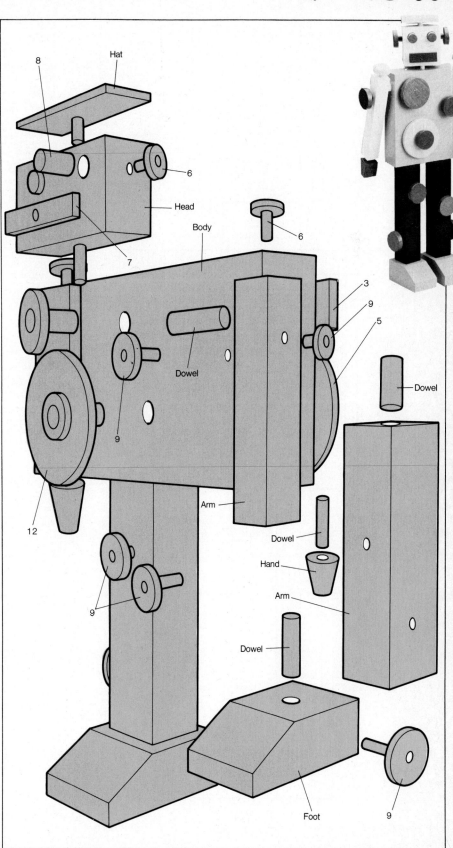

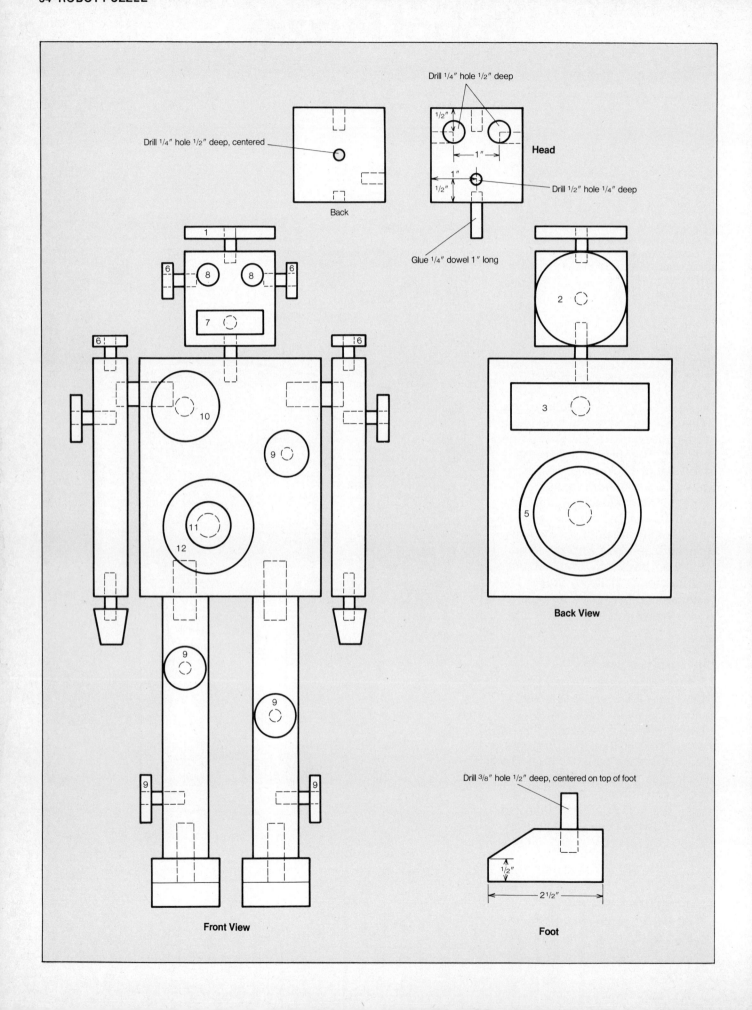

Drill ¼″ hole ½″ deep, centered

Back

Drill ¼″ hole ½″ deep

½″

1″

1″

½″

Head

Drill ½″ hole ¼″ deep

Glue ¼″ dowel 1″ long

Back View

Drill ³⁄₈″ hole ½″ deep, centered on top of foot

½″

2½″

Foot

Front View

all ¾-inch and 1-inch disks into the arms, legs, head, and body. Glue eyes in place.

STEP 3
FINISHING

Sand all pieces carefully, finishing with 220 sandpaper, and remove all dust. Since this is a puzzle and the parts are removable, care must be taken not to get paint in the open holes. The best way to do this is to insert small pieces of dowels in the holes while painting. All the pieces have dowels except the body and pieces 5 and 12, and so the easiest way to paint them is to drill holes of the proper size in a piece of scrap wood, insert the pieces, and paint. This will also protect the dowels from paint. To paint the pieces that do not have dowels, you can insert short lengths of dowel into them temporarily. Finish with two coats of nontoxic enamel of contrasting colors. For our robot puzzle, we painted the body and feet light gray, the legs black, the arms and head white, and the accessories blue, red, and yellow. You can design your own.

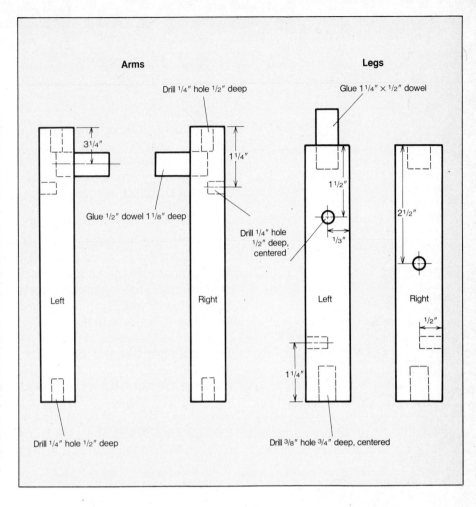

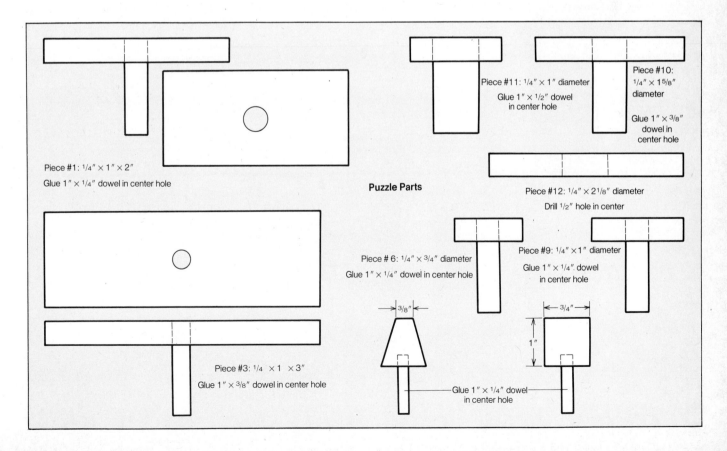

Indoor Pet House

MATERIALS LIST
Front (1), 1/2″ × 12″ × 18″, hardwood plywood
Back (1), 1/2″ × 12″ × 18″, hardwood plywood
Bottom (1), 1/2″ × 10″ × 14 1/2″, hardwood plywood
Roof (10), 1/2″ × 2″ × 16 1/2″, pine or hardwood
Sides (12), 1/2″ × 2″ × 15″, pine or hardwood
Roof beam (1), 1/2″ × 1/2″ × 14″, pine or hardwood
Brads, 1″
Yellow wood glue
Wood putty
Nontoxic paint

Tools
Table saw	Nailset
Saber saw	Drum sander
Drill	Masking tape
Router	Sandpaper, 80, 120,
Hammer	and 220

Everyone has a pet of some sort, and here's a chance to go into the real estate business and build an attractive home for small animals or stuffed toys. Kittens love to scramble on the roof and dive in the side door and out the front, and sometimes to curl up inside, away from it all. Children can arrange their stuffed bears, pandas, or elephants in this residence.

STEP 1
CUTTING THE PIECES
Cut two panels of 1/2-inch plywood 12 × 18 inches for the front and back of the house. Fasten the two panels together with masking tape, and make two 45° cuts from the center of one of the 12-inch ends of the panels. This will form the roof peak. Then make two 5° cuts 1 inch in from the bottom edge, along the long sides toward the top. This will form the bottom of the front and back panels. Next take the panels apart and cut a rabbet 1/4 inch deep and 1/2 inch high along the bottom of each panel, using the table saw or router. The bottom panel will fit into this rabbet. Then cut a 7 1/2-inch-diameter hole in the center of one of the panels 2 1/4 inches from the bottom, using the saber saw. Sand the inside of the opening with a drum sander. This panel is now the front of the house. Now cut the 1/2- × 10- × 14 1/2-inch bottom panel and bevel each of the long sides 5°. Cut the roof beam from hardwood. Sand all parts carefully.

STEP 2
ASSEMBLING ROOF AND SIDES
The roof and sides are made of 1/2- × 2-inch strips of hardwood. The roof consists of ten strips 16 1/2 inches long. Eight of these strips have a 30° chamfer 3/16 inch wide along both top edges. The other two strips have

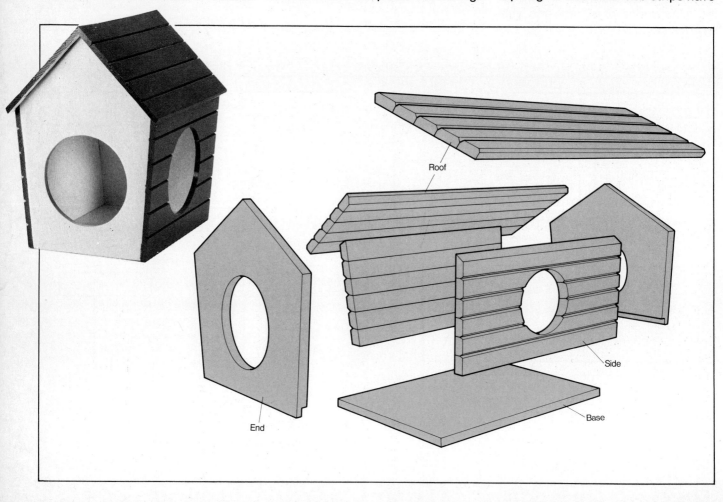

Roof

Side

Base

End

the chamfer along only one edge and a 45° bevel along the other edge. The two 45° bevels form the roof peak. The sides are made from twelve ½- × 2-inch strips that are 15 inches long. Eight of these have the same chamfer as the roof pieces, but two of the strips have the chamfer on only one edge with a 5° bevel on the other edge. The two remaining strips have the chamfer on one edge and a 50° bevel on the other edge.

To form the roof panels, glue four double-chamfered strips and one 45° beveled strip together, edge to edge, using masking tape to secure the joints until the glue is dry, and then glue the two 45° beveled edges together to form the whole peaked roof. Each side is formed with six strips, with the 5° bevel on the bottom and the 50° bevel on top. Glue them together, edge to edge. Use masking tape to hold the strips together until the glue dries. When the glue is dry, cut a 7½-inch hole in the center of the left side. Sand all parts carefully and remove all dust.

STEP 3
ASSEMBLING THE PET HOUSE
Glue the bottom panel into the rabbets in the inside bottom edges of the front and back panels, taking care that the bevel of the bottom matches the slant of the front and back panels. Glue the roof beam to the tops of the front and back panels, forming a sharp ridge on which the roof will rest. Secure the glue joints with 1-inch brads, set the brads, and fill the holes with wood putty. Glue the sides to the edges of the front and back panels and to the bottom. Glue the roof into place, with an overhang of ¾ inch front and back. Secure all joints with 1-inch brads, set the brads, and fill the holes with wood putty.

STEP 4
FINISHING
Sand all nail-hole fillings smooth, and give the whole house a final sanding with 220 sandpaper. Paint the house with two coats of nontoxic enamel in whatever colors your pet lover enjoys.

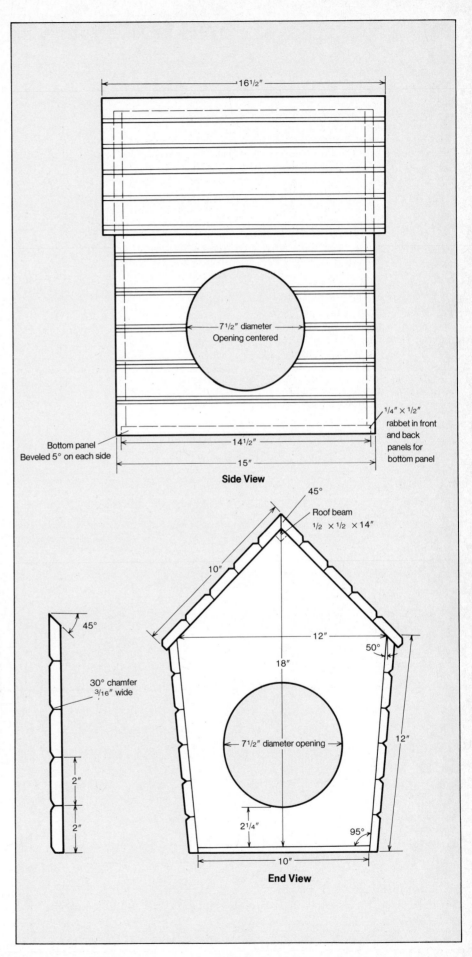

16½"

7½" diameter
Opening centered

¼" × ½" rabbet in front and back panels for bottom panel

Bottom panel
Beveled 5° on each side

14½"

15"

Side View

45°

Roof beam
½ × ½ × 14"

10"

45°

30° chamfer
3/16" wide

2"

2"

12"

50°

18"

7½" diameter opening

12"

2¼"

95"

10"

End View

Circus Train

MATERIALS LIST

Locomotive chassis (1), $1/2'' \times 3^3/4'' \times 8''$, pine
Cab top (1), $3/8'' \times 3^1/8'' \times 3^1/4''$, pine
Cab sides (2), $3/8'' \times 2^3/4'' \times 3^1/8''$, pine
Side cleats (2), $3/8'' \times 3/8'' \times 2^3/4''$, pine
Cab floor (1), $3/8'' \times 2^1/4'' \times 2^3/8''$, pine
Cab front (1), $3/8'' \times 2^1/4'' \times 3^1/8''$, pine
Boiler (1), $2'' \times 2'' \times 4^1/4''$, pine
Steam dome (1), $1^3/4'' \times 7/8''$ dowel, hardwood
Smokestack (1), $1^5/8'' \times 1^5/8'' \times 1^3/4''$, pine
Smokestack holder (1), $1'' \times 3/4''$ dowel, hardwood
Large wheels (2), $1/2'' \times 2^1/2''$ diameter, pine
Small wheels (24), $1/2'' \times 1^1/2''$ diameter, pine
Axle holders (12), $3/8'' \times 3/4'' \times 3^3/4''$, pine
Axles (12), $4^7/8'' \times 1/4''$ dowel, hardwood
Car connectors (6), $3/8'' \times 1'' \times 1^3/4''$, pine
Car hooks (5), $1'' \times 1/4''$ dowel, hardwood
Boxcar chassis (1), $1/2'' \times 3^3/4'' \times 6''$, pine
Boxcar sides (2), $3/8'' \times 3'' \times 4^1/4''$, pine
Car ends (10), $3/8'' \times 3'' \times 3^3/4''$, pine
Open-car chassis (2), $1/2'' \times 3^3/4'' \times 7''$, pine

Open-car sides (4), $3/8'' \times 3/8'' \times 11''$, pine
Cage-car chassis (2), $1/2'' \times 3^3/4'' \times 7''$, pine
Cage-car crossbars (4), $3/8'' \times 1'' \times 3^3/4''$, pine
Cage-car bar holders (4), $3/8'' \times 3/8'' \times 5^1/4''$, pine
Cage-car bars (24), $3^3/4'' \times 3/16''$ dowel, hardwood
Animals (10), $1''$ stock, pine
Brads, $5/8''$, $3/4''$, and $1''$
Yellow wood glue
Nontoxic paint
Nontoxic clear finish

Tools

Table saw
Band saw or jigsaw
Block plane
Hammer
Light wood clamps
Masking tape
Sandpaper, 80, 120, and 220

The arrival of the circus in town is a glorious event. Two ideas are combined in the circus train—transportation and the public parade through the streets to the show grounds, where the eagerly awaited performance will begin. The individual cars are detachable and interchangeable.

STEP 1
CUTTING THE PIECES

Cut all parts to dimensions shown. The locomotive chassis is beveled 45° at the front end. The cab sides have a 1-inch hole drilled in the center, 3/4 inch from the top. The sides of the boxcar are curved at the top and

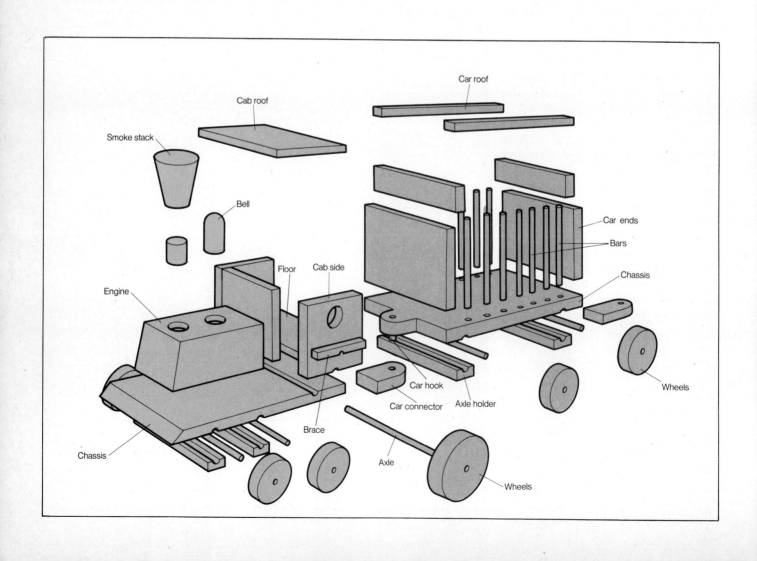

have three 1-inch holes. See plans for patterns. The five cars have a 1-inch projection as part of the chassis for the car hooks. Drill a 1/4-inch hole in each projection for the hooks. The car connectors are separate pieces that have 5/16-inch holes and are glued to the cars, including the loco-motive.

STEP 2
SHAPING THE STEAM DOME AND SMOKESTACK

The steam dome is a 7/8-inch dowel rounded with a wood rasp and sand-paper. Before shaping the boiler, lo-cate and drill the holes for the smokestack and dome. To shape the boiler, inscribe a 2-inch circle on one end of the block and cut four 45° bev-els along the 4 1/4-inch edges tangent to the circle, forming an octagon. Leave one side flat (to be glued to the chassis), and shape the 2-inch-diameter cylinder with a plane and

sandpaper. Drill a 3/4-inch hole 1/2 inch deep in the center of one end of the smokestack block. To form the smokestack, set the band saw blade at 15° and cut a truncated cone from the block with a diameter of 7/8 inch at the bottom (where the 3/4-inch hole has been drilled) and a diameter of 1 5/8 inches at the top.

STEP 3
DRILLING CAGE CARS FOR BARS

Locate and drill the holes for cage-car bars in the cage-car chassis and bar holders. These holes are 1/8 inch deep. Each of the four sides of the open cars is made up of a 3/8- × 3/8- ×

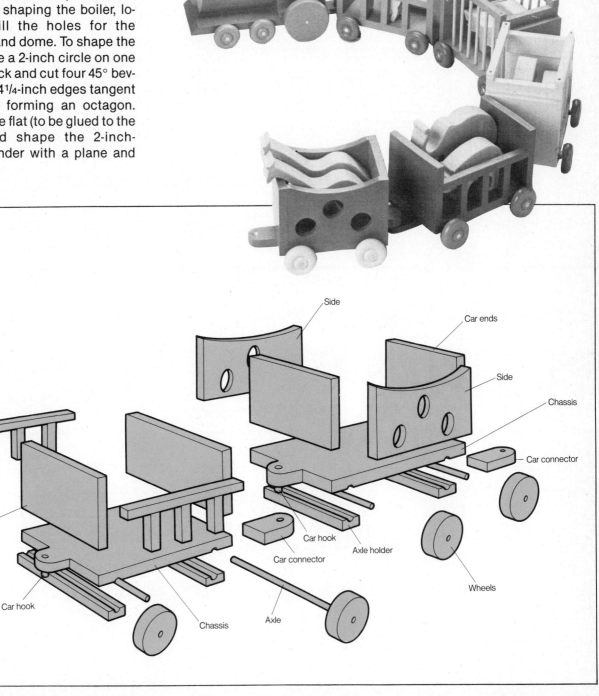

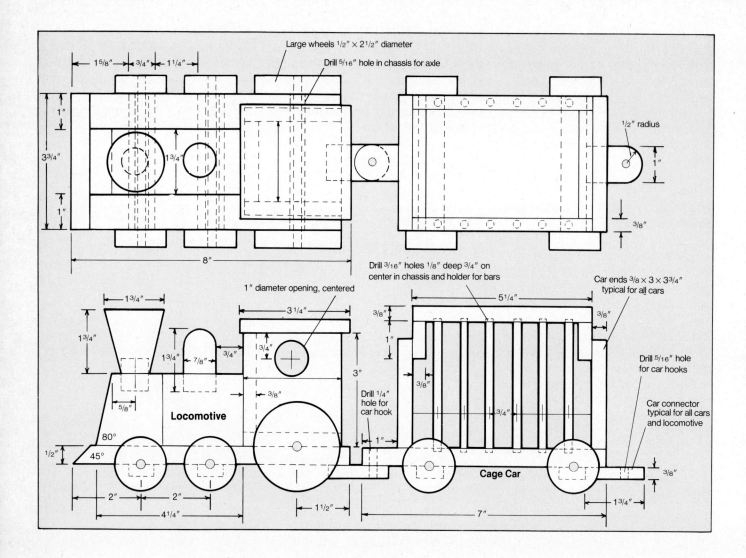

Large wheels 1/2" × 2 1/2" diameter

Drill 5/16" hole in chassis for axle

1 5/8" 3/4" 1 1/4"

1"

3 3/4"

1 3/4"

1"

8"

1/2" radius

1"

3/8"

Drill 3/16" holes 1/8" deep 3/4" on center in chassis and holder for bars

1" diameter opening, centered

Car ends 3/8 × 3 × 3 3/4" typical for all cars

5 1/4"

3/8"

3/8"

1 3/4"

1 3/4"

7/8"

3/4"

1 3/4"

3/4"

3/8"

3"

3/8"

Locomotive

Drill 1/4" hole for car hook

1"

1"

3/4"

Drill 5/16" hole for car hooks

Car connector typical for all cars and locomotive

5/8"

80°

1/2"

45°

2"

2"

Cage Car

4 1/4"

1 1/2"

7"

3/8"

1 3/4"

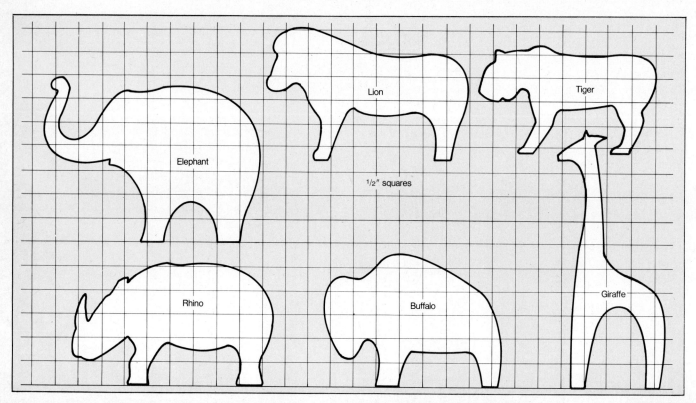

Elephant

Lion

Tiger

1/2" squares

Rhino

Buffalo

Giraffe

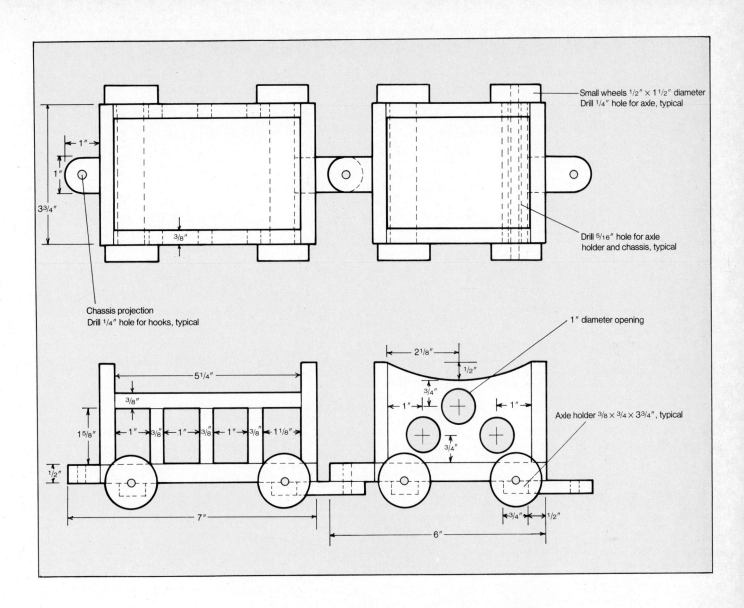

Small wheels $1/2$" $\times$ $11/2$" diameter
Drill $1/4$" hole for axle, typical

Drill $5/16$" hole for axle holder and chassis, typical

Chassis projection
Drill $1/4$" hole for hooks, typical

1" diameter opening

Axle holder $3/8 \times 3/4 \times 33/4$", typical

$5/4$-inch crossbar and three $3/8$- $\times$ $3/8$- $\times$ $15/8$-inch uprights.

STEP 4
CUTTING OUT THE ANIMALS
Sand all train parts, finishing with 220 sandpaper. The animals are cut from 1-inch pine with the grain running vertically. Enlarge and transfer the patterns to the 1-inch stock and cut out with a jigsaw. Sand all animals thoroughly and round all edges. For more animals, use the patterns for Noah's Ark animals on page 122.

STEP 5
ASSEMBLING THE PARTS
Glue the axle holders to the chassis of all cars and the locomotive. When the glue has dried, drill the $5/16$-inch axle holes through the axle holders

and chassis. Assemble the five parts of the cab unit with glue and light brads. Glue the unit to the locomotive chassis $1/4$ inch from the back end. Glue the side cleats on each side of the cab. When the glue is dry, drill the $5/16$-inch axle hole for the large wheels. Glue the boiler to the chassis and cab. Glue the four sides of the boxcar to the boxcar chassis using light brads. Glue the four ends of the open cars to the open-car chassis. Glue in the $3/8$- $\times$ $3/8$-inch bars that make up the sides of the open cars. To make the cage cars, glue the ends in place first and then the crossbars to the ends. Do not put in the bars or bar holders at this time. Glue a car connector to each car, including the locomotive. Glue a car hook to each of the chassis projections on the five cars.

STEP 6
FINISHING AND FINAL ASSEMBLY
Before the final assembly, paint all cars and wheels in bright colors of nontoxic enamel. The color of the wheels should contrast with the color of the cars. Do not paint the bars of the cage cars. The smokestack and steam dome should differ in color from the locomotive. The animals can be finished with nontoxic clear finish. When the paint is dry, glue in the smokestack and dome. Insert the bars of the cage cars in the chassis holes and into the holes in the holders. It is not necessary to glue the bars. Glue the bar holders to the crossbars, securing them with light clamps and pads so as not to mar the painted surface. Install the wheels by gluing them to the axles.

Farm Tractor and Wagon

MATERIALS LIST

Tractor

Chassis (1), $1/2'' \times 4'' \times 10^{1/2}''$
Fenders (2), $3/8'' \times 1^{3/4}'' \times 3^{7/8}''$
Motor housing (1), $1/2'' \times 2'' \times 9''$
Motor block (1), $1'' \times 1^{1/2}'' \times 4^{1/2}''$
Footboard (1), $1/2'' \times 1'' \times 3''$
Seat (1), $1/4'' \times 3/4'' \times 5''$
Steering-post holder (1), $1/2'' \times 3/4'' \times 3''$
Steering post (1), $2^{3/4}'' \times 3/16''$ dowel
Steering wheel (1), $3/16'' \times 7/8''$ diameter
Rear wheels (2), $3/4'' \times 5''$ diameter
Front wheels (2), $1/2'' \times 2^{1/2}''$ diameter
Rear axle holders (2), $1^{1/4}'' \times 1^{1/4}'' \times 1^{3/8}''$
Front axle holders (2), $3/4'' \times 1'' \times 2^{1/8}''$
Rear axle (1), $6^{5/8}'' \times 3/8''$ dowel
Front axle (1), $4^{1/8}'' \times 1/4''$ dowel
Exhaust, air intake, radiator cap, and fastening dowels, $3/16''$ and $1/4''$ dowels (as needed), hardwood

Wagon

Wagon bottom (1), $1/2'' \times 6'' \times 8^{3/4}''$
Sides (2), $1/2'' \times 3'' \times 9^{3/4}''$

Ends (2), $1/2'' \times 3'' \times 6''$
Connector holder (1), $1/2'' \times 1^{5/8}'' \times 3''$
Connector (1), $3/8'' \times 1'' \times 3''$
Connector pins (2), $1^{1/4}'' \times 3/8''$ dowel
Axle holders (2), $3/4'' \times 2'' \times 7''$
Axles (2), $9^{1/8}'' \times 1/4''$ dowel
Wheels (4), $3/4'' \times 3''$ diameter
Yellow wood glue
Nontoxic paint or clear finish
(Dimensions larger than those shown in drawings allow for saw, angle, or bevel cuts.)

Tools

Table saw
Coping saw
Saber saw
Fine-tooth backsaw
Band saw
Drill or drill press
Bar clamps
C-clamps
Fine or medium wood rasp
Masking tape
Sandpaper, 80, 120, and 220

Tractors seem to have a special appeal to youngsters, perhaps because they perform so many different tasks—mowing lawns, bringing in the hay, clearing rocks and tree stumps from a piece of land. Before starting the assembly of the tractor and wagon, *be sure to read Step 4;* the assembly will differ slightly if you decide to paint instead of using a clear finish. The wagon sides and bottom involve angle and bevel cuts, and the dimensions given include room for these cuts. This project is constructed either of pine or hardwood.

STEP 1
CUTTING THE PIECES

Cut out all pieces for the tractor and

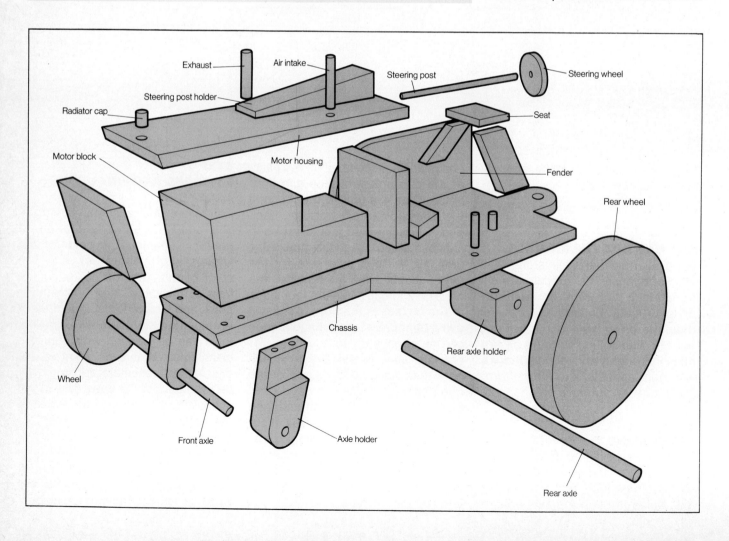

Exhaust
Air intake
Steering post
Steering wheel
Steering post holder
Radiator cap
Seat
Motor block
Motor housing
Fender
Rear wheel
Chassis
Rear axle holder
Wheel
Front axle
Axle holder
Rear axle

for the wagon to the sizes indicated in the plans and details on pages 64 and 65, using the table saw or fine-tooth backsaw. The curved parts of the tractor such as the fenders, wheels, and axle holders can be cut out on the band saw, saber saw, or coping saw. Take special care with the angle and bevel cuts of the wagon pieces. Now drill all holes in the sizes and the locations indicated. Then round the edges of all wheels with a fine or medium wood rasp and with sandpaper. Round the top edges of the seat, footboard, fenders, and motor housing. Sand all pieces well, ending with 220 sandpaper.

STEP 2
ASSEMBLING THE TRACTOR
Begin the assembly by attaching the rear and front axle holders to the chassis, using glue and 3/16-inch dowels. Note that the rear axle holders project 1/4 inch out from the chassis. The upper parts of the front axle holders are flush with the sides of the chassis, while the lower parts project 1/4 inch from the sides of the 2-inch ends of the chassis. Assemble the three parts of the motor housing, and the motor block, as a unit, using glue and securing them with light clamps or masking tape. This unit is then glued to the front end of the chassis. Next glue the steering-post holder to the top of the motor housing. Attach the fenders to the chassis, noting that the fenders are placed 1/8 inch in from the edge of the chassis. Glue in the footboard. Now assemble the three parts of the seat as a unit, and then glue it between the fenders. Insert the steering post and wheel, air intake, exhaust, and radiator cap with a bit of glue. Insert the front and rear axles through their axle holders and attach the respective wheels to them with glue, but with the axles projecting 1/4-inch from the wheels. Because the holes in the axle holders are slightly larger than the axles, each pair of wheels will turn freely as a unit.

STEP 3
ASSEMBLING THE WAGON
First glue the axle holders to the bottom of the wagon, using 3/16-inch dowels up through the holders into the wagon bottom. Next glue the two end pieces to the bottom, and then the sides to the ends and bottom, securing with masking tape and light bar clamps. Now glue the connector holder to one end of the wagon flush with the bottom. Secure it with 3/16-inch dowels. Glue one wheel to its axle, insert it into the axle holder, and then glue on the other wheel; axles should project 1/4-inch outside each wheel. There will be a 1/16-inch space between the wheels and the axle holder, for free movement. Glue the 3/8-inch dowel pins to the connector plate with a 1/8-inch projection of the pins above the plate.

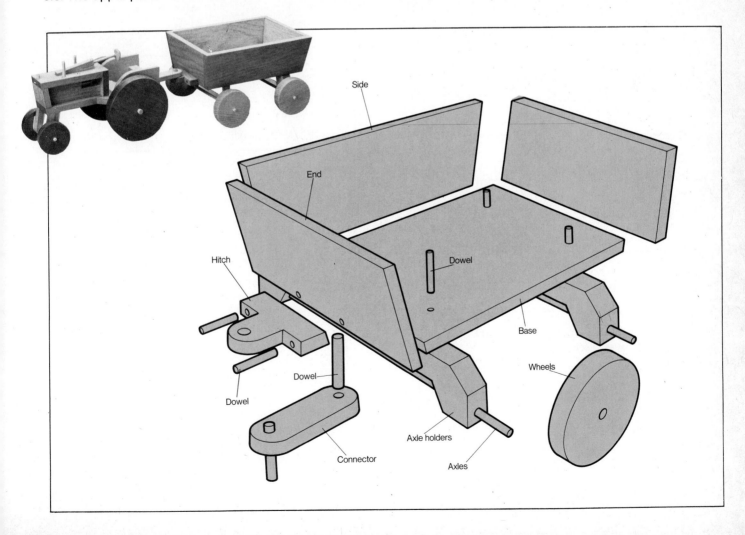

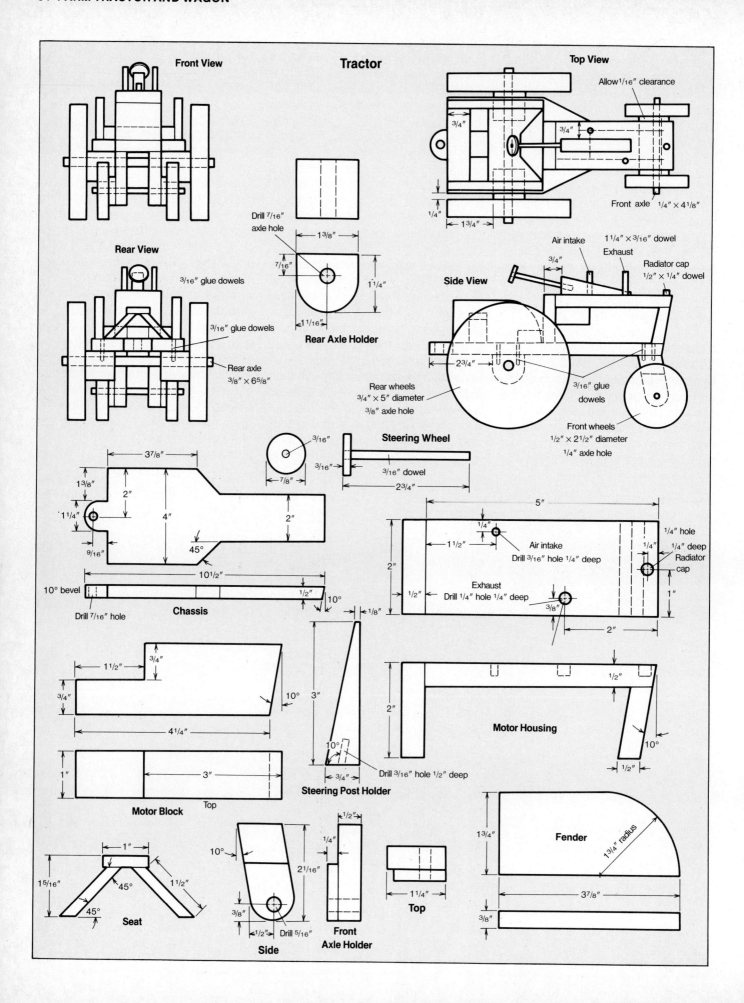

Front View

Tractor

Top View

Allow $^1/_{16}$" clearance

Rear View

Drill $^7/_{16}$" axle hole

$^3/_{16}$" glue dowels

Front axle $^1/_4$" × $4^1/_8$"

$^3/_4$"

$^3/_4$"

$1^3/_8$"

$^7/_{16}$"

$1^1/_4$"

$1^1/_{16}$"

Rear Axle Holder

$^3/_{16}$" glue dowels

Rear axle $^3/_8$" × $6^5/_8$"

Air intake

$1^1/_4$" × $^3/_{16}$" dowel

Exhaust

Radiator cap $^1/_2$" × $^1/_4$" dowel

$^3/_4$"

Side View

$^1/_4$"

$1^3/_4$"

$2^3/_4$"

Rear wheels $^3/_4$" × 5" diameter $^3/_8$" axle hole

$^3/_{16}$" glue dowels

Front wheels $^1/_2$" × $2^1/_2$" diameter $^1/_4$" axle hole

$^3/_{16}$"

Steering Wheel

$^3/_{16}$"

$^7/_8$"

$^3/_{16}$" dowel

$2^3/_4$"

$3^7/_8$"

$1^3/_8$"

$1^1/_4$"

2"

4"

2"

$^9/_{16}$"

45°

10"

5"

$^1/_4$" hole

$^1/_4$"

$1^1/_2$"

Air intake Drill $^3/_{16}$" hole $^1/_4$" deep

$^1/_4$" deep Radiator cap

2"

$^1/_2$"

Exhaust Drill $^1/_4$" hole $^1/_4$" deep

$^3/_8$"

1"

2"

$10^1/_2$"

10° bevel

$^1/_2$"

10°

$^1/_8$"

Drill $^7/_{16}$" hole

Chassis

$1^1/_2$"

$^3/_4$"

3"

$^3/_4$"

10°

$^1/_2$"

Motor Housing

$^1/_2$"

10°

$^1/_2$"

$4^1/_4$"

10°

$^3/_4$"

Drill $^3/_{16}$" hole $^1/_2$" deep

1"

3"

Steering Post Holder

Top

$1^3/_4$" radius

Fender

$1^3/_4$"

Motor Block

1"

$1^5/_{16}$"

45°

$1^1/_2$"

45°

Seat

$^1/_2$"

$^1/_4$"

10°

$2^1/_{16}$"

$^3/_8$"

$^1/_2$"

Drill $^5/_{16}$"

Side

Front Axle Holder

$1^1/_4$"

Top

$3^7/_8$"

$^3/_8$"

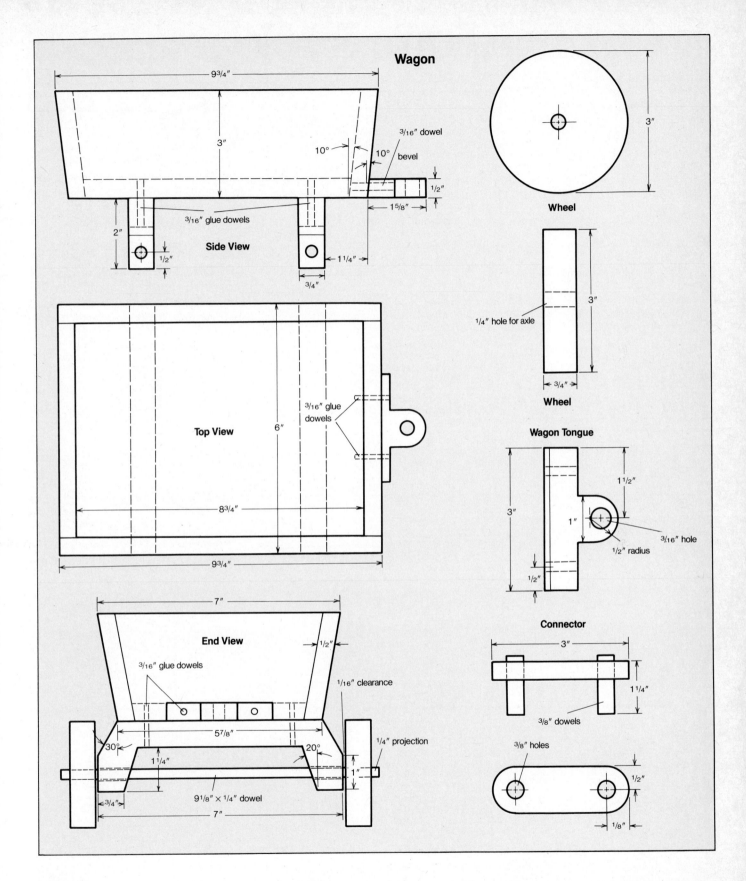

STEP 4
FINISHING THE TRACTOR AND WAGON
The assembly procedure described above should be used if the project is to be given a clear or natural finish. If you wish to paint various parts of the toy in different colors, it is best to leave those parts unglued until the paint is dry. But be sure to leave un- painted the surfaces that are to be glued so the glue can make a good bond. In either case, the parts that are attached with dowels should be glued as described above.

Farm Truck

MATERIALS LIST

Chassis (1), $1/2'' \times 4'' \times 11''$, pine
Stake bed (1), $1/2'' \times 4'' \times 6''$, pine
Hood front (1), $11/2'' \times 13/4'' \times 2''$, pine
Hood back (1), $5/8'' \times 13/4'' \times 13/4''$, pine
Cab front (1), $1/4'' \times 3'' \times 33/4''$, pine
Cab back (1), $1/4'' \times 3'' \times 33/4''$, pine
Cab sides (2), $1/4'' \times 3/4'' \times 33/4''$, pine
Cab roof (1), $1/4'' \times 3'' \times 3''$, pine
Cab-roof brace (1), $1/4'' \times 11/2'' \times 3''$, pine
Seat (1), $1'' \times 13/8'' \times 21/2''$, pine
Cab floor (1), $1'' \times 11/4'' \times 21/2''$, pine
Stake-bed front (1), $1/4'' \times 21/4'' \times 31/2''$, pine
Stake-bed sides (2), $1/4'' \times 2'' \times 21/4''$, pine
Lower horizontal braces (3), $1/8'' \times 1/2'' \times 33/4''$, pine
Upper horizontal braces (6), $1/8'' \times 1/4'' \times 33/4''$, pine
Vertical stakes (12) $1/8'' \times 1/4'' \times 21/4''$, pine
Axle holders (4), $1/2'' \times 1'' \times 11/8''$, pine
Axle-holder fasteners (8), $1'' \times 1/8''$ dowel, hardwood

Axles (2), $53/8'' \times 1/4''$ dowel, hardwood
Wheels (4), $3/8'' \times 21/2''$ diameter, pine
Steering wheel (1), $1/8'' \times 7/8''$ diameter, pine
Steering post (1), $13/4'' \times 1/8''$ dowel, hardwood
Headlights (2), $5/8'' \times 7/16''$ dowel, hardwood
Headlight holders (2), $1/2'' \times 1/8''$ dowel, hardwood
Radiator cap (1), $3/8'' \times 3/16''$ dowel, hardwood
Yellow wood glue
Nontoxic clear finish

Tools

Table saw
Band saw
Handsaw
Coping saw
Jigsaw
Light wood clamps
Spring clamps or wooden clothespins
Masking tape
Sandpaper, 80, 120, and 220

There have always been things to haul around, and in the 1920s, this stake truck was busy doing just that in the cities and countryside. It can serve a modern child's trucking needs quite well.

STEP 1
CUTTING THE PIECES

Most of the parts involve straight 90° cuts and can be cut out with the table saw or fine-tooth handsaw. Seven

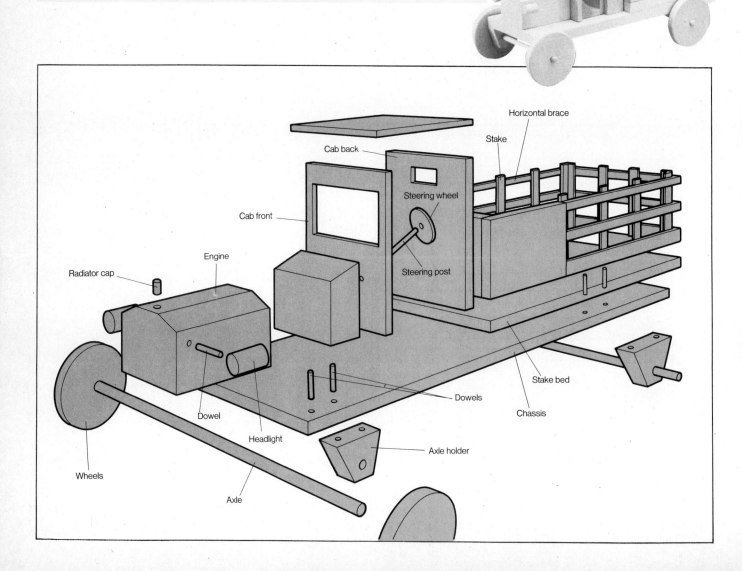

Horizontal brace
Stake
Cab back
Steering wheel
Cab front
Steering post
Engine
Radiator cap
Stake bed
Chassis
Dowels
Dowel
Headlight
Axle holder
Wheels
Axle

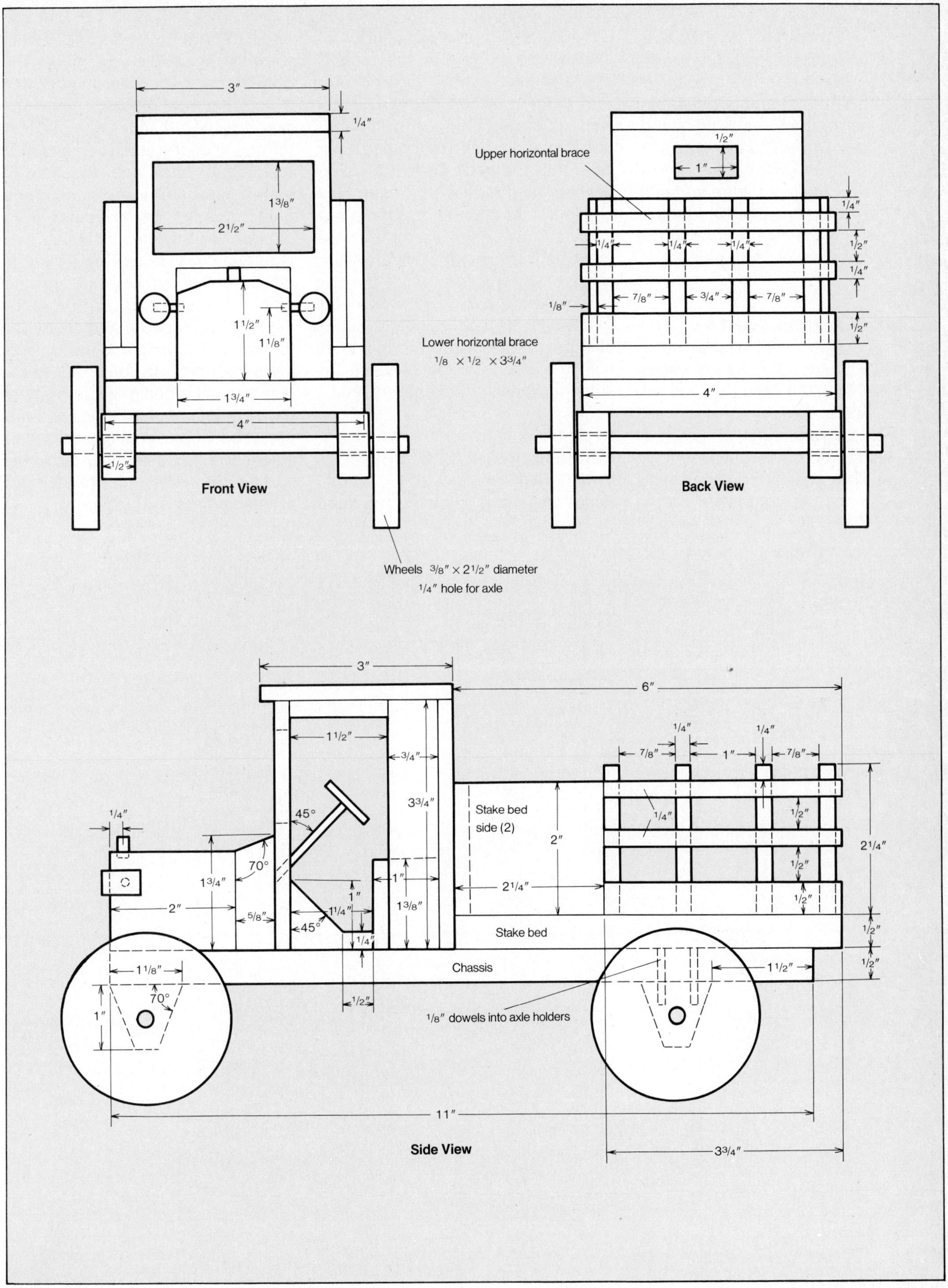

Front View

3"
1/4"
1 3/8"
2 1/2"
1 1/2"
1 1/8"
1 3/4"
4"
1/2"

Wheels 3/8" × 2 1/2" diameter
1/4" hole for axle

Back View

Upper horizontal brace
1/2"
1"
1/4"
1/4"
1/2"
1/4"
1/4" 1/4" 1/4"
7/8" 3/4" 7/8"
1/8"
1/2"
Lower horizontal brace
1/8" × 1/2 × 3 3/4"
4"

Side View

3"
6"
1/4"
1 1/2"
3/4"
3 3/4"
45°
70°
Stake bed
side (2)
1/4"
7/8" 1" 7/8"
2"
1/4"
1 3/4"
1"
1/2"
2 1/4"
2"
5/8"
1 1/4"
1/2"
1 1/4"
1/2"
1 3/8"
1/4"
Stake bed
1/2"
Chassis
1/2"
1 1/8"
70°
1"
1/8" dowels into axle holders
1 1/2"
11"
3 3/4"

pieces—the hood parts, cab floor, and axle holders—require angle cuts, but they are not difficult. The wheels and the steering wheel can be cut on the band saw, jigsaw, or coping saw. Drill all holes necessary in the wheels and axle holders, and in the hood for the headlights and radiator cap. Cut out the windshield opening and the rear-window opening with a jigsaw or coping saw.

STEP 2
ASSEMBLING THE PARTS

Sand and clean all parts, finishing with 220 sandpaper. Begin subassemblies by gluing the axle holders to the chassis. Note that they project 1/16 inch from the edge of the chassis. Secure the holders with 1/8-inch dowels. Next glue the two hood parts together, and then glue them to the cab front. Drill the 1/8-inch hole for the steering post. Glue in the radiator cap and headlights. The roof and roof brace are then glued together. Next glue the cab floor to the seat, and then glue these to the cab back. Note that the back projects 1/4 inch beyond each side of the seat. Now glue the stake-bed sides to the stake-bed front, and glue all three to the stake bed. The stake parts are glued together in three sections—the two sides and the back end. Follow the pattern shown, and use light spring clamps or wooden clothespins to hold the pieces in place. Glue the steering wheel to the steering post.

STEP 3
ASSEMBLING AND FINISHING THE TRUCK

Begin assembly by gluing the hood and cab front to the chassis. Glue in the steering wheel and post. Next glue the cab floor, seat, and cab back to the cab front–chassis subassembly. Glue the cab sides into place. After that, glue the stake bed and sides to the cab back and chassis. The stake sides and back can now be glued in place. Before gluing in the cab roof and wheels, finish all parts with two coats of nontoxic clear finish, but check to make sure any dried glue has been chipped off and that all parts are smooth and clean prior to applying the finish. When all parts are completely dry, glue on the roof and wheels. When gluing the wheels to the axles, be sure to leave a little space between each axle holder and wheel so the wheels will turn freely and the truck roll smoothly. Let glue dry, and you're ready to go.

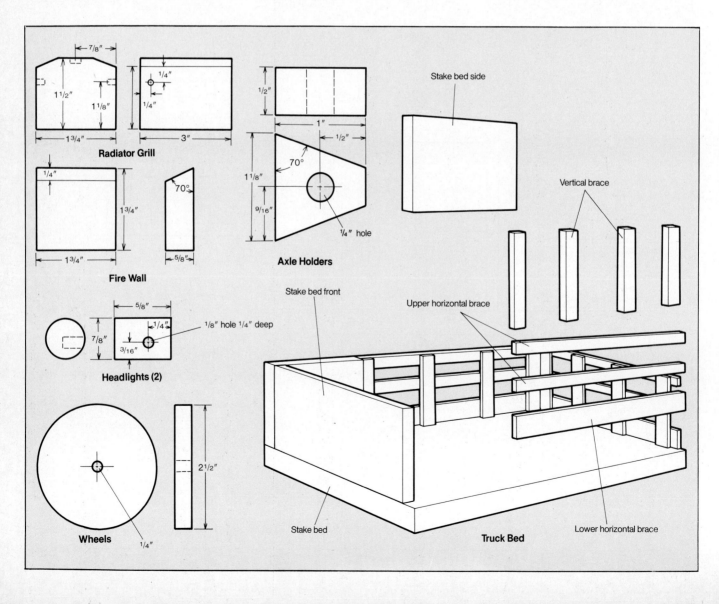

Radiator Grill

Fire Wall

Axle Holders

1/4" hole

Stake bed side

Vertical brace

Headlights (2)

1/8" hole 1/4" deep

Stake bed front

Upper horizontal brace

Wheels

Stake bed

Truck Bed

Lower horizontal brace

Ambulance

MATERIALS LIST
Chassis (1), 1/2″ × 4″ × 10″, pine
Hood (1), 1 1/2″ × 2″ × 3″, pine
Sides (2), 1/4″ × 4 1/2″ × 7 3/4″, pine
Roof (1), 1/4″ × 4″ × 7 3/4″, pine
Sub-roof (1), 1/4″ × 2″ × 4″, pine
Front roof brace (1), 1/4″ × 1/2″ × 3 1/2″, pine
Rear roof brace (1), 1/4″ × 1/4″ × 3 1/2″, pine
Back panel (1), 1/4″ × 2 1/2″ × 3 1/2″, pine
Rear floorboard (1), 1/4″ × 1″ × 3 1/2″, pine
Rear floor brace (1), 1/4″ × 1/4″ × 3 1/2″, pine
Seat back (1), 1/4″ × 3 1/2″ × 4 1/2″, pine
Seat (1), 1/4″ × 1 1/4″ × 3 1/2″, pine
Seat brace (1), 1/4″ × 1″ × 3 1/2″, pine
Front floorboard (1), 1/4″ × 1 1/2″ × 3 1/2″, pine
Dashboard (1), 1/4″ × 1 7/8″ × 4″, pine
Axle holders (2), 1/2″ × 1″ × 4″, pine
Wheels (4), 3/8″ × 2 1/2″ diameter, pine

Axles (2), 5 3/8″ × 1/4″ dowel, hardwood
Steering wheel (1), 3/16″ × 3/4″ diameter, pine
Steering post (1), 2 1/2″ × 3/16″ dowel,
   hardwood
Radiator cap (1), 3/8″ × 1/4″ dowel, hardwood
Headlights (2), 5/8″ × 3/8″ dowel, hardwood
Headlight holders (2), 1/2″ × 1/8″ dowel,
   hardwood
Yellow wood glue
Nontoxic clear finish

Tools
Table saw or backsaw
Band saw or coping saw
Drill or drill press
Light wood clamps, spring clamps
Masking tape
Sandpaper, 80, 120, and 220

It's a far cry from our modern ambulance with its sophisticated equipment, but this 1912 Maxwell did heroic service in its day. It will provide many hours of imaginative fun for any child.

STEP 1
CUTTING THE PIECES
Cut out the chassis and axle holders. The holders have a 20° chamfer along each side. Glue the holders to the chassis. Cut out the hood and dashboard. Note the chamfer cuts on each. The remaining body pieces all have straight cuts. Cut out the windows with a coping saw. Cut out the wheels and steering wheel, using the band saw or coping saw. When the glue is dry on the chassis and axle holders, drill the 5/12-inch axle holes through both pieces as shown in the drawings. This is best done on the drill press or with some sort of drill guide to keep the holes straight.

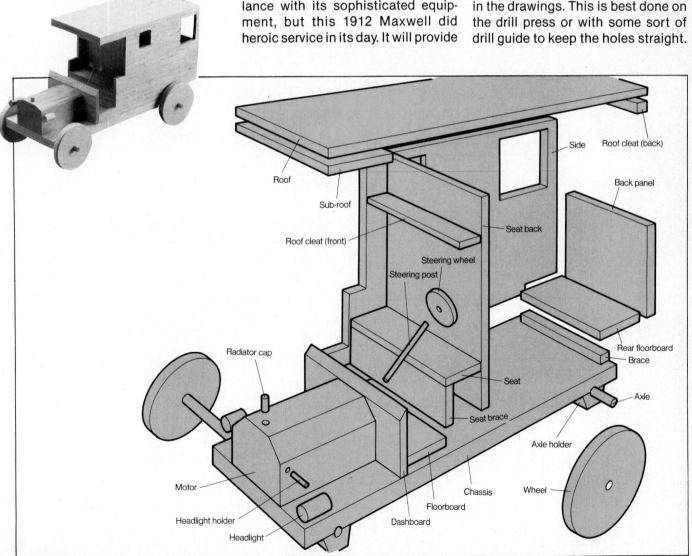

Roof

Sub-roof

Roof cleat (front)

Side

Roof cleat (back)

Back panel

Seat back

Steering wheel

Steering post

Rear floorboard

Brace

Radiator cap

Seat

Axle

Seat brace

Axle holder

Motor

Chassis

Wheel

Headlight holder

Floorboard

Dashboard

Headlight

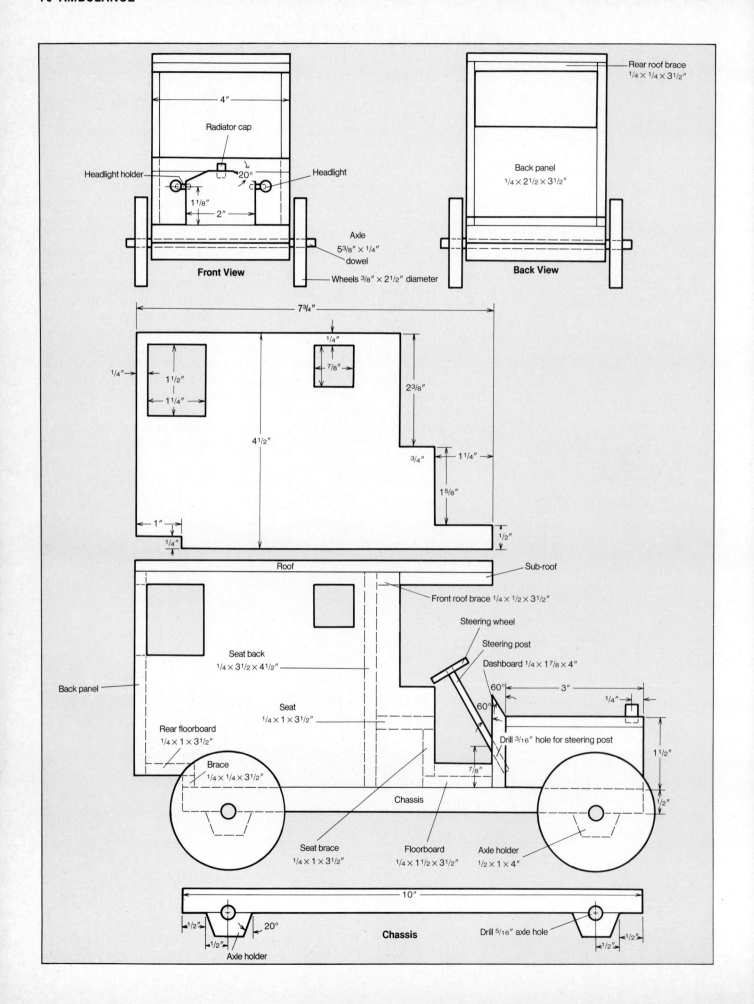

Radiator cap

Headlight holder

Headlight

20°

1 1/8"

2"

4"

Front View

Axle
5 3/8" × 1/4"
dowel

Wheels 3/8" × 2 1/2" diameter

Rear roof brace
1/4 × 1/4 × 3 1/2"

Back panel
1/4 × 2 1/2 × 3 1/2"

Back View

7 3/4"

1/4"

1/4"

7/8"

1 1/2"

1 1/4"

4 1/2"

2 3/8"

3/4"

1 1/4"

1 5/8"

1"

1/4"

1/2"

Roof

Sub-roof

Front roof brace 1/4 × 1/2 × 3 1/2"

Steering wheel

Steering post

Dashboard 1/4 × 1 7/8 × 4"

60°

60°

3"

1/4"

Seat back
1/4 × 3 1/2 × 4 1/2"

Back panel

Seat
1/4 × 1 × 3 1/2"

Rear floorboard
1/4 × 1 × 3 1/2"

Drill 3/16" hole for steering post

1 1/2"

Brace
1/4 × 1/4 × 3 1/2"

7/8"

1/2"

Chassis

Seat brace
1/4 × 1 × 3 1/2"

Floorboard
1/4 × 1 1/2 × 3 1/2"

Axle holder
1/2 × 1 × 4"

10"

1/2"

20°

1/2"

Chassis

Drill 5/16" axle hole

1/2"

1/2"

Axle holder

Drill the holes in the hood for the radiator cap and headlights.

STEP 2
ASSEMBLING THE PARTS

First sand all parts carefully. Round the edges of the wheels with 80 sandpaper on a sanding block. Finish all pieces with 220 sandpaper, and then remove all dust. Begin the subassemblies by gluing the dashboard to the hood, using light clamps or masking tape. Next glue the front floorboard, the seat brace, seat, and seat back together. These can be done all together or one at a time, whichever you find easier. Now glue the rear floorboard and its brace to the rear end of the chassis, but be sure that these are set 1/4 inch in from each side of the chassis. Glue the sub-roof to the underside of the front end of the roof.

STEP 3
ASSEMBLING THE AMBULANCE

When the glue is dry on the subassemblies, you can begin putting the units together. First drill the 3/16-inch hole for the steering post at an angle of 60° into the dashboard 1/2 inch deep. Then glue the hood and dashboard to the chassis. Next glue the seat and floorboard unit to the chassis and dashboard. Now glue one of the sides to the chassis, seat unit, and rear floorboard. The back panel is then glued to the side and rear floorboard. After you have done this, glue the other side in place, and then glue in the front and rear roof braces. Glue in the steering wheel, headlights, and radiator cap. Do not put the roof or wheels in place now.

STEP 4
FINISHING THE AMBULANCE

Check the assembly for any glue that might have been squeezed out. Chip it off and re-sand. Finish with two coats of clear finish, including the roof and wheels. When the finish is dry, glue on the roof and attach the wheels by gluing them to the axles, with the axle projecting 1/4 inch on each side. For free turning, there should be a clearance of 1/16 inch between the wheels and the chassis.

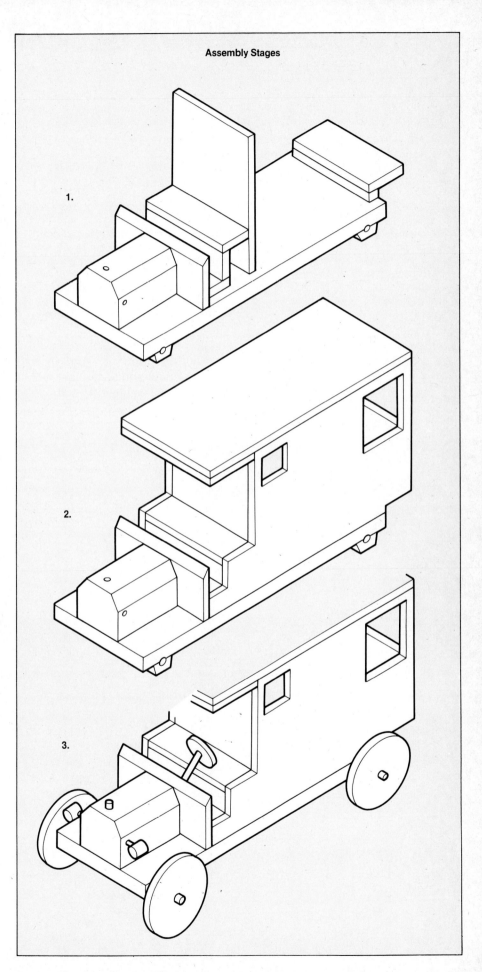

Assembly Stages

1.

2.

3.

Racing Car

MATERIALS LIST

Chassis (1), 3/8″ × 2¼″ × 9″, hardwood
Axle holders (2), 5/8″ × 1″ × 2½″, hardwood
Hood (1), 1³/8″ × 1³/8″ × 2½″, hardwood
Dashboard (1), 3/8″ × 1½″ × 2¼″, hardwood
Seats (2), 1/2″ × 7/8″ × 7/8″, hardwood
Seat backs (2), 1/4″ × 7/8″ × 1¼″, hardwood
Fuel tank (1), 2¼″ × 7/8″ dowel, hardwood
Fuel-tank holder (1), 1/2″ × 1⅛″ × 2¼″, hardwood
Front fenders (2), 3/16″ × 1/2″ × 4⅛″, hardwood
Front fender braces (2), 3/16″ × 3/4″ × 1³/4″, hardwood
Running boards (2), 3/16″ × 1/2″ × 2½″, hardwood

Running board braces (2), 3/16″ × 5/8″ × 3/4″, hardwood
Trunk (1), 7/8″ × 1½″ × 2¼″, hardwood
Rear fenders, front part (2), 3/16″ × 1/2″ × 2″, hardwood
Rear fenders, back part (2), 1/2″ × 1³/8″ × 2½″, hardwood
Wheels (4), 1/4″ × 2½″ diameter, hardwood
Axles (2), 3¼″ × 1/4″ dowel, hardwood
Radiator cap (1), 1/2″ × 1/4″ dowel, hardwood
Headlights (2), 5/8″ × 1/2″ dowel, hardwood
Headlight holders (2), 3/8″ × 1/8″ dowel, hardwood
Spotlight (1), 5/8″ × 3/8″ dowel, hardwood

Spotlight holder (1), 3/8″ × 1/8″ dowel, hardwood
Steering post (1), 2″ × 1/8″ dowel, hardwood
Steering wheel (1), 1/8″ × 7/8″ diameter, hardwood
Yellow wood glue
Nontoxic clear finish

Tools

Table saw
Band saw
Drill or drill press
Light wood clamps
Wood rasp

Masking tape
Sandpaper, 80, 120, and 220

This rakish, stylish 1913 Mercer Raceabout is a forerunner of modern sports and racing cars. One can imagine racing about on a beautiful day in this open car; but in bad weather, driver and passenger would require considerable fortitude, to say nothing of helmets, goggles, and driving gloves.

STEP 1
CUTTING THE PARTS

Cut out all parts to dimensions shown, noting the angle cuts of the

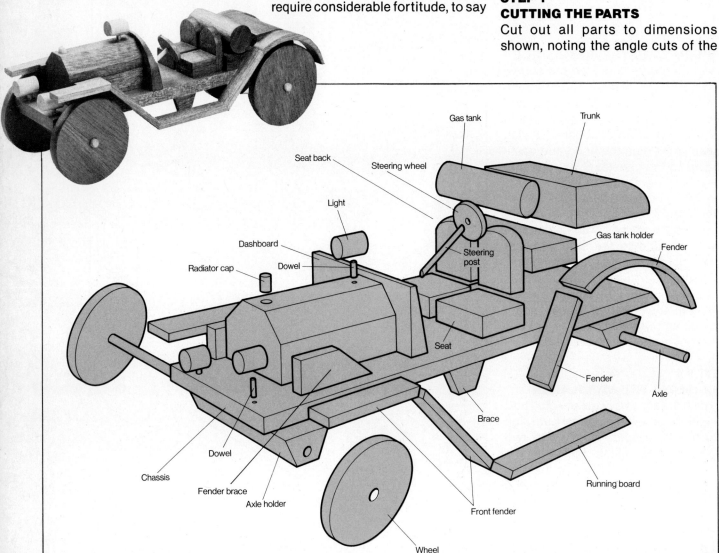

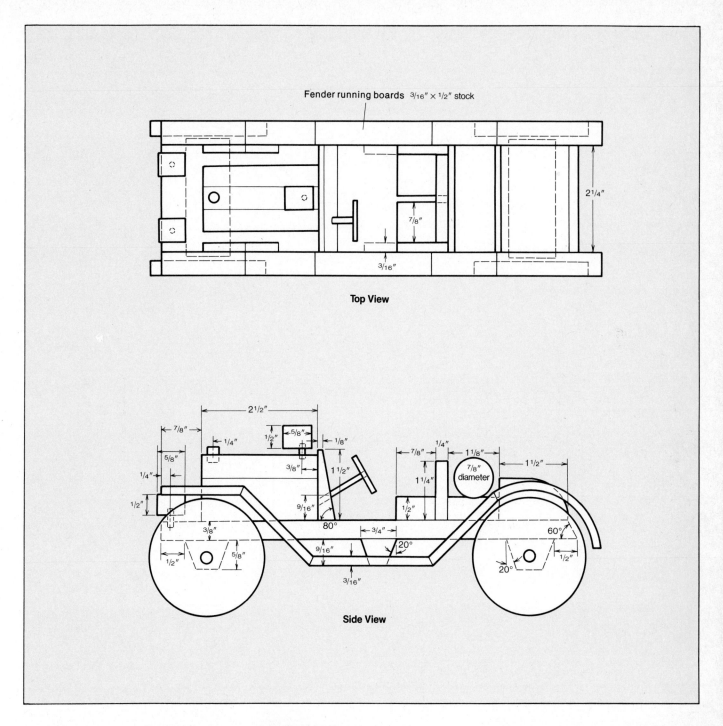

Fender running boards 3/16″ × 1/2″ stock

Top View

Side View

chassis, hood, axle holders, fenders, running boards, and braces. The dashboard is sloped at 10°. The curved section of the rear fender is laid out on the block and cut out on the band saw. The fuel-tank holder is slightly rounded along the center line with a wood rasp and sandpaper to receive the fuel tank. Drill the necessary holes in the chassis, hood, dashboard, and axle holders for the spotlight, radiator cap, headlights, steering post, and axles. Cut and drill the spotlight and headlights.

STEP 2
ASSEMBLING AND FINISHING THE RACE CAR

Sand all parts carefully, finishing with 220 sandpaper, and remove all dust. Begin assembly by gluing the axle holders to the chassis. Then glue the trunk to the chassis, followed by the fuel-tank holder, the fuel tank, seat backs, and seats. Glue the hood in place, 7/8 inch from the front of the chassis. The dashboard is glued to the hood and the chassis. The front fender braces and the run-

ning-board braces are secured to the chassis. The fender parts and the running boards should be glued together as a unit. This whole assembly is glued to the car at several points—at the braces, the chassis, the fuel-tank holder, and the trunk. Glue in the spotlight, radiator cap, headlights, and steering post. Glue the steering wheel in place. Before putting the wheels on, finish all parts with two coats of nontoxic clear finish. When dry, the wheels are glued to the axles.

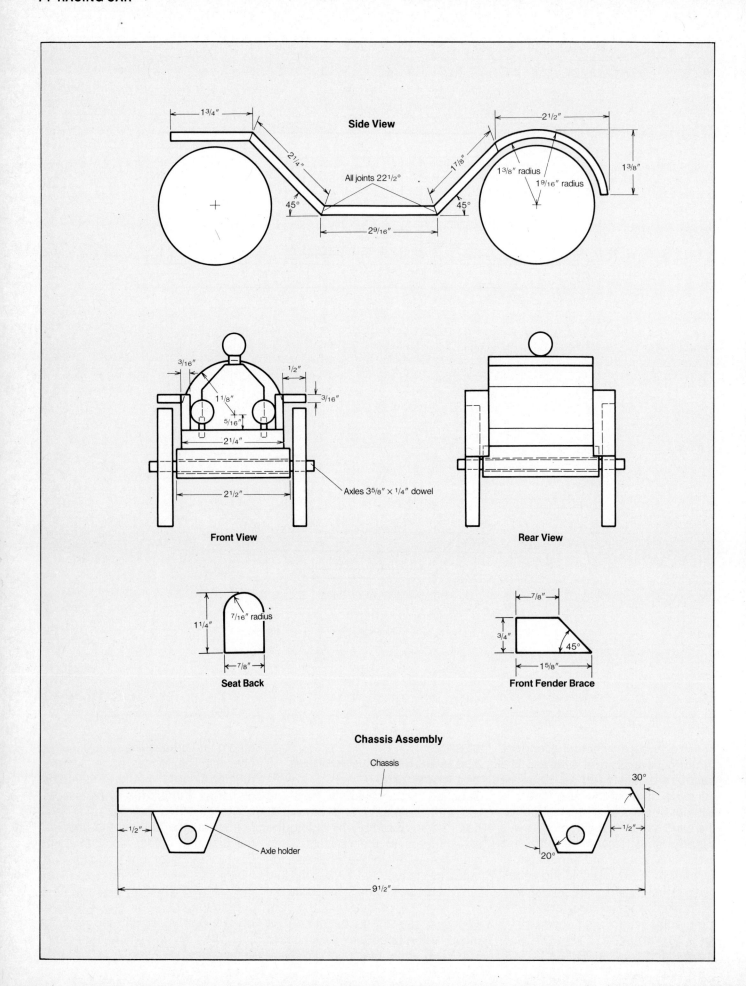

Side View

1 3/4"

2 1/4"

All joints 22 1/2°

45°

2 9/16"

45°

1 7/8"

2 1/2"

1 3/8" radius

1 9/16" radius

1 3/8"

Front View

3/16"

1/2"

1 1/8"

3/16"

5/16"

2 1/4"

2 1/2"

Axles 3 5/8" × 1/4" dowel

Rear View

Seat Back

1 1/4"

7/16" radius

7/8"

Front Fender Brace

7/8"

3/4"

45°

1 5/8"

Chassis Assembly

Chassis

Axle holder

1/2"

30°

1/2"

20°

9 1/2"

Model T Ford

MATERIALS LIST

Chassis (1), 3/4″ × 4″ × 91/8″, pine
Hood (1), 13/4″ × 13/4″ × 3″, pine
Front (1), 1/4″ × 35/8″ × 4″, pine
Back (1), 1/4″ × 35/8″ × 4″, pine
Sides (2), 1/4″ × 2″ × 53/4″, pine
Front fenders (2), 1/4″ × 1/2″ × 5″, pine
Front fender braces (2), 1/4″ × 13/8″ × 27/8″, pine
Roof (1), 1/4″ × 4″ × 61/2″, pine
Running boards (2), 1/4″ × 1/2″ × 33/8″, pine
Rear fenders, front part (2), 1/2″ × 11/2″ × 15/8″, pine
Rear fenders, back part (2), 1/4″ × 1/2″ × 13/8″, pine
Front seat, back (1), 1/4″ × 21/2″ × 31/2″, pine

Front seat (1), 1/4″ × 11/4″ × 31/2″, pine
Front seat brace (1), 1/4″ × 1″ × 31/2″, pine
Rear seat, back (1), 1/4″ × 23/4″ × 31/2″, pine
Rear seat (1), 1/4″ × 11/2″ × 31/2″, pine
Rear seat brace (1), 1/4″ × 11/8″ × 31/2″, pine
Wheels (4), 1/4″ × 21/2″ diameter, pine or hardwood
Axles (2), 47/8″ × 1/4″ dowel, hardwood
Front lamps (2), 3/8″ × 1/4″ dowel, hardwood
Headlights (2), 5/8″ × 7/16″ dowel, hardwood
Radiator cap (1), 3/8″ × 3/16″ dowel, hardwood
Steering wheel (1), 3/16″ × 7/8″ diameter, pine or hardwood
Steering post (1), 11/2″ × 3/16″ dowel, hardwood

Yellow wood glue
Nontoxic clear finish
(Dimensions larger than those shown in drawings allow for saw, angle, or bevel cuts.)

Tools
Table saw
Band saw or jigsaw
Coping saw
Drill or drill press
Smooth wood rasp
Coarse wood rasp
Light wood clamps
Masking tape
Sandpaper, 80, 120, and 220

The Model T, affectionately known as the original "tin lizzie," needs no introduction. "Model T" became almost synonymous with "automobile" because it was the first inexpensive mass-produced model, and thus *the* first car for many people, who taught themselves to drive and personally experienced the new form of locomotion. For a place to park your Model T, look at the next project.

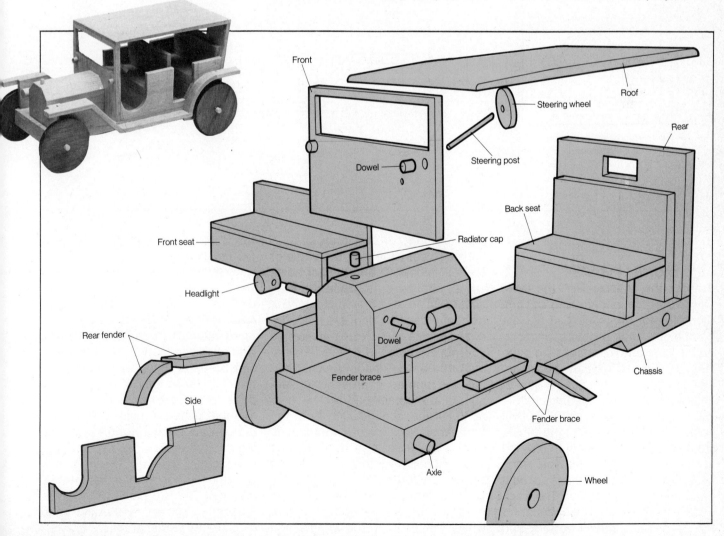

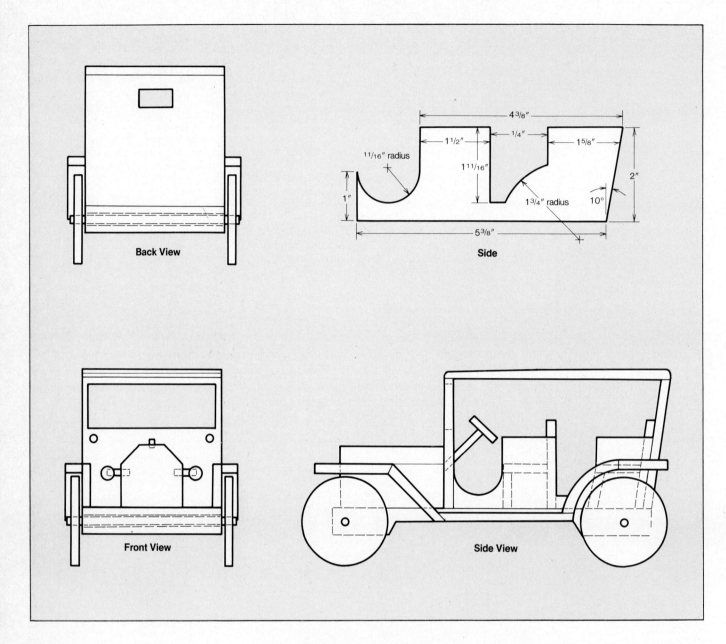

Back View

Side

Front View

Side View

STEP 1
CUTTING THE PIECES
Cut out the chassis with the table saw to the dimensions given and drill the holes for the axles. Cut out the hood block, and drill holes for the radiator cap and headlight holders. Next cut out the front and back panels, and then use the coping saw or jigsaw to cut out the openings for the windshield and rear window. Drill holes in the front panel for the lamps. Note that the back panel is beveled at 10° top and bottom. The sides have several cuts, and these are best done with the band saw. The back ends are cut at 10°. The opening for the front has a curved bottom, and

the opening for the rear seat is curved to coincide with the curve of the rear fender. The front-seat parts are all straight cuts, while the rear-seat parts are all beveled at 10°. The front and back fenders are made up of two pieces each. Note the beveled and curved cuts. After the fenders, cut out the front fender brace. Then cut the running boards, which are square at the back end and beveled at 45° at the front. Next cut out the roof panel. Note that the roof slopes toward the front. Use a wood rasp and sandpaper for this. Now cut out the dowels for the headlights, headlight holders, radiator cap, steering post, and axles. Cut out the steering wheel. Then cut out the wheels, drill

the axle holes, and sand slightly around the edges.

STEP 2
ASSEMBLING THE MODEL T
Sand all parts carefully, finishing with 220 sandpaper. Several parts can be assembled as units before the final assembly. First glue the three parts of the front and rear seats together. Glue the headlights and radiator cap to the hood. Glue the lamps to the front panel and the hood to the center of the front panel. Glue the two parts of the rear fenders together. The two parts of the front fenders are glued together and then glued to the fender braces.

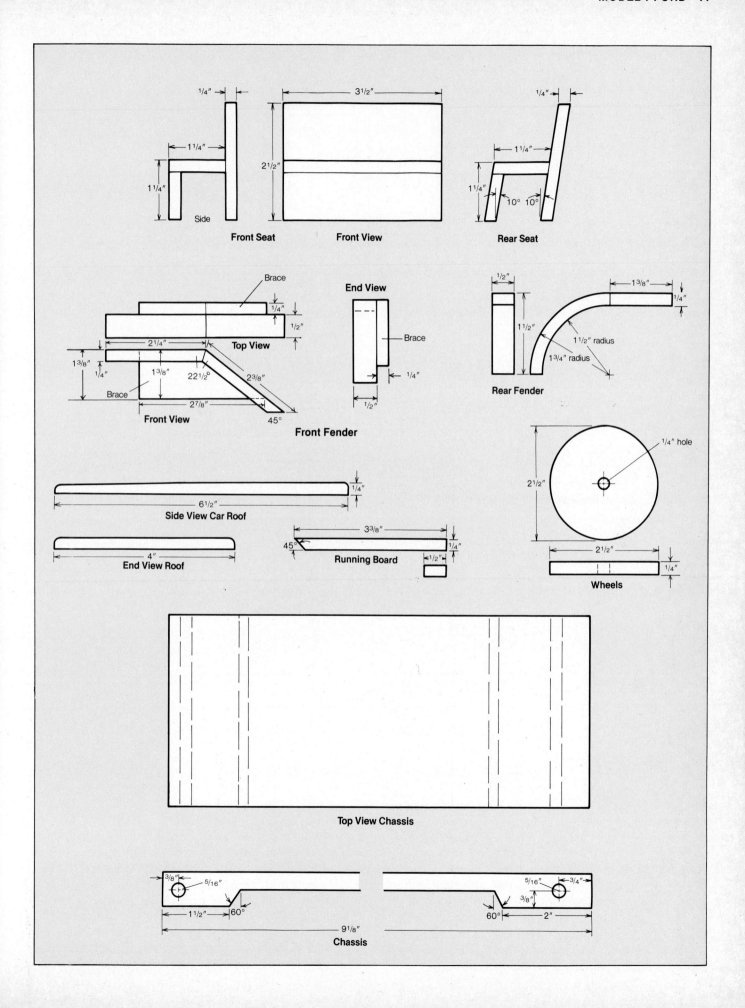

1/4"
1 1/4"
1 1/4"
Side
Front Seat

3 1/2"
2 1/2"
Front View

1/4"
1 1/4"
1 1/4"
10° 10°
Rear Seat

Brace
1/4"
1/2"
Top View
2 1/4"
1 3/8"
1/4"
1 3/8"
22 1/2°
2 3/8"
Brace
2 7/8"
Front View
45°
Front Fender

End View
Brace
1/4"
1/2"

1/2"
1 1/2"
1 3/8"
1 3/4" radius
1 1/2" radius
1/4"
Rear Fender

1/4" hole
2 1/2"
2 1/2"
1/4"
Wheels

1/4"
6 1/2"
Side View Car Roof

4"
End View Roof

3 3/8"
45°
1/4"
Running Board
1/2"

Top View Chassis

3/8"
5/16"
1 1/2"
60°
9 1/8"
Chassis

5/16"
3/4"
3/8"
60°
2"

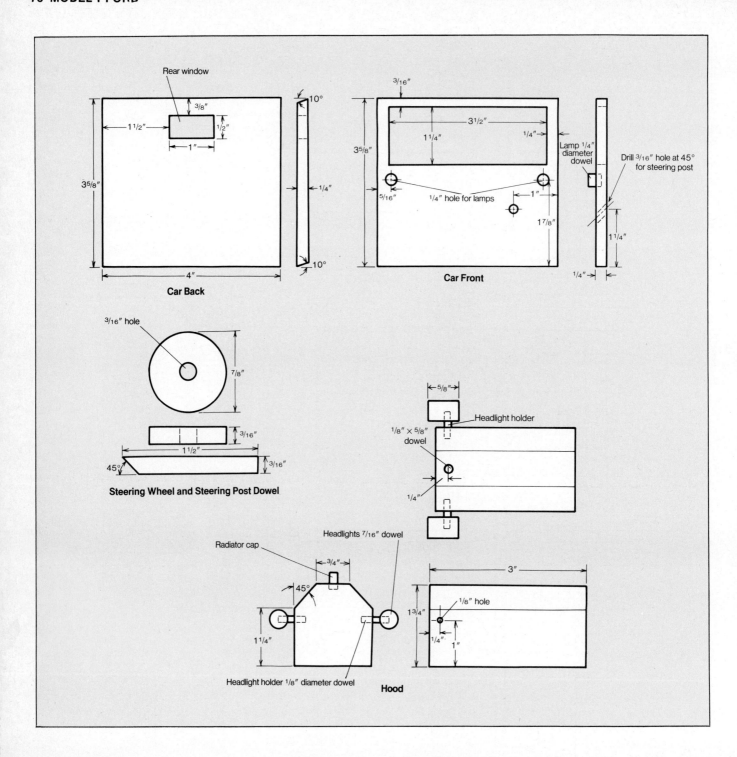

Rear window

3/8″

1½″ 1/2″

1″

3⁵/8″

4″

Car Back

10°

1/4″

10°

3/16″

3½″

1¼″ 1/4″

3⁵/8″

5/16″ 1/4″ hole for lamps 1″

1⁷/8″

Lamp 1/4″ diameter dowel

Drill 3/16″ hole at 45° for steering post

1¼″

1/4″

Car Front

3/16″ hole

7/8″

3/16″

1½″

45° 3/16″

Steering Wheel and Steering Post Dowel

5/8″

Headlight holder

1/8″ × 5/8″ dowel

1/4″

Radiator cap

Headlights 7/16″ dowel

3/4″

45°

1¼″

Headlight holder 1/8″ diameter dowel

3″

1³/4″ 1/8″ hole

1/4″ 1″

Hood

STEP 3
ASSEMBLY
When the glue is dry, begin the assembly by drilling the hole for the steering post in the front panel. Then glue the hood and front panel to the chassis. Next glue the right side to the front panel and the chassis. Follow this by gluing the back panel to the right side and to the chassis. Use masking tape to hold the pieces in place as you proceed. Next glue the rear seat assembly to the chassis, the back panel, and the right side. The front seat unit can now be glued in place, and after that, the left side. Glue the steering post and wheel into position. Complete this phase of the assembly by gluing the fender units and running boards in place. Let the glue dry completely before finishing the car.

STEP 4
FINISHING
Before gluing on the roof and wheels, finish all parts with two or more coats of nontoxic clear finish. When the finish is completely dry, glue the roof in place. Finally, glue the wheels to the axles, with the axles projecting 1/4 inch on each side, and with a 1/16-inch space between the chassis and each wheel.

Garage for Model T

MATERIALS LIST

Floor (1), 1/4″ × 71/2″ × 111/2″, plywood
Framing (1), 3/8″ × 3/8″ × 19′, pine
Planking (1), 1/4″ × 3/4″ × 50″, pine
Door frames (2), 1/4″ × 3/8″ × 38″, pine
Door header (1), 1/4″ × 3/8″ × 71/2″, pine
Door bar (1), 1/4″ × 1/2″ × 71/2″, pine
Door-bar holders (2), 1/2″ × 11/2″ × 1/2″, pine
Brads, 1/2″, 3/4″ —18 or 19 gauge
Brass hinges (2 pairs), 3/4″ × 5/8″
Yellow wood glue
Nontoxic paint
Wood putty

Tools

Table saw
Block plane
Hammer
Screwdriver
Light bar clamps

C-clamps or light
   spring clamps
Masking tape
Sandpaper, 80, 120,
   and 220

A lot of Model T's were kept in barns and sheds, but in the changing city, garages soon made their appearance in response to the increasing number of motorized vehicles. This one is designed for the flivver which is described on page 75.

STEP 1
CUTTING FRAMES, PLANKS, AND FLOOR

Cut all framing members, planking, and the floor to the sizes shown, including the two vertical planks for either side of the doors and the door header. See page 81 for side frames, front and back frames, and the two parts of roof framing. Take care with all angle cuts to ensure a good fit. The planks can be cut from 1/4– × 3/4– inch lattice strips.

STEP 2
ASSEMBLING THE FRAME

Assemble the frame in sections: the two side frames, the two end frames (front and back), and the two roof frames. This can be done with glue and masking tape, light bar clamps, or light brads. When the glue is dry, glue the frame to the floor. Begin with the sides, attaching them to the floor with glue and light brads, C-clamps, or spring clamps. Then glue in the front and back framing, and finally, the roof unit.

STEP 3
ASSEMBLING THE PLANKS

Before assembling the planks, chamfer the two top edges of each plank with a small block plane or sandpaper wrapped around a block

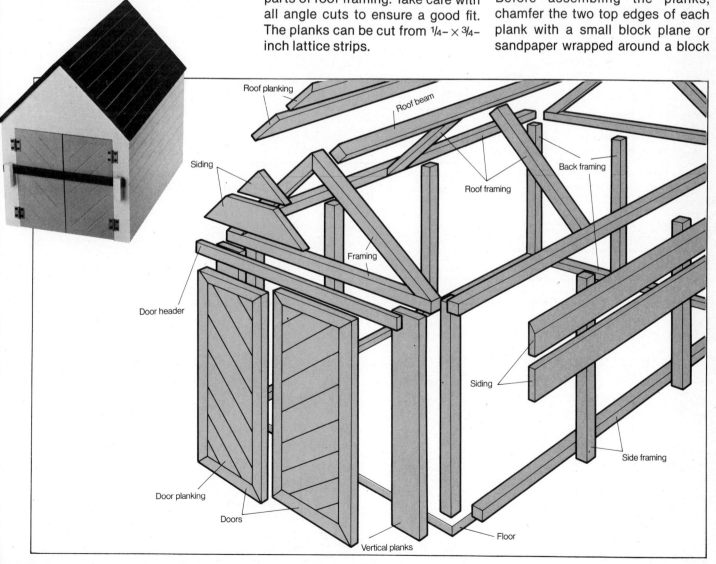

of wood. Assemble the planks in sections, as with the frame: the sides, front and back, and the roof. First put all planks for a unit face down on the workbench. Then put a strip of masking tape along each joint. Now reverse the section and spread it fanwise, using the tape as a hinge. Put a thin bead of glue between each pair of planks, close the fan, and allow to dry. Use tape to hold the unit while drying. You are now ready to attach the planking to the frame. Do the back first, then the front, and finally, the sides. Again, you can use

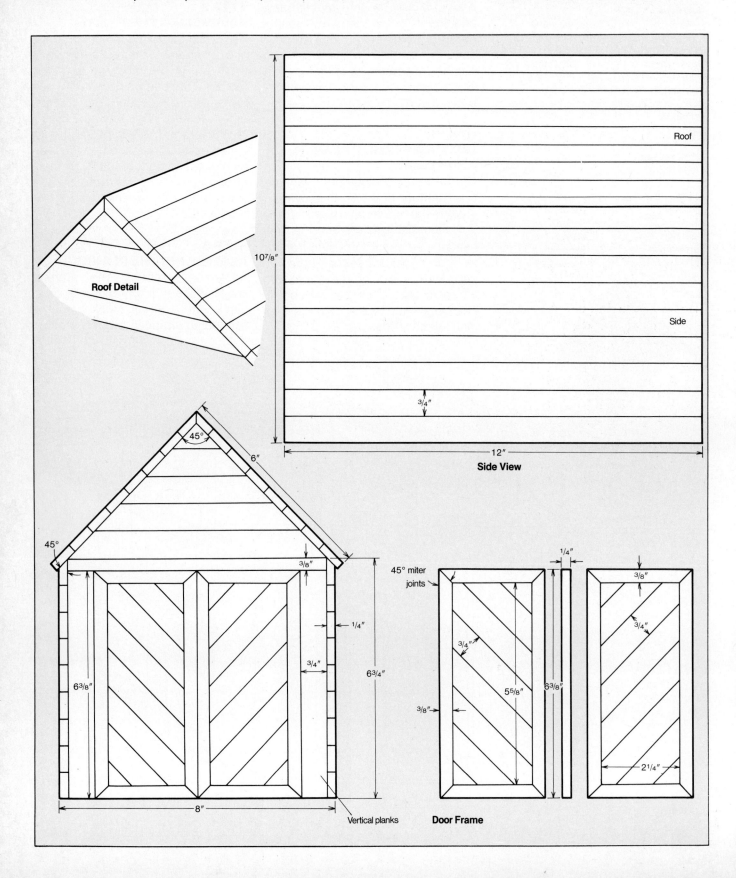

Roof Detail

$10^{7/8}''$

Roof

Side

$3/4''$

$12''$

Side View

$45°$

$6''$

$45°$

$3/8''$

$1/4''$

$3/4''$

$6^{3/4}''$

$6^{3/8}''$

$8''$

Vertical planks

$45°$ miter joints

$1/4''$

$3/8''$

$3/4''$

$5^{5/8}''$

$6^{3/8}''$

$3/8''$

$3/4''$

$2^{1/4}''$

Door Frame

glue and secure with tape or brads. The roof planking should be made in two sections and then glued together along the ridge line later. If you want to paint the roof a different color from the rest of the garage, do not glue it into place at this time.

STEP 4
ASSEMBLING THE DOORS
The doors are made with a 1/4- × 3/8-inch frame and chamfered plank pieces cut at 45° to form a herringbone pattern. First make the panel of plank pieces, and then fit around it the 1/4- × 3/8-inch frame with mitered corners. When the glue is dry, fit the door in the door opening and locate the hinges. Next glue the two door-bar holders to the vertical planking on each side of the doors. Cut and fit the door bar.

STEP 5
FINISHING
Finish the garage with two coats of nontoxic enamel after sanding and cleaning. We used three colors: one for the roof, one for the garage, and one for the doors. If you like detail, draw some tools on the walls inside. When the paint is dry, glue the roof in place, attach the doors, and your garage is ready for use.

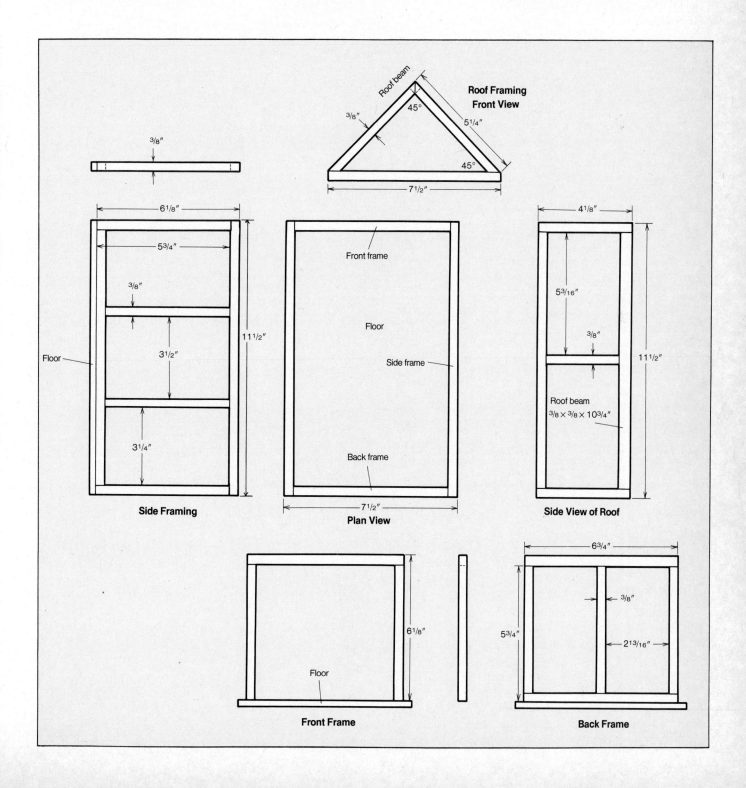

Windmill

MATERIALS LIST

Base top (1), 1/2″ × 7″ × 10″, plywood or hardwood

Base sides (2), 1/2″ × 1 1/2″ × 10″, plywood or hardwood

Base ends (2), 1/2″ × 1 1/2″ × 7″, plywood or hardwood

Front panel (1), 1/2″ × 8″ × 16″, plywood or hardwood

Back panel, top section (1), 1/2″ × 4 3/4″ × 6″, plywood or hardwood

Back panel, mid-section (1), 1/2″ × 6″ × 6 3/4″, plywood or hardwood

Back panel, bottom section (1), 1/2″ × 4″ × 8″, plywood or hardwood

Side panels (2), 1/2″ × 4″ × 14 3/4″, plywood or hardwood

Roof (1), 1/4″ × 5 1/2″ × 7 1/4″, plywood or hardwood

Vanes (4), 1/4″ × 3 1/4″ × 7″, plywood or hardwood

Upper shaft (1), 6 1/2″ × 1/2″ dowel, hardwood

Lower shaft (1), 5 1/4″ × 1/2″ dowel, hardwood

Crank handle (1), 1 3/4″ × 1/2″ dowel, hardwood

Door (1), 1/4″ × 2″ × 4″, plywood or hardwood

Pulleys, securing rings, and crank, 1/4″, 3/16″, and 1/2″ stock (as needed), plywood or hardwood

Heavy rubber bands

No. 6 × 1″ flat head wood screws

No. 6 × 1/2″ pan head sheet metal screws

Yellow wood glue

Nontoxic paint

(Dimensions larger than those shown in drawings allow for saw, angle, or bevel cuts.)

Tools

Table saw

Band saw

Drill or drill press

Wood rasp

Screwdriver

Masking tape

Sandpaper, 80, 120, and 220

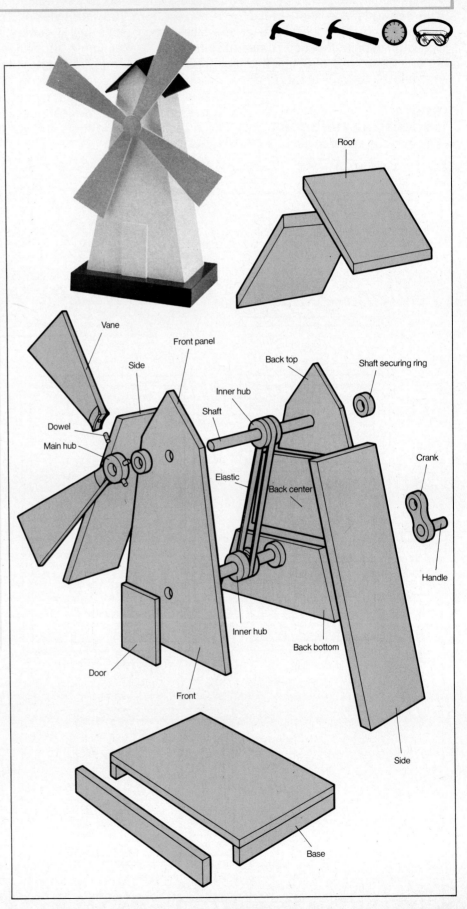

Windmills go back to the seventh century in Asia and the Middle Ages in Europe. Although now they strike us as merely picturesque, through the centuries they have performed a number of useful functions—pumping water, driving sawmills, and grinding grain—providing energy at relatively low cost. No Dutch land-

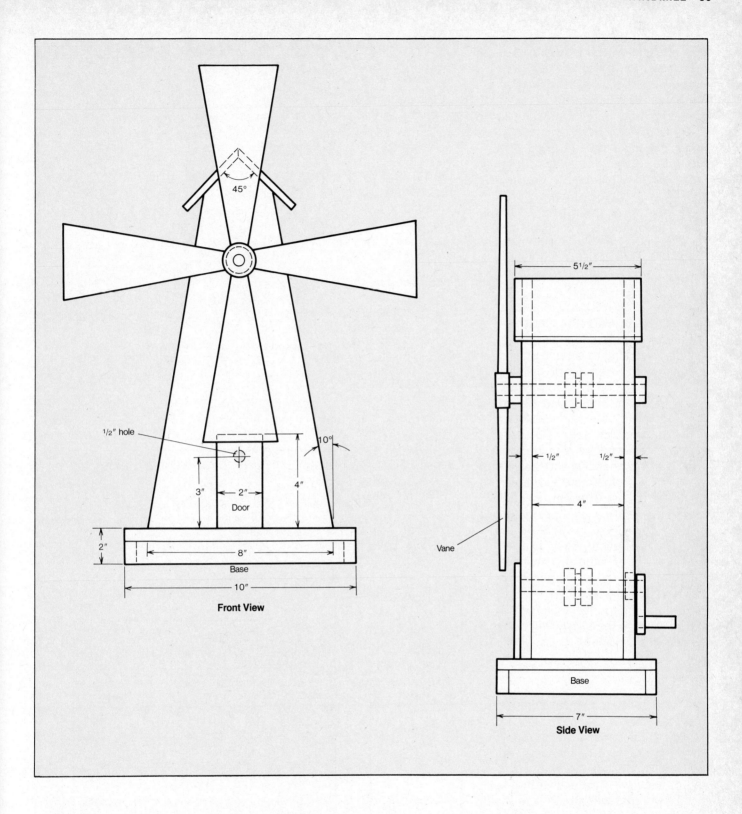

Front View

45°

1/2" hole

3"   2"   4"
Door

10°

2"

8"
Base

10"

5 1/2"

1/2"   1/2"

4"

Vane

Base

7"

Side View

scape would be complete without its typical windmills, and we're familiar with the high steel towers and metal wheels that stand in stately isolation on the prairies of the American West. "Tilting at windmills" is a handy phrase that we owe to Don Quixote and his heroic sortie against what he saw as outrageous giants inhabiting the Spanish countryside.

Perhaps our hand-powered model will give children the imaginative experience of capturing the power of the wind. In reading the instructions for making the windmill, note that there is a test assembly of the moving parts, and then a dismantling for painting, before final assembly.

STEP 1
CUTTING AND ASSEMBLY
Cut the base parts to sizes shown and glue them together to form the windmill base. Cut the panels for the main structure to the given sizes and shapes. Tape the front panel and the upper and lower parts of the back panel together in the proper posi-

tions and drill the ½-inch shaft holes in both front and back at the same time to ensure that they will line up. Then glue the side panels to the inside of the front panel. Glue the two sections of the back panel to the sides, making sure that the shaft holes line up and that the removable center section fits properly. This section will be secured to the sides with the two 1-inch wood screws. Glue the door to the bottom center of the front panel, covering the lower shaft hole. Cut the two roof panels and glue them together on the 45° bevel.

STEP 2
HUBS, RINGS, AND PULLEYS
The best way to form the disks used for hubs, securing rings, and pulleys is to draw the diameter of the disk with a compass on a scrap of wood of the proper thickness. (The dimensions of the various disks are shown in the drawings on page 85.) Using the compass mark as a guide, drill the ½-inch hole needed, and then cut the disk out on the band saw to the required diameter. Glue the inner hub disk to the front panel, making sure the holes are lined up. Glue up the three parts of each pulley (the two outer wheels and the inner wheel), carefully lining up the center holes. Drill one side of each pulley and the two securing rings for setscrews to secure them to the shaft. Drill holes in main hub for vanes.

STEP 3
VANES
Cut the four vanes to size. Glue two small blocks of 3/16-inch stock (¾ × 1 inch) to the small end of each vane. Shape the blocks as shown, with rasp and sandpaper. Drill the bottom end of each vane to receive the ¼-inch dowel that will attach it to the main hub. Slightly round the bottom of each vane with rasp and sandpaper so as to fit the main hub. Glue vanes to main hub.

STEP 4
ASSEMBLY
Glue the upper shaft to the main hub and vane assembly, aligning the end of the shaft flush with the front of the

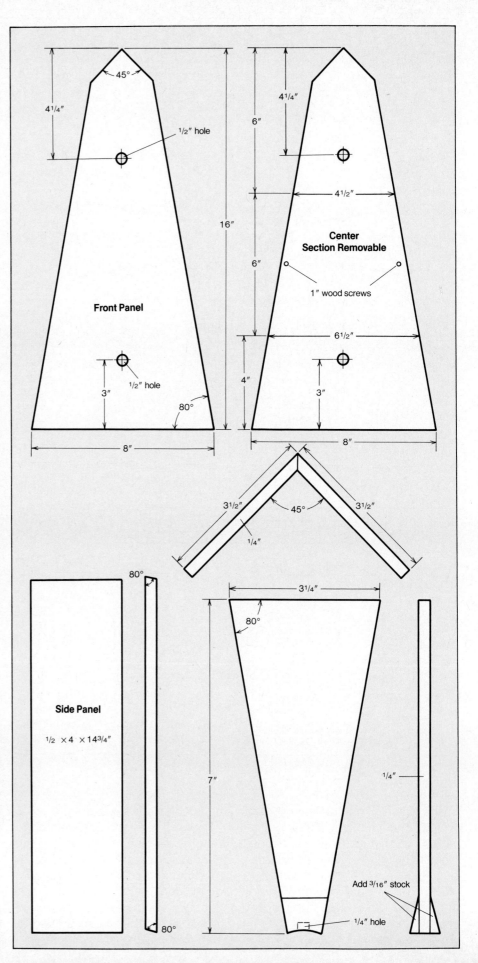

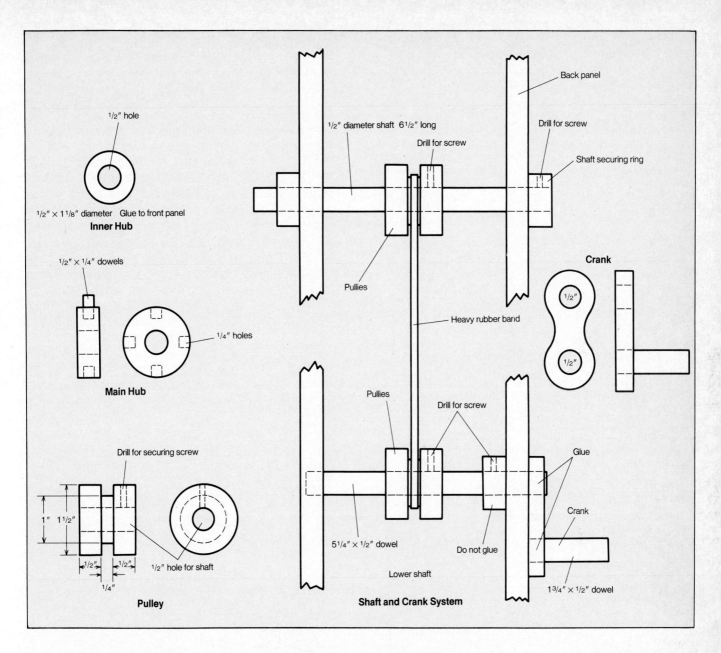

Inner Hub
1/2" hole
1/2" × 1 1/8" diameter   Glue to front panel

Main Hub
1/2" × 1/4" dowels
1/4" holes

Pulley
Drill for securing screw
1" 1 1/2"
1/2" 1/2"
1/4"
1/2" hole for shaft

Shaft and Crank System
1/2" diameter shaft 6 1/2" long
Drill for screw
Back panel
Drill for screw
Shaft securing ring
Pullies
Heavy rubber band
Pullies
Drill for screw
Glue
5 1/4" × 1/2" dowel
Do not glue
Lower shaft
Crank
1 3/4" × 1/2" dowel

Crank
1/2"
1/2"

hub. Insert the upper shaft through the inner hub and the front panel. Slip a heavy rubber band over one pulley and onto the shaft; push the shaft through the upper hole in the back panel. Secure the shaft with one of the securing rings. Secure the pulley to the center of the shaft with a setscrew.

Assemble the crank and glue it to the lower shaft. Insert the shaft through the lower hole in the back panel and then through the securing ring and the pulley. Before inserting the shaft into the hole in the front panel, slip the rubber band over the pulley. Secure the shaft with the securing ring, but be sure to leave a slight space between the ring and

the back panel for free movement. Secure the pulley to the center of the lower shaft with the setscrew. Now turn the handle to make sure the shafts turn freely and the vanes spin. You may have to experiment with rubber bands until you get the proper tension. When everything works, disassemble the unglued parts, removing the setscrews from the securing rings, for painting.

STEP 5
PAINTING
After sanding and cleanup, paint the parts separately. You may wish to follow this color scheme: main structure white with brown door; roof brown; vanes yellow; base green; and

upper securing ring and handle white or brown. Or you may prefer to select your own colors. Do not paint the shafts, pulleys, and lower securing ring. After the paint is dry, make sure the shaft holes are clear of paint. If necessary to clear them, use a piece of sandpaper wrapped around a dowel.

STEP 6
FINAL ASSEMBLY
Glue the main structure to the base, and the roof to the main structure. Insert the shafts, pulleys, rings, and rubber bands in proper order (see Step 4). Secure the shafts and then the removable back panel. The windmill is ready to turn.

Locomotive

MATERIALS LIST
Main frame (1), 3/8″ × 3¹/2″ × 10¹/4″, pine
Boiler, cab section (1), 1¹/2″ × 2¹/8″ × 2¹/2″, hardwood
Boiler, center section (1), 1³/4″ × 1³/4″ × 5″, hardwood
Boiler, front section (1), 1¹/4″ × 1³/4″ × 1³/4″, hardwood
Cab roof (1), 3/16″ × 4¹/4″ × 3³/4″, hardwood
Cab sides (2), 1/4″ × 2¹/2″ × 3″, hardwood
Cab front (1), 1/4″ × 3″ × 3¹/2″, hardwood
Steam whistle (1), 1³/4″ × 7/8″ dowel, hardwood
Steam dome (1), 1¹/2″ × 7/8″ dowel, hardwood
Bell (1), 1¹/8″ × 1/2″ dowel, hardwood
Smokestack, upper part (1), 1³/4″ × 2″ × 2″, pine
Smokestack, lower part (1), 1¹/8″ × 3/4″ dowel, hardwood
Lantern (1), 5/8″ × 5/8″ × 1″, pine
Lantern holders (2), 5/8″ × 1/8″ dowel, hardwood
Catwalk, front part (2), 3/16″ × 1/2″ × 4″, pine
Catwalk, back part (2), 3/16″ × 3/4″ × 4″, pine

Front braces (2), 3/16″ × 3/16″ × 1³/4″, hardwood
Rear wheels (4), 1/4″ × 2¹/2″ diameter, hardwood
Rear axles (2), 4¹/8″ × 1/4″ dowel, hardwood
Rear axle holders (2), 3/4″ × 7/8″ × 3¹/2″, pine
Front truck plate (1), 1/4″ × 3¹/2″ × 3¹/2″, pine
Back truck-axle holders (2), 1/2″ × 1″ × 1¹/8″, pine
Front truck-axle holders (2), 1/2″ × 1″ × 1³/8″, pine
Truck wheels (4), 1/4″ × 1¹/4″ diameter, hardwood
Truck axles (2), 4¹/8″ × 3/16″ dowel, hardwood
Truck oilers (2), 1/2″ × 5/8″ × 1″, pine
Cowcatcher (1), 1″ × 1¹/2″ × 3¹/2″, hardwood
Brace (1), 1/4″ × 5/8″ × 2¹/2″, pine
Yellow wood glue
Nontoxic clear finish

Tools
Table saw
Band saw
Coping saw
Drill or drill press
Lathe

Block plane
Wood rasp
Light wood clamps
Masking tape
Sandpaper, 80, 120, and 220

Making a model of the *General* is a project resonant with historical associations. This famous locomotive was owned by Georgia's Western and Atlantic Railroad and used by the Confederacy during the Civil War. In April 1862, twenty Union soldiers hijacked the *General* but were furiously pursued by the *Texas,* a second Confederate locomotive, which steamed backward in a frantic attempt to recapture the stolen prize. Children who have watched reruns of the silent movie with Buster Keaton or Walt Disney's *The Great Locomotive Chase* are familiar with the exploit. This wooden model keeps the history alive.

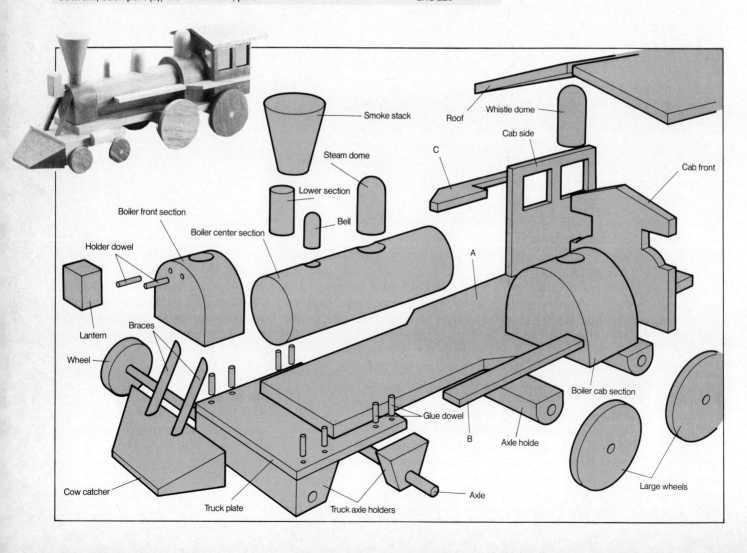

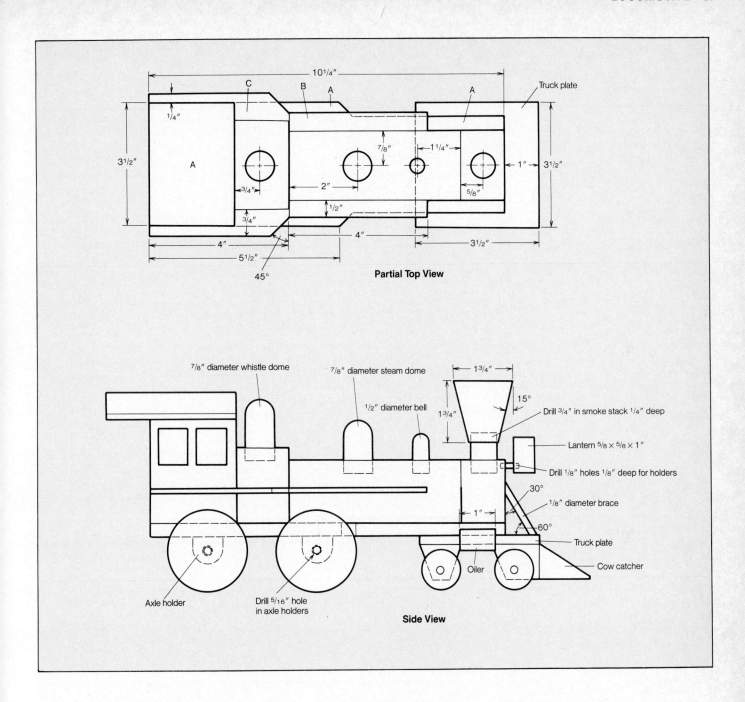

Partial Top View

Side View

STEP 1
CUTTING THE PIECES

Cut out the three parts of the boiler to the dimensions shown. While the blocks are still square, drill the holes for the whistle, dome, bell, and smokestack. The sections can now be cut to their final shapes. The center section is a cylinder with a diameter of 1³/4 inches. This can be turned on a lathe or formed with the table saw and a plane. To use the table saw, first draw a circle with a diameter of 1³/4 inches on one end of the block. Then cut four 45° bevels along the 5-inch sides of the block tangent to the circle, forming an octagon shape. Leave one of the eight sides flat (to be glued to the main frame) and shape the other edges to the 1³/4-inch diameter with a block plane and sandpaper. Cut the block for the smokestack (upper part) and drill the ³/4-inch hole for the lower part. To form the smokestack, set the blade of the band saw to 15° and cut out a truncated cone with a lower diameter of ⁷/8 inch and an upper diameter of 1³/4 inches. Glue in the ³/4-inch dowel and finish shaping with sandpaper.

The rounded tops of the whistle, dome, and bell are formed with a wood rasp and sandpaper. Cut and drill the rear axle holders. The rear axle holders and truck oilers are shaped with the plane and sandpaper. The remaining pieces have straight or angle cuts and can be cut out on the table or band saw. Drill axle holes in the truck-axle holders.

STEP 2
ASSEMBLING THE PARTS

Sand all parts carefully, finishing with 220 sandpaper. Glue the three

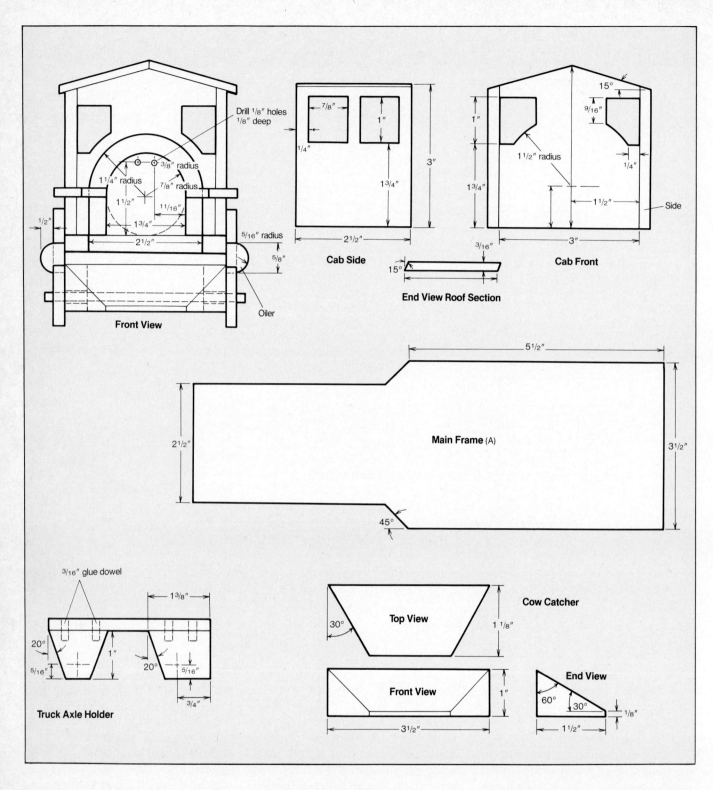

parts of the boiler together and secure with light wood clamps or masking tape. Glue in the whistle, dome, bell, smokestack, and lantern. Next glue the five parts of the cab together. The truck-axle holders are glued to the truck plate using 1/2-inch lengths of 3/16-inch dowels. Glue in the cowcatcher brace between the front truck-axle holders. Glue in the cowcatcher and oilers. The rear axle holders are glued to the main frame.

STEP 3
ASSEMBLING AND FINISHING THE LOCOMOTIVE
If you prefer, the various subassemblies can be finished before the final assembly. Do not finish surfaces to be glued together. Begin assembly by gluing the truck assembly to the front end of the main frame. Then glue the cab to the other end of the main frame. The boiler unit is fastened in place next. Glue in the catwalk parts and the front diagonal braces. The wheels are glued to the axles. Finish the locomotive with two coats of clear finish.

Barn Toy Chest

MATERIALS LIST

Chest bottom (1), 1/2″ × 19″ × 29″, plywood
Front and back (2), 1/2″ × 12″ × 30″, plywood
Lower sides (2), 1/2″ × 12″ × 19″, plywood
Upper side panels (2), 1/2″ × 91/4″ × 19″, plywood
Roof (1), 1/2″ × 34″ × 30″, plywood
Cupola body (1), 1″ × 2″ × 81/4″, pine
Cupola roof (1), 1/4″ × 11/2″ × 81/4″, pine
Doors (4), 1/4″ × 3/8″ × 17″, pine
Tray bottom (1), 1/4″ × 183/8″ × 283/8″, plywood
Tray frame (1), 1/2″ × 21/2″ × 8″, plywood
Tray cleats (2), 1/2″ × 1″ × 29″, plywood
Combination hinge and lid support (1 pair)*, 3/4″ × 21/2″ × 41/2″
Roof handle (1), 3/4″ × 13/4″ × 30″, pine
Plate casters (4), 11/4″ (optional)
Yellow wood glue
Brads, 11/4″
Wood putty

Nontoxic paint
(Dimensions larger than those shown in drawings allow for saw, angle, or bevel cuts.)
*If you are unable to locate this item locally, you can obtain it from:

The Woodworkers' Store
21801 Industrial Blvd.
Rogers, Minnesota 55374

Carlson Capitol Mfg. Co.
P.O. Box 6165
Rockford, Illinois 61125

Tools
Table saw
Band saw
Hammer
Screwdriver
Masking tape
Sandpaper, 80, 120, and 220

With this attractive receptacle, you can help prevent overstuffed closets and scattered or lost toys. If you decide to put the barn on wheels, it can easily be moved to a play area and then off to one side. Putting things away becomes a game, and a room can be made tidy in minutes. When making the roof, note that the dimensions given are for all six parts and that they allow room for cutting and beveling.

STEP 1
CUTTING THE PIECES
First, cut out the five pieces for the lower part of the barn—the bottom,

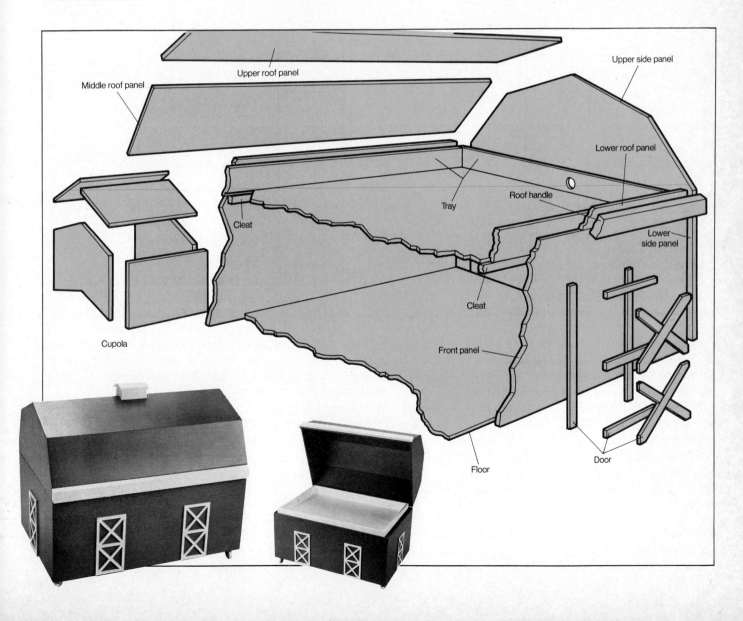

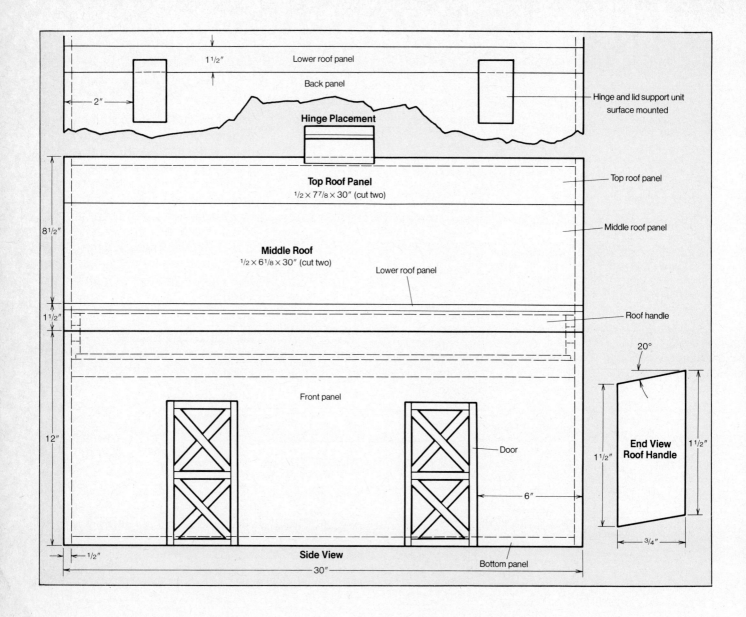

front, back, and two lower sides. The roof panels have bevel cuts and care must be taken with these to ensure a good fit (see Side View plan). The lower roof panels have straight cuts, but the upper side panels must be cut at angles to conform to the roof panels. Lay out the shape of the upper side panel, as shown in Section A, directly onto the wood and cut out on the band saw or table saw. If you attach the two pieces of plywood together with light brads, you can saw both panels at the same time. Cut out the tray cleats and the roof handle to size.

STEP 2
ASSEMBLING THE TRAY
Cut the sides of the tray to size as shown with a 45° cut at each end for a mitered joint. Cut a 1/4- × 1/4-inch rabbet along the bottom edge of each side to accept the bottom panel. Drill a 1-inch finger hole into each end of the tray. Cut the bottom panel from 1/4-inch plywood. Assemble the tray sides with glue and light brads. Glue the bottom panel into the rabbets and secure with light brads. Set all brads and fill the holes with wood putty. When dry, sand smooth.

STEP 3
ASSEMBLING THE DOORS
The doors are decorative and are made of 1/4-inch stock 3/8 inch wide. Cut all pieces to size, assemble with glue, and secure with masking tape. When dry, sand all doors smooth.

STEP 4
ASSEMBLING THE CUPOLA
The cupola is made of two pieces of 1-inch stock beveled on each side at 20°. The roof is cut from 1/4-inch stock with the same bevels. Assemble all parts with glue, and secure with masking tape. When dry, sand smooth.

STEP 5
ASSEMBLY
Begin the assembly by attaching the tray cleats to the inside of the front and back panels, 1½ inches from the top and ½ inch in from either end, with glue and light brads. Next, fasten the lower side panels to the bottom panel with glue and brads. Complete the lower part of the chest

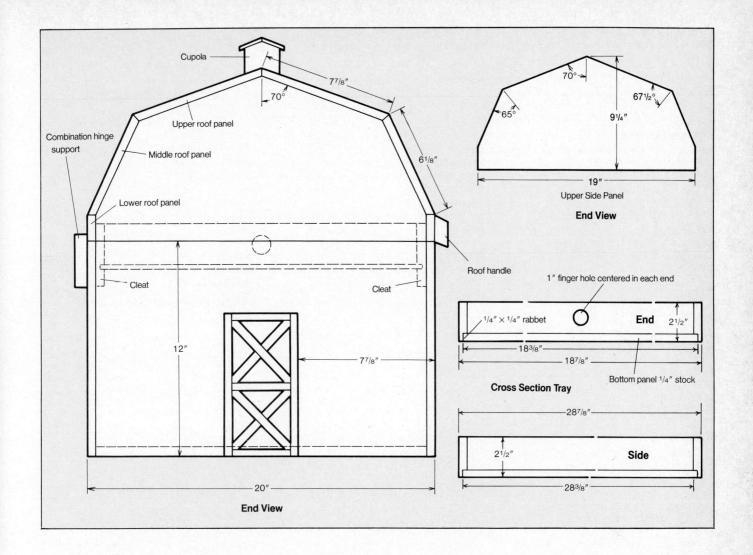

Cupola

70°

7⁷/₈"

Upper roof panel

Middle roof panel

Combination hinge support

Lower roof panel

6¹/₈"

Cleat

Roof handle

Cleat

12"

7⁷/₈"

20"

End View

70°

65°

67¹/₂°

9¹/₄"

19"

Upper Side Panel

End View

1" finger hole centered in each end

¹/₄" × ¹/₄" rabbet

End

2¹/₂"

18³/₈"

18⁷/₈"

Bottom panel ¹/₄" stock

Cross Section Tray

28⁷/₈"

2¹/₂"

Side

28³/₈"

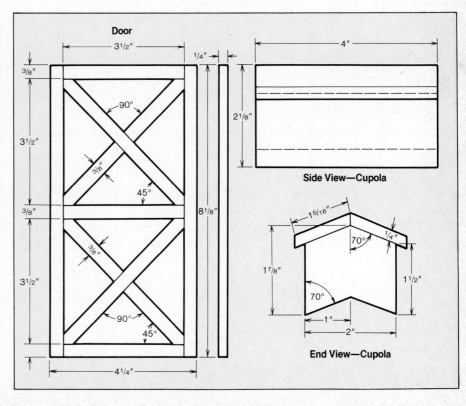

Door

3¹/₂"

¹/₄"

3/8"

3¹/₂"

90°

3/8"

45°

3/8"

3/8"

3¹/₂"

3/8"

90°

45°

8¹/₈"

4¹/₄"

4"

2¹/₈"

Side View—Cupola

1⁵/₁₆"

70°

¹/₄"

17/8"

70°

1¹/₂"

1"

2"

End View—Cupola

by gluing the front and back panels to the sides and bottom. Assemble the roof by gluing the roof panels to the end and to each other. Use brads to secure the panels to the ends, and put strips of masking tape across the roof panels until the glue dries. Set all brads and fill with wood putty. The roof is attached to the body of the chest by a surface-mounted combination hinge and lid support, affixed to the outside of the roof and body with the screws that come with the product. The roof handle can be put on now, or later if you wish to paint it a different color. The same is true of the doors and the cupola. When all glue and wood putty are dry, sand the chest, remove all dust, and it is ready for painting. We painted our barn red and the cupola, doors, and handle white. Use two coats of a nontoxic enamel. If you decide to put the barn on wheels, attach the plate casters.

Village

MATERIALS LIST

Building sides and floors, $1/4''$ stock, plywood
Church roof pieces (2), $1/4'' \times 2^1/2'' \times 5''$, plywood
Church steeple, lower part (1), $1^1/4'' \times 1^1/4'' \times 1^1/4''$, pine
Church steeple, upper part (1), $1'' \times 1'' \times 2^1/2''$, pine
General-store roof pieces (4), $1/4'' \times 1^1/2'' \times 4''$, plywood
Saltbox-house roof (1), $1/4'' \times 4'' \times 6''$, plywood
Octagon-house roof (1), $1/4'' \times 3^1/2'' \times 3^1/2''$, plywood

Octagon cupola (1), $7/8'' \times 1'' \times 1''$, pine
Schoolhouse roof (1), $2^1/4'' \times 4'' \times 4''$, pine
Schoolhouse cupola (1), $3/4'' \times 1'' \times 1^1/4''$, pine
Victorian mansion roof (1), $1^1/2'' \times 2^1/2'' \times 3''$, pine
Victorian tower roof (1), $1'' \times 1^3/4'' \times 1^3/4''$, pine
Bank roof (1), $1^1/2'' \times 3^1/2'' \times 3^1/2''$, pine
Shed-house roof (1), $1^1/2'' \times 3'' \times 3''$, pine
Shed-house addition (1), $1^1/2'' \times 1^3/4'' \times 3''$, pine
Office-building roof (1), $1^1/2'' \times 3'' \times 4''$, pine
House A roof (1), $1'' \times 2'' \times 3^1/2''$, pine
House B roof (1), $1'' \times 2'' \times 4''$, pine

House C roof (1), $7/8'' \times 2^3/4'' \times 4''$, pine
Doors, windows, $3/16''$ stock
Yellow wood glue
Nontoxic paint

Tools

Table saw
Band saw
Backsaw
Wood rasp
Light wood clamps
Masking tape

Sandpaper, 80, 120, and 220

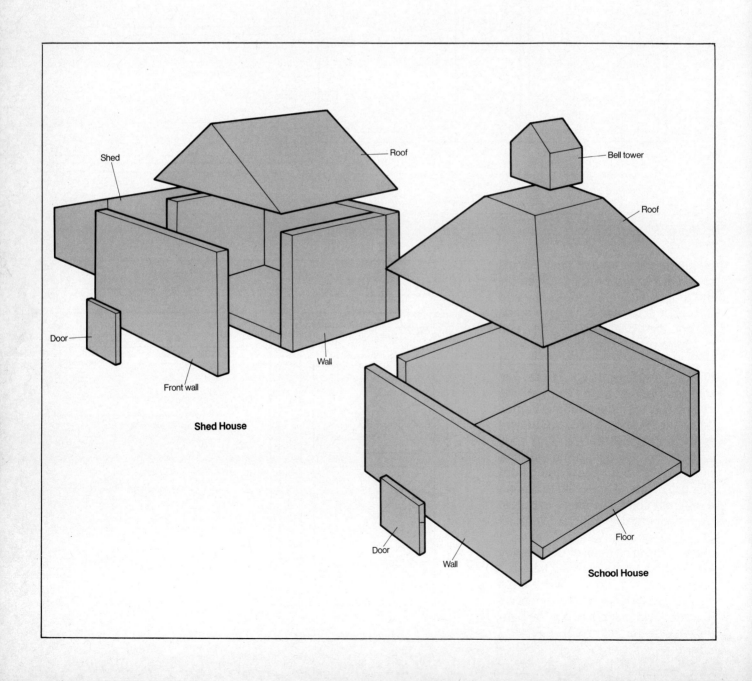

Shed House

School House

With these structures young settlers can found a model community of their own. The village is loosely based on architecture from the northeastern United States of various periods. The saltbox house recalls the Adams house in Quincy, Massachusetts. The octagon house is modeled after one that was built in New York State, and the house with shed attached was common to many towns. For variety's sake, there's also a Victorian mansion. Additional houses, a bank, a general store, an office building, the little red schoolhouse, and the steepled New England church complete the ensemble. If they are so minded, kids can make signs for the general store and the doctor's or lawyer's office.

STEP 1
CUTTING THE PIECES

The sides and floors of all buildings are made from ¼-inch plywood. Cut these out on the table saw to the dimensions given. The roofs of the church, general store, saltbox house, and octagon house are made from ¼-inch plywood and require different angle cuts as indicated. The roofs of

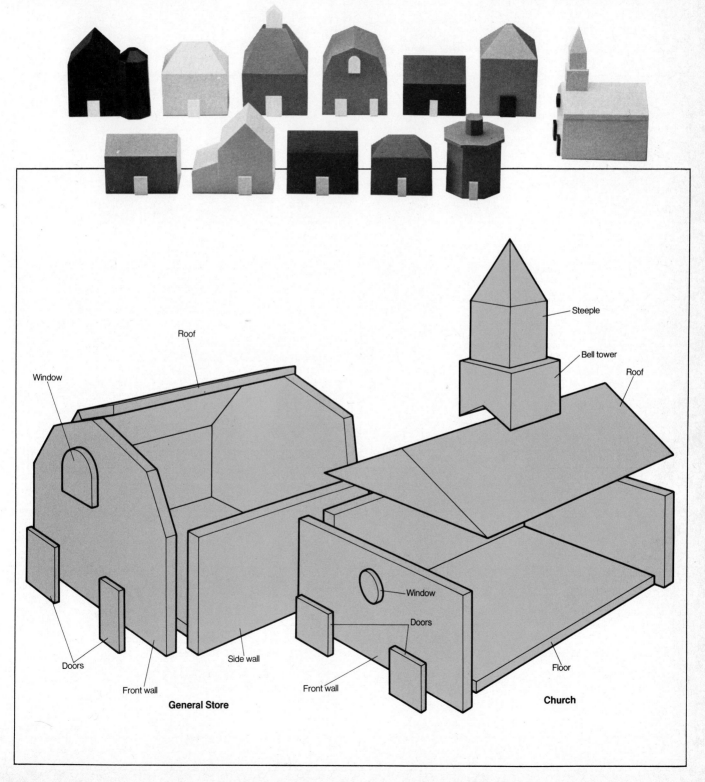

General Store

Church

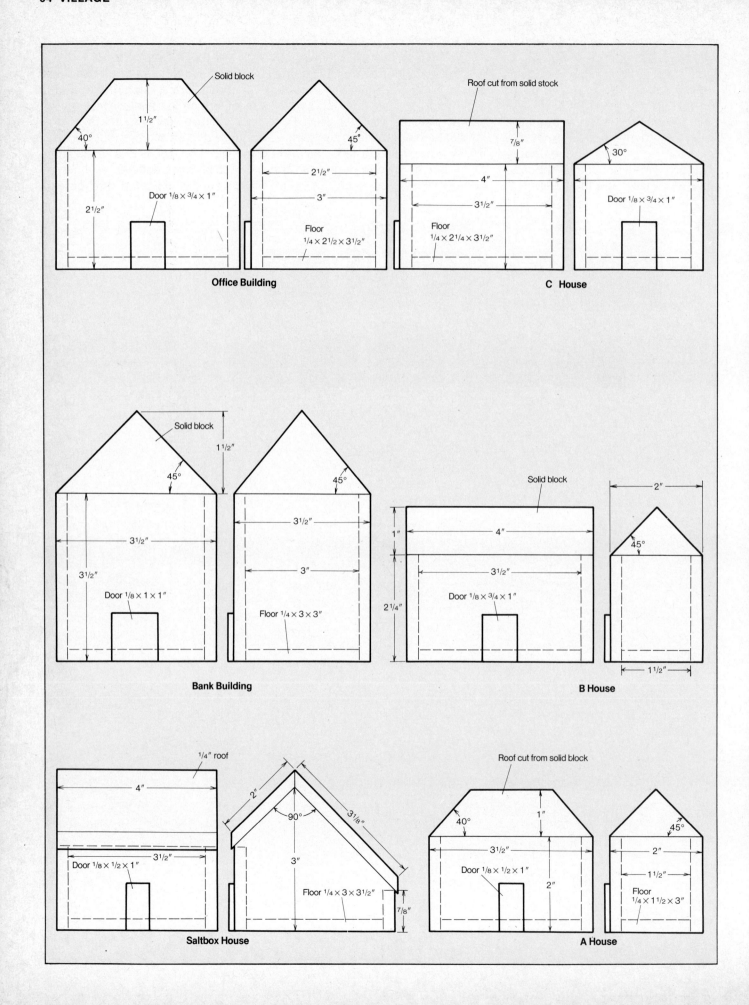

Office Building

Solid block
1 1/2"
40°
2 1/2"
Door 1/8 × 3/4 × 1"

45°
2 1/2"
3"
Floor
1/4 × 2 1/2 × 3 1/2"

C House

Roof cut from solid stock
7/8"
4"
3 1/2"
Floor
1/4 × 2 1/4 × 3 1/2"

30°
Door 1/8 × 3/4 × 1"

Bank Building

Solid block
1 1/2"
45°
3 1/2"
3 1/2"
Door 1/8 × 1 × 1"

45°
3 1/2"
3"
Floor 1/4 × 3 × 3"

B House

Solid block
1"
4"
2 1/4"
3 1/2"
Door 1/8 × 3/4 × 1"

2"
45°
1 1/2"

Saltbox House

1/4" roof
4"
3 1/2"
Door 1/8 × 1/2 × 1"

2"
90°
3 1/8"
3"
Floor 1/4 × 3 × 3 1/2"
7/8"

A House

Roof cut from solid block
40°
1"
3 1/2"
Door 1/8 × 1/2 × 1"
2"

45°
2"
1 1/2"
Floor
1/4 × 1 1/2 × 3"

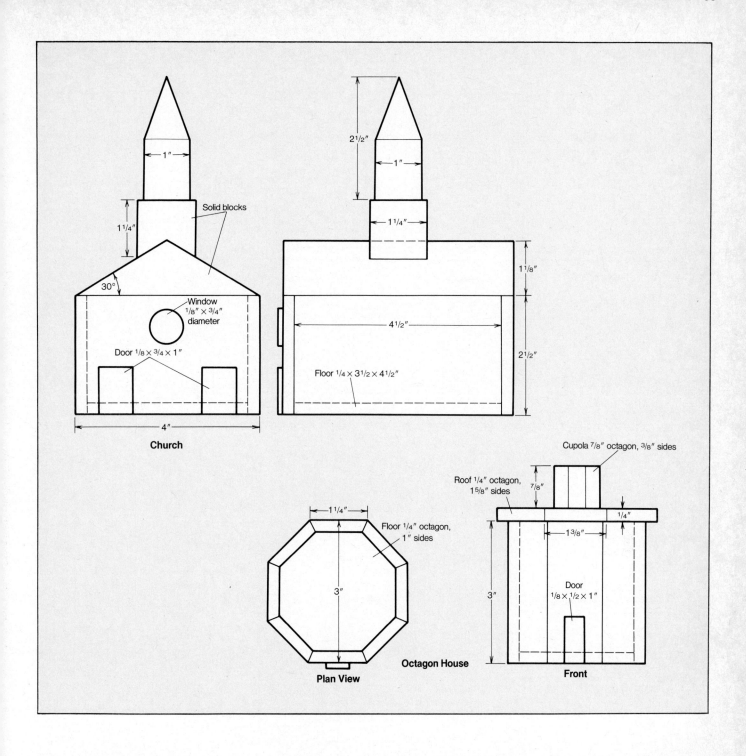

Church

Plan View

Octagon House

Front

the remaining structures are solid blocks of pine and are cut at various angles as shown. The church steeple is made in two parts, the lower part being angled to fit the slope of the roof. The octagon-house cupola is a small octagonal block that can be cut with a backsaw. The roof of the Victorian tower is also an octagon, which is sloped with the wood rasp and sandpaper. The schoolhouse cupola is cut from 3/4-inch stock. The shed for the shed house is cut from 1 1/2-inch stock. The doors and windows for all structures are cut from 3/16-inch stock to the sizes indicated.

STEP 2
ASSEMBLING AND FINISHING THE BUILDINGS

For each building, glue the floor, sides, and roof together, securing the pieces with masking tape or light wood clamps. Glue in the church steeple and octagon-house cupola.

Do not glue on the schoolhouse cupola, or any doors and windows at this time. When the glue is dry, sand all buildings thoroughly and remove all dust. Finish the village with two coats of nontoxic enamels in bright colors. We used white for the church and red for the schoolhouse, with a white cupola. The other buildings can be whatever colors you choose. The doors, windows, and schoolhouse cupola should be painted separately and glued on later.

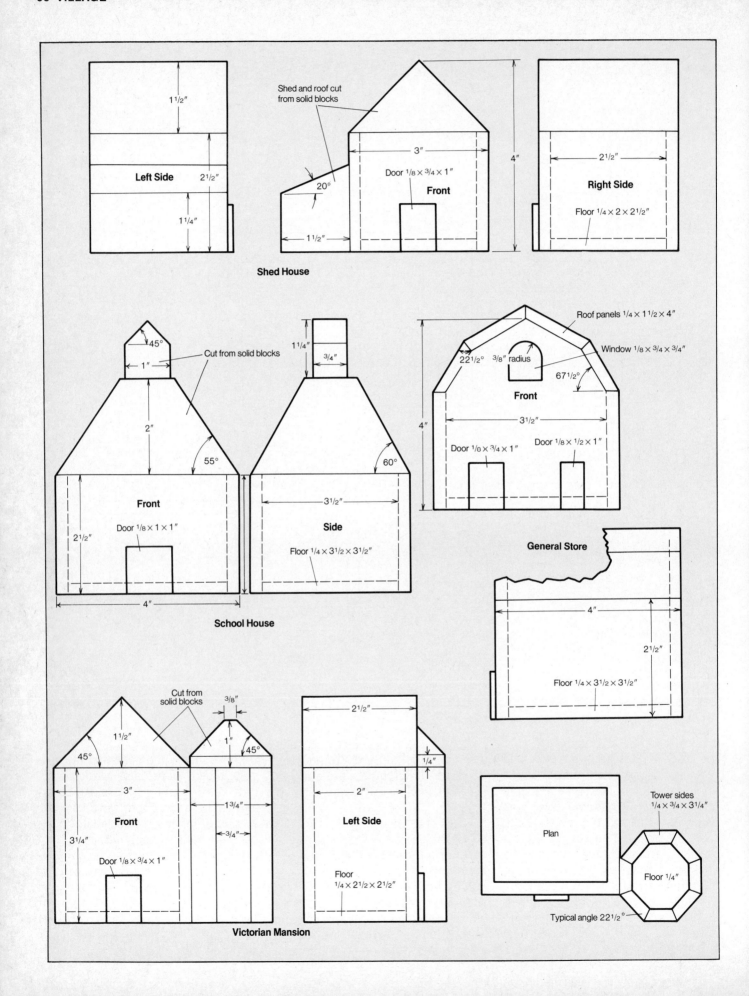

Shed House

Left Side
1¹/₂″
2¹/₂″
1¹/₄″

Shed and roof cut from solid blocks
20°
3″
4″
Door ¹/₈ × ³/₄ × 1″
Front
1¹/₂″

Right Side
2¹/₂″
Floor ¹/₄ × 2 × 2¹/₂″

School House

45°
1″
Cut from solid blocks
2″
55°
Front
Door ¹/₈ × 1 × 1″
2¹/₂″
4″

1¹/₄″
³/₄″
60°
3¹/₂″
Side
Floor ¹/₄ × 3¹/₂ × 3¹/₂″

General Store

Roof panels ¹/₄ × 1¹/₂ × 4″
Window ¹/₈ × ³/₄ × ³/₄″
22¹/₂°   ³/₈″ radius
67¹/₂°
Front
4″
3¹/₂″
Door ¹/₈ × ³/₄ × 1″   Door ¹/₈ × ¹/₂ × 1″

4″
2¹/₂″
Floor ¹/₄ × 3¹/₂ × 3¹/₂″

Victorian Mansion

Cut from solid blocks
³/₈″
1¹/₂″
45°
45°   1″
3″
1³/₄″
³/₄″
Front
3¹/₄″
Door ¹/₈ × ³/₄ × 1″

2¹/₂″
¹/₄″
2″
Left Side
Floor ¹/₄ × 2¹/₂ × 2¹/₂″

Tower sides ¹/₄ × ³/₄ × 3¹/₄″
Plan
Floor ¹/₄″
Typical angle 22¹/₂°

Color Tower (page 17). Toddlers like playing with the colored rings of this easy toy.

Crayon and Pencil Holder (page 18). Make a faithful keeper of writing and drawing tools.

Animal Puzzles (page 19). You cut and paint them; the kids put them together.

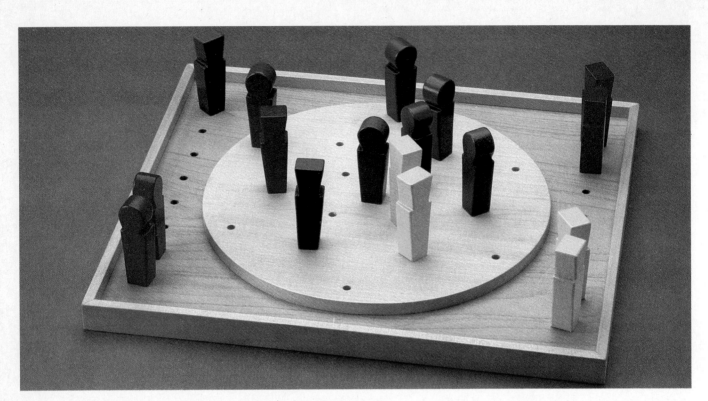

People Game (page 20). A simple game to make for younger players.

Giant Checkerboard (pages 21-22). The old favorite, here hand-crafted on a large scale.

Photo Puzzle (page 23). Make children's puzzles from pictures of your own choosing.

Face Puzzle (page 27). With different parts, this puzzle becomes several faces.

Animal Pull Toys (pages 24-26). Every young child likes pull toys, the simpler the better.

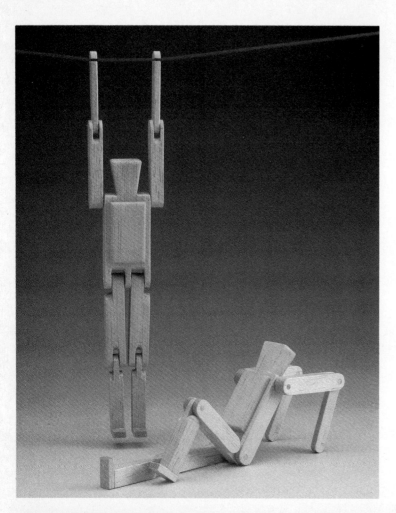

Loose-Jointed Doll (pages 28-29). If you decide to try this doll, plan to make more than one. Kids love them.

Doll Seesaw (pages 30-31). The Loose-Jointed Doll can sit neatly in the seesaw's seat, as can other small creatures.

Doll Swing (pages 32-33). With the Doll See-saw, this is part of a doll-sized playground.

Doll Cradle (pages 34-36). Care will make this cradle the pride of any doll's parent.

Cat Play Clock (pages 45-47). This clock doesn't keep time, but it helps children learn to tell time.

Giant Tic Tac Toe (page 48). A universal favorite with children, this shiny board with wooden Xs and Os will get a lot of use.

Tugboat (pages 43-44). Designed to bathtub specifications, this workhorse tugboat floats rightside up.

Circus Train (pages 58-61). A rolling trainload of fun for a playroom.

Noah's Ark and Noah's Animals (pages 117-123). The top lifts off this child-size ark so the animals can be stored neatly inside.

Shuffleboard (page 49). The outdoor game in a tabletop version.

Disk Bowling Game (page 50). A scaled-down game that's just right for junior bowlers.

Indoor Pet House (pages 56-57). Stuffed animals, live cats, and small dogs all find this house comfortable, maybe because the angled walls give it a jaunty air.

Farm Tractor and Wagon (pages 62-65). Perfect for hauling produce on the playroom floor.

Farm Truck (page 66-68). The wooden cars and trucks in this book are taken from the early 1900s to beguile space-age kids.

Ambulance (page 69-71). This one has a clear finish to show the wood. You can also paint it, as well as the other clear finished projects in this book, bright colors.

Racing Car (pages 72-74). A drill press makes rolling toys easy to put together.

Model T Ford (pages 75-78). With careful cutting, the car that put people on wheels reappears as a rugged wood toy.

Garage for the Model T (pages 79-81). Frame and slat construction make this garage a sturdy home for the Model T.

Windmill (pages 82-85). The vanes on the windmill turn by a crank in the back and rubber bands on wheels inside.

Barn Toy Chest (page 89-91). Its large volume and lift-out tray make this chest ideal for stabling the young ones' toys.

Village (pages 92-96). Cutting, gluing, and painting for a few hours produces a collection of little buildings where youngsters can go to town.

Carousel (pages 137-140). A smooth-turning carousel in the grand style for year-round play.

Fire Engine (pages 128-132). The ladders on this engine are a nice test of craftsmanship.

Ferris Wheel (pages 133-136). Make this favorite fairground ride along with the carousel for a working playroom amusement park.

Locomotive (pages 86-88). This steamer is modeled on the famous *General* which ran the rails in the 1860s.

Ox Cart and Oxen (pages 113-116). You can take the yokes off these oxen, unhitch the cart, and take off its sides.

Riverboat (pages 124-127). A stately side-wheeler with paddles that turn freely will take young imaginations on long river trips.

Rocking Horse (pages 141-144). No home with young children should be without a rocking horse—preferably one this sturdy.

Three-Wheel Horse Cart (pages 145-147). Designed to last, this all-time favorite will roll smoothly under a succession of young riders.

Soap Box Racer (pages 148-151). Good for coasting or a push from a friend, this classic racer turns with a tug on the steering rope.

Red Rack Wagon (page 152-155). With its removable racks, this wagon can be adapted to a variety of important childhood expeditions.

Ox Cart and Oxen

MATERIALS LIST

Oxen:
Oxen (2), $1^{1}/8'' \times 5'' \times 8''$, pine or hardwood
Yokes (2), $^{1}/2'' \times 1^{1}/4'' \times 5^{1}/2''$, pine or hardwood
Yoke pins (4), $1^{5}/8'' \times ^{1}/4''$ dowel, hardwood
Wheels (4), $^{1}/4'' \times 1''$ diameter, pine or hardwood
Axles (4), $1^{1}/8'' \times ^{1}/8''$ dowel, hardwood

Cart:
Cart bed (1), $^{3}/8'' \times 6'' \times 9''$, pine or hardwood
Sides (4), $^{1}/4'' \times 1^{1}/2'' \times 7^{1}/2''$, pine or hardwood
Ends (4), $^{1}/4'' \times 1^{1}/2'' \times 5''$, pine or hardwood
Side braces (4), $^{1}/2'' \times ^{1}/2'' \times 1^{1}/2''$, pine or hardwood
Stakes (8), $^{1}/4'' \times ^{1}/2'' \times 3''$, pine or hardwood

Stake holders (16), $^{3}/8'' \times ^{1}/2'' \times 1^{1}/2''$, pine or hardwood
Axle holders (2), $1'' \times 1'' \times 2''$, pine or hardwood
Axle (1), $9'' \times ^{3}/8''$ dowel, hardwood
Axle pins (2), $^{3}/4'' \times ^{1}/8''$ dowel, hardwood
Wheels (2), $^{3}/4'' \times 5''$ diameter, pine or hardwood
Wheel braces (4), $^{1}/4'' \times ^{3}/4'' \times 3^{1}/4''$, pine or hardwood
Cart tongue, $^{3}/8'' \times ^{5}/8'' \times 9''$, pine or hardwood
Cart-tongue holders (2), $^{3}/8'' \times ^{5}/8'' \times 2''$, pine or hardwood
Tongue pin, $1^{1}/8'' \times ^{1}/4''$ dowel, hardwood

Glue dowels (as needed), $^{3}/16''$ dowel, hardwood

Screw eyes (4), #214 $^{1}/2''$
Metal rings (2), $^{1}/2''$ diameter
S hooks (2), $^{3}/4''$
Yellow wood glue
Nontoxic clear finish or paint

Tools
Table saw ⎯ Backsaw
Band saw ⎯ Jigsaw
Drill or drill press
Fine or medium wood rasp
Round rasp
Awl
Light bar clamp, C-clamp, or spring clamp
Masking tape
Sandpaper, 80, 120, and 220

Oxen have been used for plowing and hauling for centuries and are still a mainstay of life and work in many parts of the world. Children will enjoy weaving tales around this pair of strong, patient beasts. The oxen here are used to pull this oxcart, but they can be unhitched for other work and play. The cart has removable sides for different loads.

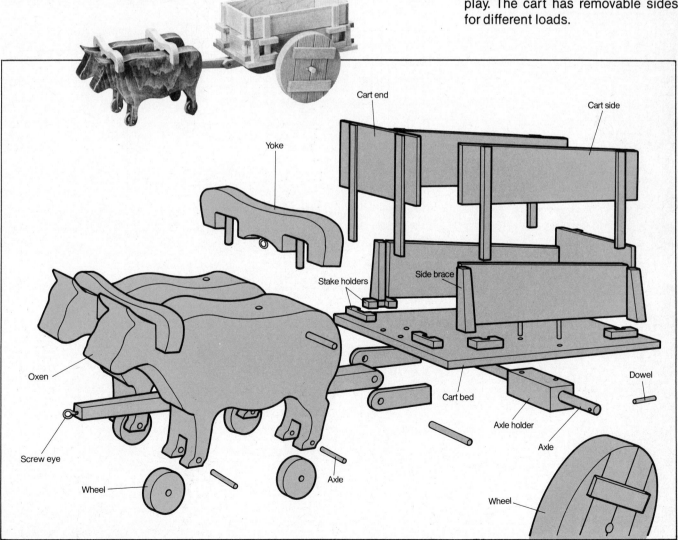

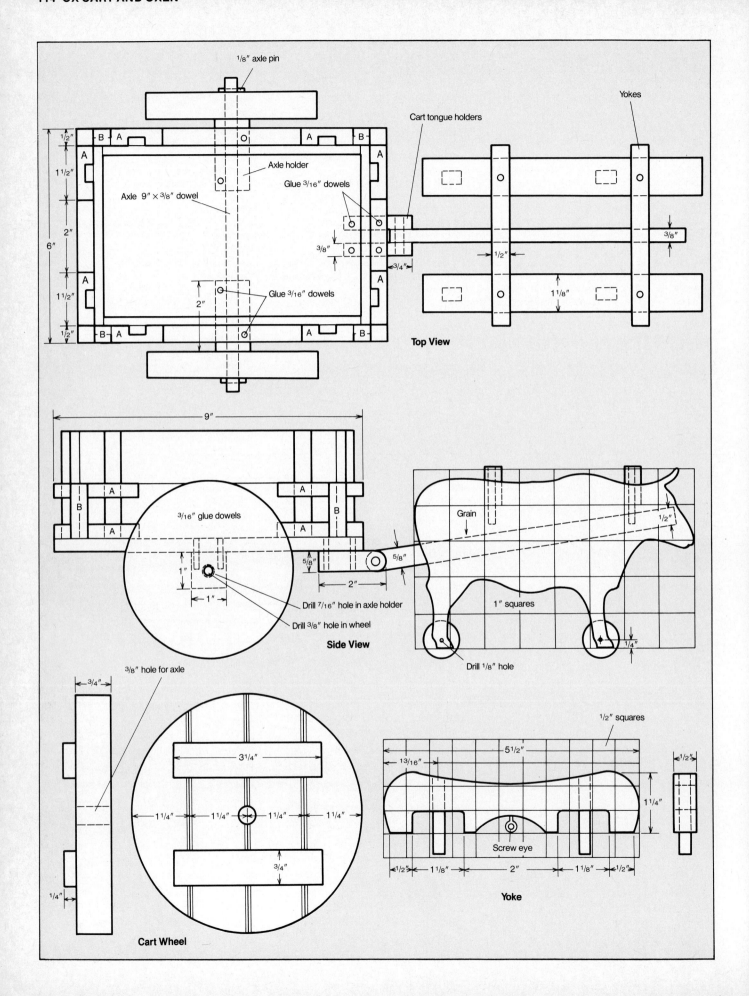

1/8" axle pin

Yokes

Cart tongue holders

B A A A B

A A

Axle holder

Axle 9" × 3/8" dowel

Glue 3/16" dowels

6"

1/2"
1 1/2"
2"
1 1/2"
1/2"

3/8"

3/8"

1/2"

1 1/8"

2"

A A

Glue 3/16" dowels

B A A A B

3/4"

Top View

9"

A A

B B

A A

3/16" glue dowels

1"

1"

1"

Drill 7/16" hole in axle holder

Drill 3/8" hole in wheel

5/8"

2"

5/8"

Grain

1" squares

1/2"

1/4"

Drill 1/8" hole

Side View

3/4"

3/8" hole for axle

3 1/4"

1 1/4"   1 1/4"   1 1/4"   1 1/4"

3/4"

1/4"

Cart Wheel

1/2" squares

5 1/2"

13/16"

1 1/4"

1/2"

Screw eye

1/2" 1 1/8" 2" 1 1/8" 1/2"

Yoke

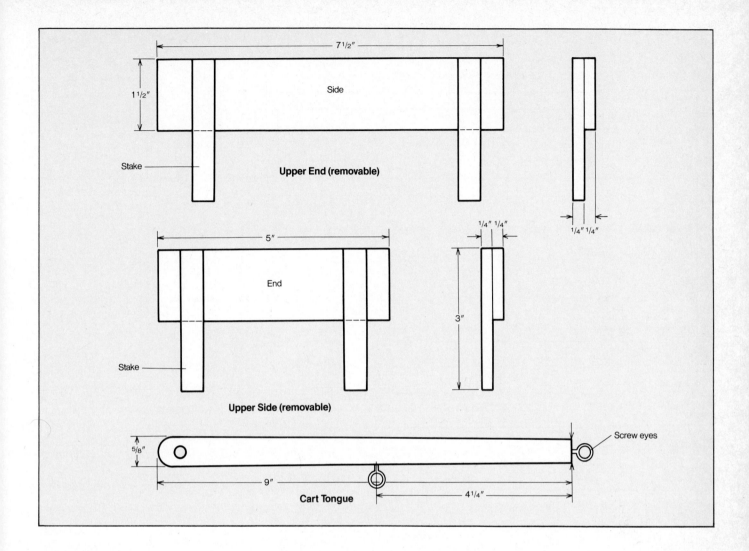

STEP 1
MAKING THE OXEN

Cut out the 5- × 8-inch blocks of 1 1/8-inch stock for the oxen, making sure the grain runs vertically along the 5-inch side. Next, cut a groove in each block 5/16 inch wide × 7/8 inch deep; this groove is to accommodate the oxen wheels and should be cut in the center of the 1 1/8-inch thickness of one edge of the 8-inch sides. Then enlarge the drawing of the ox, trace it onto each of the grooved blocks, and cut out two oxen on the band saw or jigsaw. Now drill the 1/8-inch holes in the oxen legs for the axle. Put a piece of scrap wood in the space between the legs when drilling, to prevent breakage. This is best done on the drill press. The wheels can be cut from 1/4-inch stock or purchased from one of many suppliers. Drill 3/16-inch holes in the four oxen wheels. The holes will be larger than the dowel diameter, to permit their turning on the axle. Sand the oxen, rounding the edges with a fine rasp and sandpaper.

STEP 2
MAKING AND ATTACHING THE YOKES

Trace the yoke shape onto 1/2-inch stock and cut out the yokes on the band saw or jigsaw. The inside of the yokes, which fit over the oxen, can be cut square or rounded to fit the rounded backs of the oxen. Sand the yokes smooth. Drilling the holes for the holding pins through the yokes into the oxen can be tricky. It is best done on the drill press this way: Cut a block of scrap wood exactly 2 inches wide and clamp it between the oxen, making sure the heads and rear ends of the oxen line up. Now put the front yoke in place and mark the locations of the holes—centered on the thickness of the yoke, directly over the centers of the backs of the oxen. Hold the yoke steady with your hand and drill the holes through the yoke and into the oxen. Repeat for the rear yoke. The holes should be 1 1/8 inches deep in the oxen. Enlarge the holes in the oxen slightly with a round rasp or sandpaper wrapped around a dowel. Make them just large enough so that the yoke pins, which are glued to the yokes, can be easily removed from the oxen when they are unhitched.

STEP 3
CUTTING THE CART PIECES

Cut all pieces for the cart to size as shown in the plans. The stake holders are cut from one piece of 3/8-inch stock. The 1/4-inch-deep, 1/2-inch-wide recess is cut with the table saw or band saw and must be done carefully so that the stakes will move smoothly in and out. The wheels are

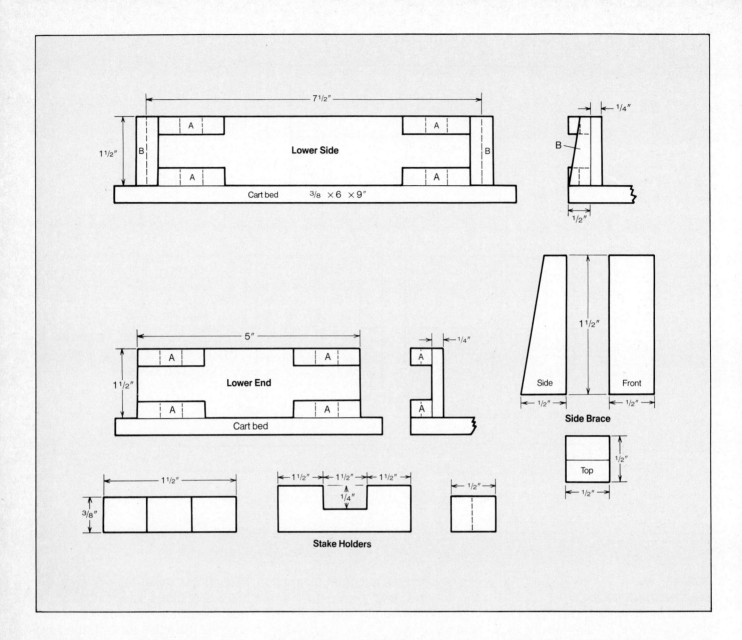

built up of four pieces of ³/₄- × 1¹/₄-inch stock glued edge to edge. Before gluing, chamfer the straight edges of all the pieces. The wheel braces are glued across the joints. Next drill the holes in the two axle holders and two tongue holders. The tongue is cut from ³/₈-inch stock 9 inches long, tapered from ⁵/₈ inch at the cart end to ¹/₂ inch at the front. Sand all pieces carefully.

STEP 4
ASSEMBLING THE CART
Begin assembly of the cart by gluing the axle holders to the cart bed. These holders project ¹/₄ inch from the edge of the cart bed. Next glue the tongue holders to the bed ³/₈ inch apart and projecting ³/₄ inch out from

the edge. Secure all holders with ³/₁₆-inch dowels. The lower cart sides and ends, side braces, and stake holders are best glued together and then glued as a unit to the cart bed. To do this, glue the two lower sides to the two lower ends, with the side pieces inside the shorter end-pieces. Next glue on the four tapered side braces (B) and finally, the stake holders (A). Use one of the stakes as a guide when gluing the holders to make sure they line up. When the glue is dry, you are ready to glue the whole unit to the cart bed. Then insert the stakes into the stake holders, after sanding them slightly to ensure easy in-and-out movement. When the fit is right, glue the stakes to the upper sides and upper ends,

holding them with spring clamps or small C-clamps. Next glue the cart tongue between the tongue holders, using the ¹/₄-inch dowel pin at a 10° angle. For the wheel assembly, drill ¹/₈-inch holes in the axle ⁵/₁₆ inch from each end to take the axle pins. Insert the axle into the axle holders, glue a wheel and pin to each end, and the cart is ready to be hitched. To hitch up the oxen, insert a small screw eye and a ¹/₂-inch ring in the lower center of each yoke and a screw eye S hook into the tongue. Open up the ends of the S hooks away from the screw eyes a little, so they can easily be slipped on and off the rings. Finish the cart and oxen with clear finish or nontoxic paint, as you prefer.

Noah's Ark

MATERIALS LIST
Main Hull:
Hull bottom (1), 1/2″ × 6″ × 15 1/2″, pine
Bow planks (16), 1/2″ × 3/4″ × 5″, pine
Bow planks (2), 1/2″ × 1″ × 5″, pine
Middle hull planks (16), 1/2″ × 3/4″ × 10″, pine
Left-side window spacers (6), 1/2″ × 1/2″ × 1″, pine
Right-side window spacers (4), 1/2″ × 3/4″ × 1″, pine
Right-side window spacers (2), 1/2″ × 1″ × 1″, pine
Stern panels (9), 1/2″ × 1 1/4″ × 7″, pine
Bow brace (1), 1/2″ × 1″ × 7″, pine
Door (1), 1/2″ × 3″ × 4″, pine
Door stop (1), 1/4″ × 3/8″ × 3 1/2″, pine
Door bar (1), 3/16″ × 1/2″ × 4″, pine
Door-bar cleats (2), 3/16″ × 3/8″ × 1 1/2″, pine
Deck cleat (1), 3/8″ × 3/8″ × 38″, pine

Upper Deck and Deckhouse:
Upper deck, 1/2″ × 6″ × 15 1/2″, pine
Side planks (8), 1/4″ × 3/4″ × 9 1/2″, pine
Vertical planks (10), 1/4″ × 3/4″ × 3 3/4″, pine
Vertical planks (2), 1/4″ × 3/4″ × 1″, pine
Window spacers (8), 1/4″ × 3/4″ × 1″, pine
Window spacers (4), 1/4″ × 3/4″ × 7/8″, pine
Roof cleats (2), 1/4″ × 1/2″ × 4″, pine
Roof panels (5), 1/4″ × 1 3/16″ × 10 1/2″, pine
Roof braces (12), 1/4″ × 3/4″ × 1 1/8″, pine
Yellow wood glue
Nontoxic stain
Nontoxic clear finish

Tools
Table saw
Wood rasp
Light wood clamps, spring clamps, or C-clamps
Masking tape
Sandpaper, 80, 120, and 220

For generations children have listened with fascination to the story of Noah building the ark and the flood of waters that covered the earth. Although our model does not adhere to the actual specifications in Genesis (more windows, for example), it does have the door in the side and the space above the windows and the suggestion of several levels. The ark is plank-built, with two storage spaces. Plans for a removable ramp, for Noah to shepherd in his pairs of every living thing, are given in the Noah's Ark Animals and Ramp project, page 122.

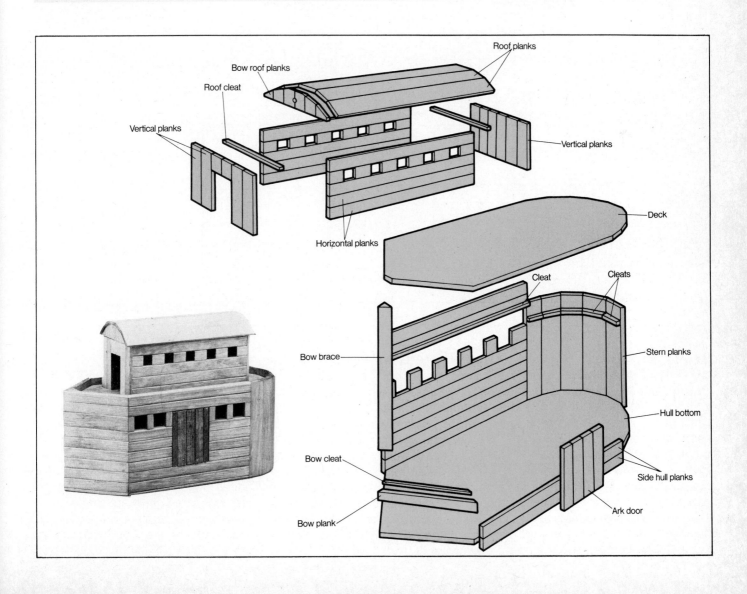

Roof planks
Bow roof planks
Roof cleat
Vertical planks
Vertical planks
Horizontal planks
Deck
Cleat
Cleats
Bow brace
Stern planks
Hull bottom
Bow cleat
Side hull planks
Ark door
Bow plank

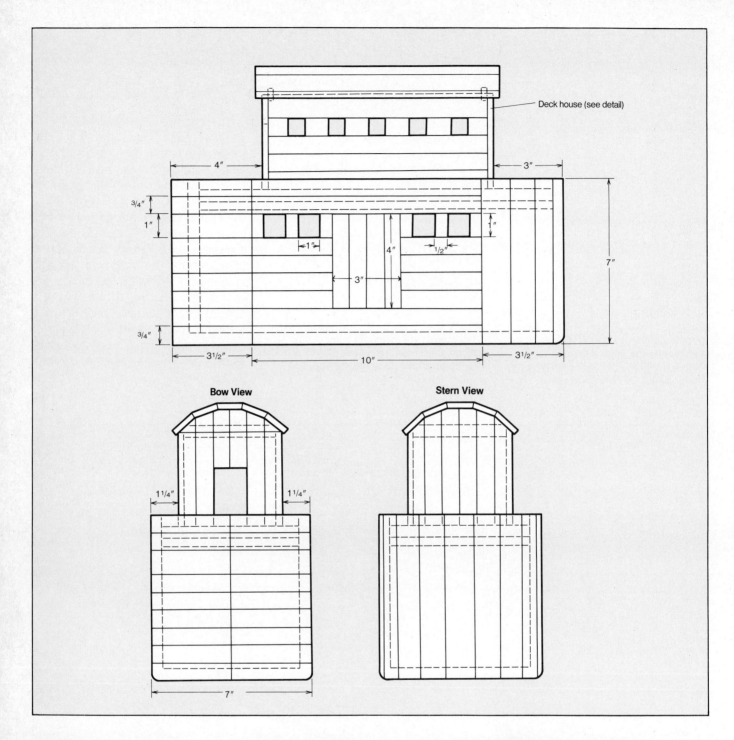

Deck house (see detail)

Bow View

Stern View

STEP 1
CUTTING THE PIECES

Cut out the hull bottom and deck, which are the same size and shape. Cut out the bow planks, which are cut at 45° at one end and 22½° at the other. The middle hull planks have a 22½° cut at the bow end and a 90° cut at the stern end. The nine stern panels are beveled at 10° along each side. The five roof panels are also beveled at 10°. The roof braces are cut to fit the inside curve of the roof

panels. The deck cleats are cut at the same angles as the bow, hull, and stern planks. The bow brace is a triangular piece cut at 45°. The door can be made of four ³/₄-inch planks (the same as the side planks) or of one piece of wood scored to look like planks. All other pieces have square cuts and can be cut to size as indicated. Bevel the edges of planks and window spacers to emphasize the "planking," and give it a hand-hewn appearance.

STEP 2
ASSEMBLING THE BOW, STERN, AND SIDES

Sand all pieces carefully and remove all dust. This project requires a large amount of gluing. Use the glue sparingly. Apply it with a small brush and try to keep it away from the very edges of the pieces. The bow and the hull sides and stern are made up of planks glued together, edge to edge. Each side of the bow consists of eight ³/₄-inch planks and one 1-inch

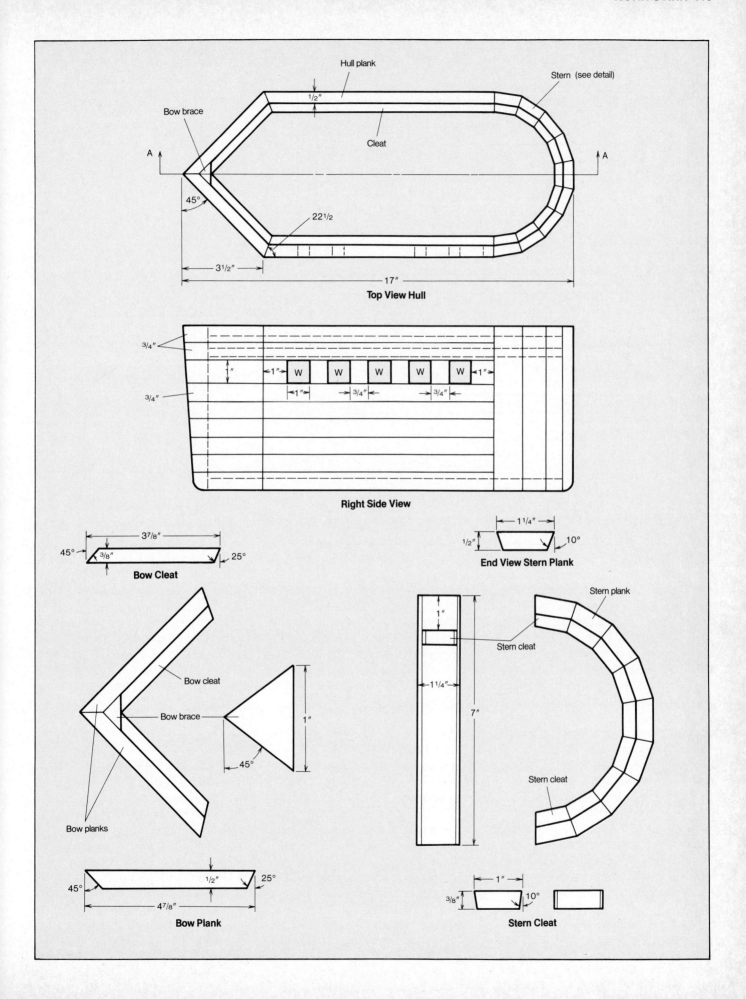

Hull plank

Stern (see detail)

Bow brace

1/2"

Cleat

A

A

45°

22 1/2

3 1/2"

17"

Top View Hull

3/4"

1"

1"

W W W W W

1"

3/4"

1"

3/4"

3/4"

Right Side View

1 1/4"

3 7/8"

1/2"

10°

45°

3/8"

25°

End View Stern Plank

Bow Cleat

Stern plank

Bow cleat

Bow brace

1"

1"

Stern cleat

45°

1 1/4"

7"

Bow planks

Stern cleat

1/2"

25°

1"

45°

3/8"

10°

4 7/8"

Bow Plank

Stern Cleat

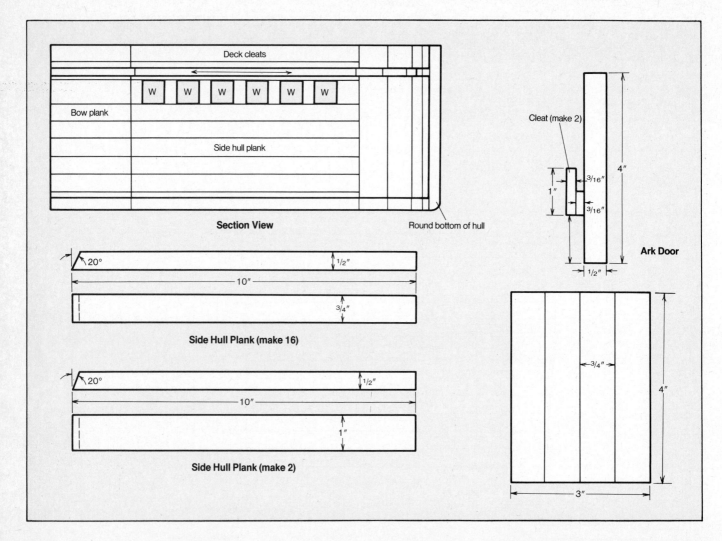

Deck cleats

Bow plank

Side hull plank

W W W W W W

Section View

Round bottom of hull

20° 1/2"
10"
3/4"

Side Hull Plank (make 16)

20° 1/2"
10"
1"

Side Hull Plank (make 2)

Cleat (make 2)

3/16"
1"
3/16"
4"
1/2"

Ark Door

3/4"
4"
3"

plank. The 1-inch plank is placed third from the top to coincide with the 1-inch window spacers in the hull sides. Glue the bow planks together, using masking tape as a clamp. Make sure the angled ends line up. Glue the side hull planks together with the window spacers third from the top. Make sure the short planks and window spacers line up around the door opening on the left side. Glue the stern planks together. Smooth down the sharp angle where the edges meet, and score the joint to show the individual planks. Glue the planks together that make up the bow and stern ends of the deckhouse. These planks are used vertically. Glue the horizontal planks and window spacers together to form the two sides of the deckhouse.

STEP 3
ASSEMBLING THE ROOF
Glue the five roof panels together

and smooth down the sharp edges. Glue roof cleats to the top of the bow and stern ends of the deckhouse. The cleats should project 1/4 inch above them. Glue the roof braces together and shape them to fit the roof curve. Do not glue them to the roof at this time. Glue the door-bar cleats to the back of the door.

STEP 4
ASSEMBLING THE HULL
The ark is made in three units that are not glued together; the deck and roof can be removed, and the inside of the ark can be used for storage. The three units are: the hull; the deck and deckhouse; and the deckhouse roof. Inspect all glue joints. If any glue has squeezed out, scrape it off and resand the area. Try a dry assembly of all parts of the main hull before gluing. Begin assembly by gluing the two sides of the bow to the bow brace. Then glue the hull bottom to

the bow and brace. Glue the sides to the hull bottom and the bow. The stern section is glued to the hull bottom and the sides. Use masking tape to hold the sections together. The deck-cleat pieces can now be glued in place all around the inside of the hull, 1 inch from the top. Use spring clamps, light wood clamps, or C-clamps. The hull section is complete.

STEP 5
ASSEMBLING THE DECKHOUSE
Glue the four walls of the deckhouse together, noting that the sides fit inside of the end walls. Glue the deckhouse to the center of the deck 2 1/2 inches from the stern end. This section is now complete. Glue the roof braces to the roof, making sure they fit smoothly over the roof cleats so that the roof is removable. Again inspect all glue joints and clean up if necessary. The door is fitted into its opening and barred from the inside.

It cannot be opened from the outside. The deck and deckhouse unit must be removed to open it. The ark can now be stained with a light brown stain for aging if desired, and finished with two coats of nontoxic clear finish. Check for any spots that need sanding before proceeding with the finish.

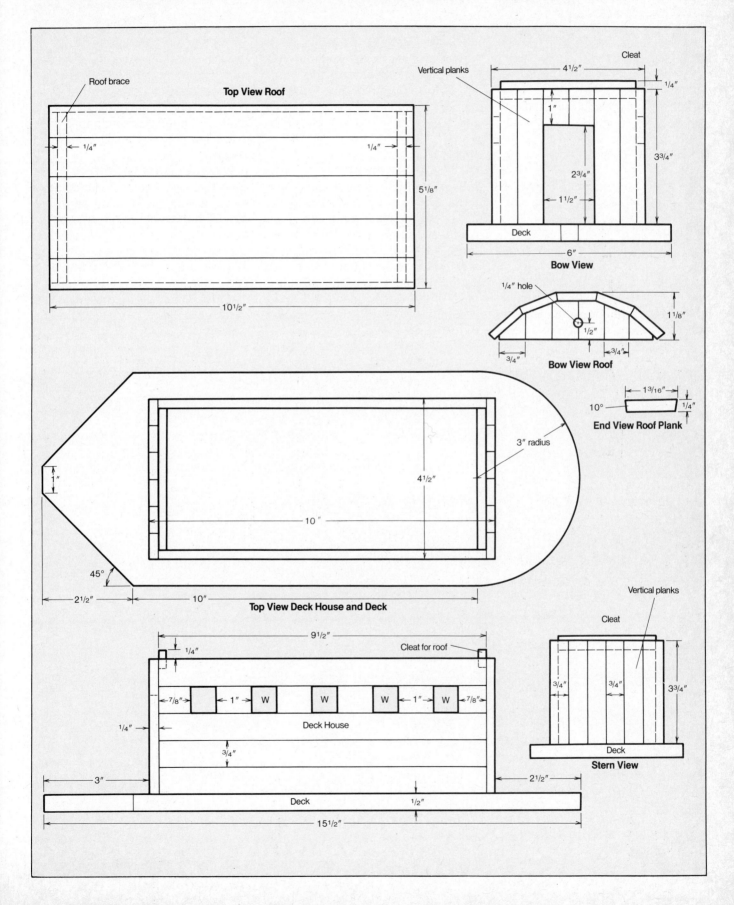

Noah's Animals

MATERIALS LIST
Animals (28), 3/4″ stock, pine or hardwood
Animals (2), 1″ stock, pine or hardwood
Ramp planks (4), 1/4″ × 3/4″ × 8″, pine
Ramp steps (4), 3/16″ × 1/4″ × 3″, pine
Ramp cleat (1), 3/16″ × 3/8″ × 3″, pine
Yellow wood glue
Nontoxic clear finish

Tools
Table saw
Band saw or jigsaw
Light spring clamps
Masking tape
Sandpaper, 80, 120, and 220

Two by two, they came to fill the ark, and what is the ark without its inhabitants? We have chosen a variety of creatures, some common and some not so common, so that different types are represented—the stork, the tortoise, and the ibex, for example. The ramp is attached to Noah's Ark (page 117) for the animals' entry.

STEP 1
CUTTING THE PIECES
Enlarge and transfer the animal patterns to 3/4-inch stock and cut out on the jigsaw or band saw with a fine blade. Note that the tortoise is cut from 1-inch stock. Also note that all animals are of the silhouette type except the tortoise. Make sure the grain of the wood runs vertically for all animals except the hippo and the tortoise. The grain should run horizontally for these two. Sand all animals thoroughly, and round all edges with sandpaper. The ramp parts are cut from pine. Bevel the edges of the planks slightly with sandpaper.

STEP 2
ASSEMBLY AND FINISHING
Glue the four planks together, edge to edge, with the beveled edges on top. Glue the cleat to one end of the ramp on the bottom. The cleat is used to hook the ramp onto the ark. The four steps are glued to the ramp and secured with light spring clamps. Finish all animals and the ramp with two coats of nontoxic clear finish.

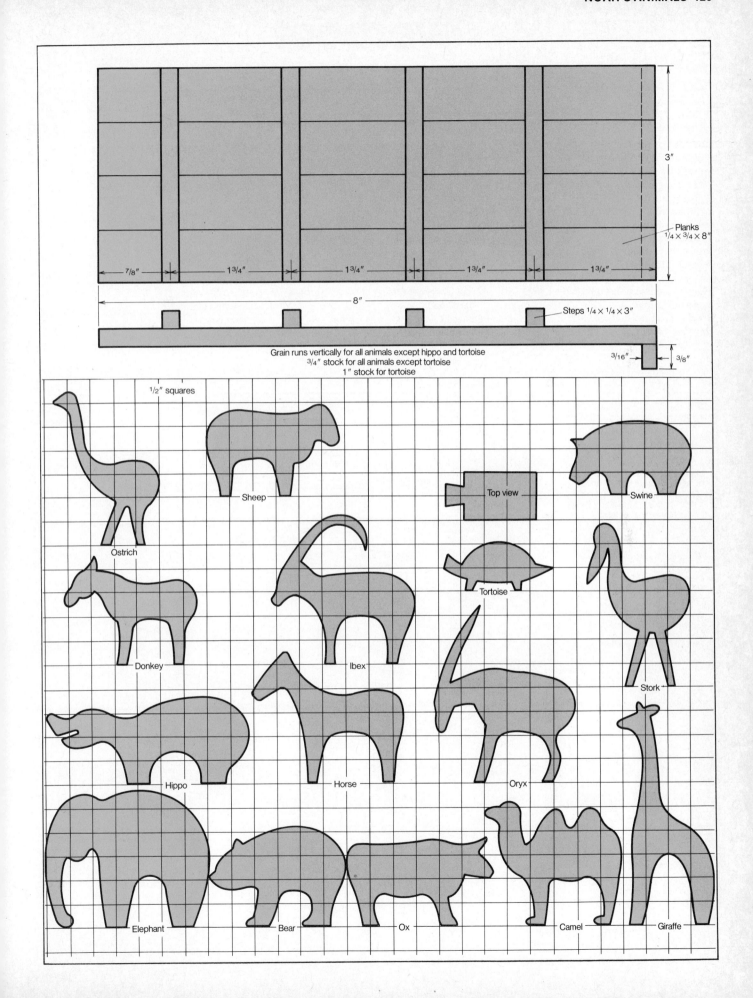

3"

Planks
$^1/_4 \times {}^3/_4 \times 8"$

$^7/_8"$ $1^3/_4"$ $1^3/_4"$ $1^3/_4"$ $1^3/_4"$

8"

Steps $^1/_4 \times {}^1/_4 \times 3"$

Grain runs vertically for all animals except hippo and tortoise
$^3/_4"$ stock for all animals except tortoise
1" stock for tortoise

$^3/_{16}"$ $^3/_8"$

$^1/_2"$ squares

Ostrich

Sheep

Top view

Swine

Donkey

Ibex

Tortoise

Stork

Hippo

Horse

Oryx

Elephant

Bear

Ox

Camel

Giraffe

Riverboat

MATERIALS LIST

Hull (1), 3/4″ × 51/2″ × 20″, hardwood
Hull rail (bow) (1), 1/2″ × 21/2″ × 51/2″, pine
Hull rail (stern) (1), 1/2″ × 11/4″ × 4″, pine
Hull rail (sides), 1/4″ × 1/2″ × 281/2″, pine
Main cabin (1), 2″ × 51/2″ × 133/4″, pine
Second and third decks (2), 1/4″ × 51/2″ × 17″, hardwood
Second-deck cabin (1), 1″ × 2″ × 133/4″, pine
Second- and third-deck rails (ends) (4), 1/4″ × 11/4″ × 4″, pine
Second- and third-deck rails (sides), 1/4″ × 1/4″ × 64″, pine
Third-deck platform (1), 1/2″ × 2″ × 133/4″, pine
Third-deck cabin (1), 7/8″ × 11/2″ × 9″, hardwood

Third-deck cabin roof (1), 3/16″ × 13/4″ × 91/4″, pine
Wheelhouse (1), 3/4″ × 1″ × 11/4″, hardwood
Wheelhouse roof (1), 1/8″ × 11/4″ × 11/2″, pine
Front staircase (1), 1/4″ × 1/2″ × 16″, hardwood
Top step (1), 1/4″ × 1/4″ × 15/8″, hardwood
Smokestacks (2), 10″ × 1/2″ dowel, hardwood
Paddle-wheel housing (fronts and backs) (4), 1/4″ × 33/4″ × 4″, hardwood
Paddle-wheel housing (centers) (2), 1/2″ × 33/4″ × 4″, hardwood
Paddle-wheel centers (2), 1/2″ × 2″ diameter, hardwood
Paddles (32), 1/8″ × 1/2″ × 3/4″, pine
Paddle-wheel axles (2), 1″ × 1/4″ dowel, hardwood

Small-boat supports (2), 3/4″ × 11/2″ × 21/2″, hardwood
Small boats (2), 3/8″ × 5/8″ × 11/4″, hardwood
No. 4 × 1/2″ round head brass screw
Yellow wood glue
Nontoxic clear finish

Tools

Table saw
Band saw
Backsaw
Drill or drill press
Light wood clamps
Spring clamps
Screwdriver

Masking tape
Sandpaper, 80, 120, and 220

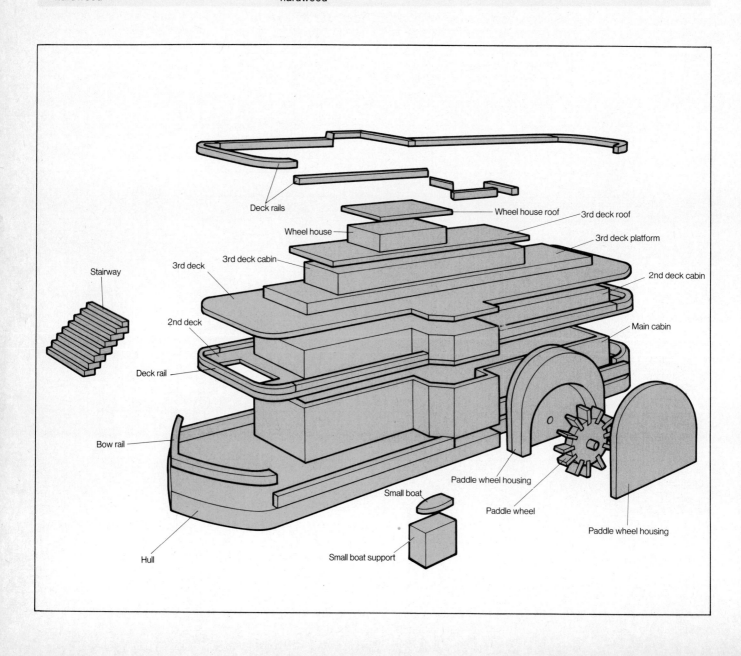

Deck rails

Wheel house roof

3rd deck roof

Wheel house

3rd deck platform

3rd deck cabin

3rd deck

2nd deck cabin

Stairway

2nd deck

Main cabin

Deck rail

Bow rail

Paddle wheel housing

Small boat

Paddle wheel

Hull

Small boat support

Paddle wheel housing

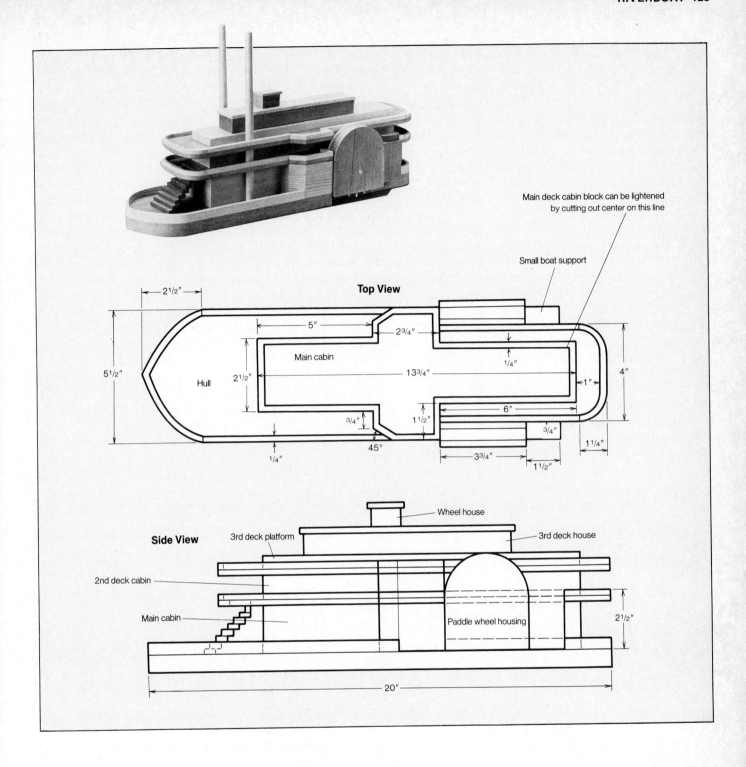

Main deck cabin block can be lightened by cutting out center on this line

Small boat support

Top View

2½"

5"

2¾"

Main cabin

2½"

13¾"

¼"

4"

1"

Hull

5½"

¾"

1½"

6"

¾"

45°

¼"

3¾"

1¼"

1½"

Side View

Wheel house

3rd deck platform

3rd deck house

2nd deck cabin

Paddle wheel housing

2½"

Main cabin

20"

Steam-powered paddle-wheel boats, some stern-wheelers, some side-wheelers, were once a lively fact of life on the great American waterways. They carried goods, passengers, and news. Great skill and knowledge of every shoal, sandbar, and bend in the river were required of their pilots, who also had to keep an eye out for small-boat traffic. Huck Finn, on the Mississippi, knew that steamboats and rafts were natural enemies. Pilots liked to show their prowess by skimming a raft, laughing when the paddle wheel bit off an oar. Our model is based on a famous side-wheeler, the *Robert E. Lee.*

STEP 1
CUTTING THE PIECES
Enlarge and transfer the pattern for the hull to ¾-inch stock and cut out on the band saw. The hull rail is made in sections. The hull pattern is used to shape the bow and stern sections. The remaining sections of the rail are cut from straight pieces of ¼- × ½-inch stock. The main cabin is cut from a 2-inch block, which can be laminated from thinner stock. The center of the block can be cut out, leaving a "wall" about ¼ inch thick to make it lighter. This can be done with a jigsaw, saber saw, or band saw. The second and third decks are the same and are cut from ¼-inch

stock. Locate and drill the 1/2-inch holes in the two decks for the smoke-stacks. The second deck has an opening for the stairway. The pattern for the second and third decks is used to cut the 1/4-inch rail sections. The second-deck cabin and third-deck platform, cabin, wheelhouse, and roofs are all cut from solid stock. Cut out the three sections of the paddle-wheel housing as shown. Locate and drill the 1/4-inch holes in the fronts and backs of the housing for the wheel axles. The paddle wheel is made from a 2-inch disk with sixteen equally spaced notches for the paddles. From the center of the disk lay out sixteen lines, 22 1/2 inches apart. At the outer edge of each line, cut a notch on the band saw, table saw, or backsaw. The notches should be 1/8 inch wide and 1/4 inch deep to accept the paddles. Cut out the small boats and small-boat supports. The stairway has steps of different lengths, which are glued to one another.

STEP 2
ASSEMBLING THE PARTS
Begin by sanding the inside of all rail sections and the tops and bottoms of the decks and hull until they are smooth. Then glue the rails into position, securing with light clamps, spring clamps, or masking tape. When the glue is dry, sand the outside of the rails and the decks and hulls together. Next glue the main cabin to the hull. Glue the second-deck cabin to the second deck. To the third deck, glue the platform, deck-house and roof, and wheelhouse and roof. Glue the backs of the paddle-wheel housing to the center sections. Place the fronts of the housing on the center sections and drill two small holes, one on each side, to accept small brass round head screws. This will allow the housing cover to be removed for access to the paddle wheel. Glue the small boats to their supports. Form the stairway by gluing the steps together.

STEP 3
FINISHING AND ASSEMBLING THE RIVERBOAT
Make sure all units are sanded. Finish all units with two coats of non-toxic clear finish. Do not finish the top of the main cabin and the top of the second-deck cabin. When all parts are completely dry, begin the final assembly by gluing the second deck to the main cabin. Before gluing the third deck to the second-deck cabin, insert the smokestacks through the deck holes to make sure they are lined up. Glue in the smoke-stacks. Glue in the stairway. The paddle-wheel housing back-and-center unit is glued to the three decks. The axle is glued to the back of the housing. The paddle wheel is placed on the axle, and the front of the housing is fastened to the center with the brass screws. The axle should project about 1/8 inch. Finally, glue in each boat support with its small boat.

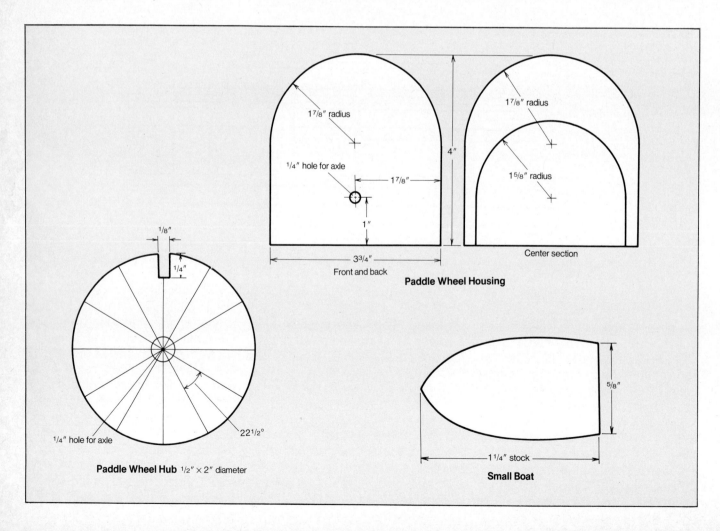

1 7/8" radius

1 7/8" radius

1/4" hole for axle

1 5/8" radius

4"

1 7/8"

1"

3 3/4"

Front and back

Center section

Paddle Wheel Housing

1/8"

1/4"

22 1/2°

1/4" hole for axle

Paddle Wheel Hub 1/2" × 2" diameter

5/8"

1 1/4" stock

Small Boat

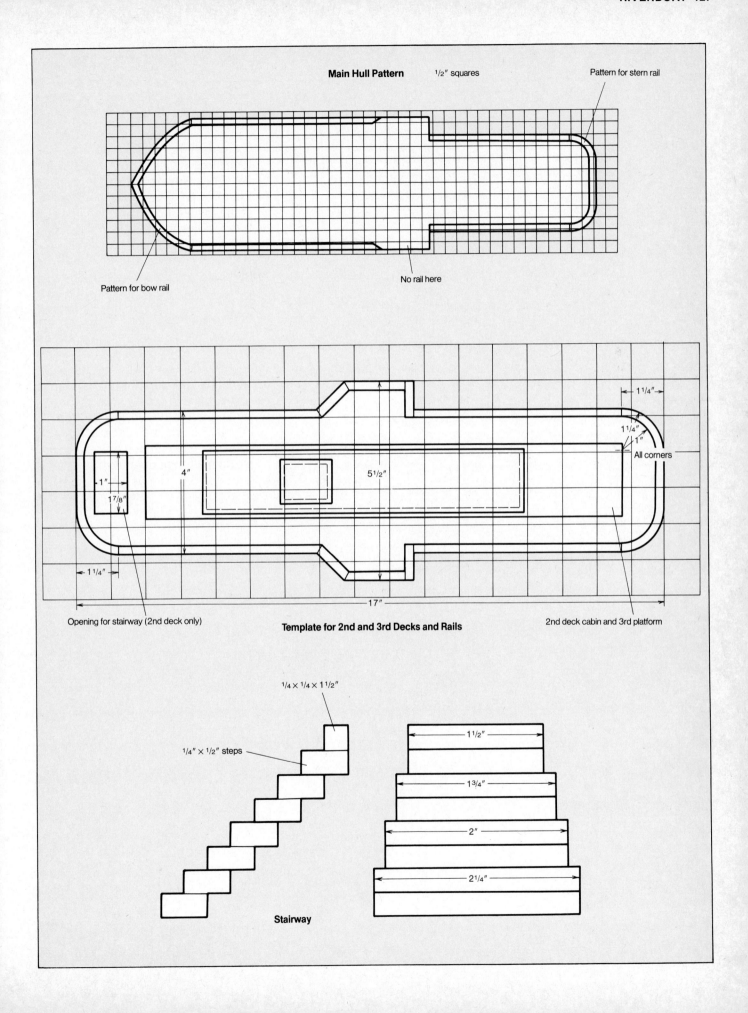

Main Hull Pattern ¹/₂″ squares

Pattern for stern rail

Pattern for bow rail

No rail here

1¹/₄″

1¹/₄″
1″
All corners

4″

1″

1⁷/₈″

5¹/₂″

1¹/₄″

17″

Opening for stairway (2nd deck only)

Template for 2nd and 3rd Decks and Rails

2nd deck cabin and 3rd platform

¹/₄ × ¹/₄ × 1¹/₂″

¹/₄″ × ¹/₂″ steps

1¹/₂″

1³/₄″

2″

2¹/₄″

Stairway

Fire Engine

MATERIALS LIST

Chassis (1), 1/2″ × 3″ × 18 1/2″, pine
Axle holders (2), 1/2″ × 1″ × 3″, pine
Sides (2), 1/2″ × 3 1/4″ × 10 3/4″, pine
Top (1), 1/4″ × 3 1/2″ × 10 3/4″, pine
Pivot block (1), 2 1/2″ × 3″ × 3″, pine
Pivot disk (1), 1/2″ × 3″ diameter, pine
Pivot post (1), 2 3/4″ × 3/4″, hardwood dowel
Cab bottom (1), 1/4″ × 2 1/2″ × 4″, pine
Cab sides (2), 1/4″ × 3 1/4″ × 4 1/2″, pine
Cab back (1), 1/4″ × 2 1/2″ × 3 1/4″, pine
Cab front (1), 1/4″ × 1 3/4″ × 2 1/2″, pine
Windshield (1), 1/4″ × 1 1/2″ × 2 1/2″, pine
Seat (1), 1/4″ × 1 1/2″ × 2 1/2″, pine
Seat brace (1), 1/4″ × 1″ × 2 1/2″, pine
Fenders (2), 1/4″ × 1/2″ × 4″, pine
Headlights (2), 3/8″ × 3/8″ dowel, hardwood
Main-ladder holders (2), 1/2″ × 1″ × 1″, pine
Holder spacer (1), 1/4″ × 1″ × 1 7/8″, pine
Main-ladder support (front) (1), 1/4″ × 1 1/2″ × 3″, pine
Side-ladder rails (4), 1/4″ × 1/4″ × 9 1/2″, pine
Side-ladder rungs (24), 1″ × 1/8″ dowel, hardwood
Side-ladder hangers (4), 5/8″ × 1/8″ dowel, hardwood
Main-ladder rails (2), 1/4″ × 3/8″ × 18″, pine

Main-ladder braces (6), 1/4″ × 1/4″ × 5/8″, pine
Main-ladder end braces (4), 1/4″ × 1/4″ × 7/8″, pine
Main-ladder tops (2), 1/4″ × 1/2″ × 17 1/4″, pine
Top braces (2), 1/4″ × 1/4″ × 7/8″, pine
Main-ladder spacer (1), 3/8″ × 3/4″ × 1 3/8″, pine
Main-ladder rungs (17), 1 5/8″ × 3/16″ dowel, hardwood
Extension-ladder rails (2), 1/4″ × 1/4″ × 18″, pine
Extension-ladder rungs (18), 1″ × 1/8″ dowel, hardwood
Extension-ladder hooks (2), 5/8″ × 1/8″ dowel, hardwood
Extension-ladder stop (1), 3/16″ × 1/2″ × 1 3/8″, pine
Wheels (4), 1/2″ × 2″ diameter, pine
Axles (2), 4 1/2″ × 1/4″ dowel, hardwood
Thumbscrew, 1/4—20 × 1 1/4″
Carriage bolt, wing nut, and washers, 3/16—24 × 3 1/2″
Yellow wood glue
Nontoxic paint
Nontoxic clear finish

Tools

Table saw
Band saw
Drill or drill press
Light wood clamps
Masking tape
Sandpaper, 80, 120, and 220

Toy engines are attractive with their long lines and bright colors. Kids can have fun playing with this one and imitating what are apt to be their favorite civic officials. The engine features swiveling extension ladders, which young firefighters can maneuver in their rescue operations.

STEP 1
CUTTING THE PIECES

Cut out all parts to dimensions shown, noting the angle and bevel cuts on the cab parts, fenders, and ladder parts. The sides are beveled at 45° along each end, and a 1/4- × 1 1/4-inch rabbet is cut along the length of the side at the top. Locate and drill holes for side-ladder holders. Note the semicircular opening cut into the rear bottom of each side for the wheels. Drill a 3/4-inch hole in the

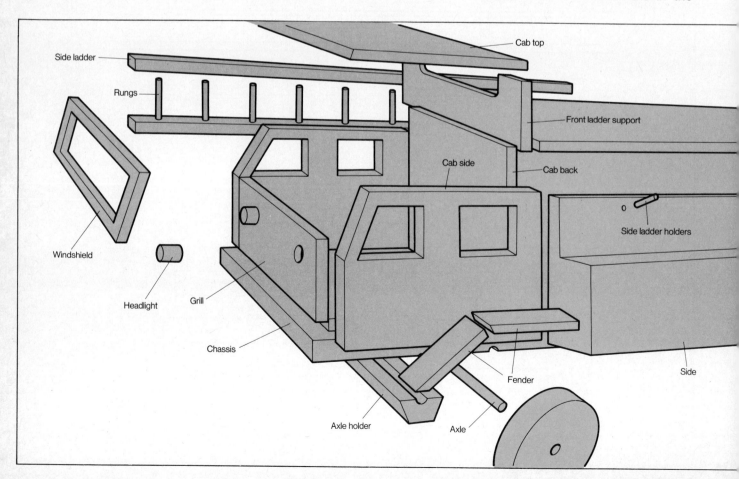

center of the pivot disk. The pivot block is made of glued-up stock, and a ¾-inch hole is drilled through the block at the center for the pivot post. Drill a ³⁄₁₆-inch hole in the center of the back of the pivot block through to

the pivot-post hole for the thumbscrew. The thumbscrew will cut its own threads as you screw it in. If you prefer, you can use a metal insert with ¼-inch—20 threads. The thumbscrew will secure the extension-ladder assembly in any position. Drill the main-ladder holders to

accommodate the ³⁄₁₆-inch securing bolt. Locate and drill all holes in ladder rails for ladder rungs. This is best done on a drill press with a depth stop. Cut all ladder rungs to length. Drill axle holes in axle holders.

STEP 2
ASSEMBLING THE PARTS
Sand all parts carefully and remove all dust. Start by gluing the axle holders to the chassis. Next glue the

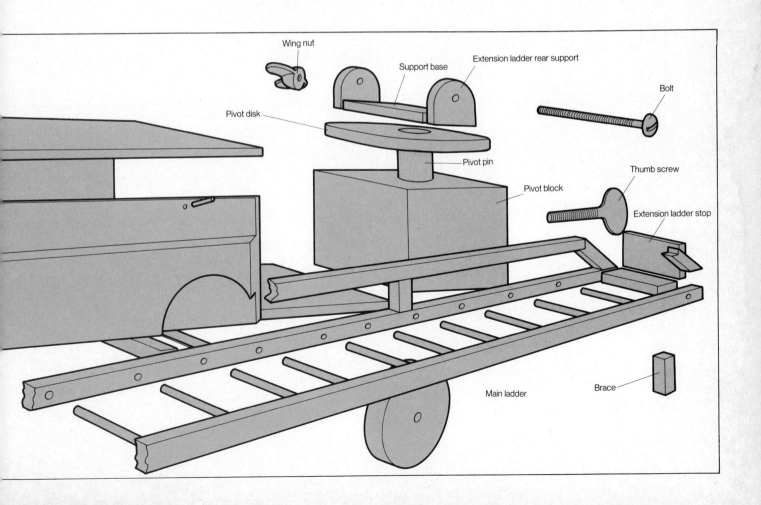

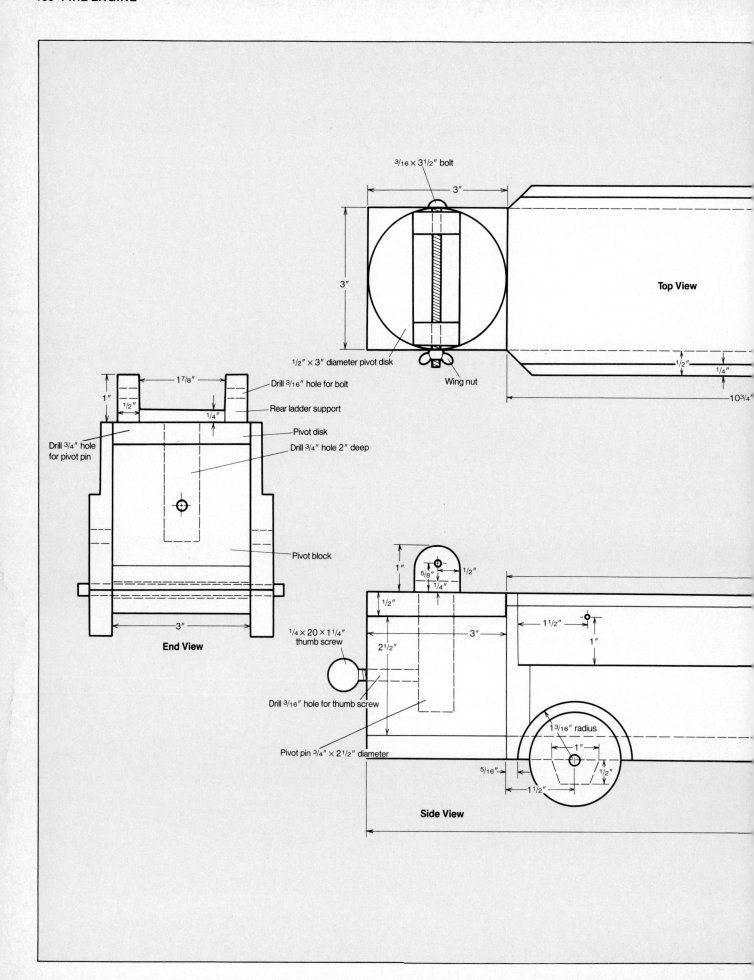

$3/16 \times 3^{1/2}''$ bolt

3"

3"

Top View

$1/2'' \times 3''$ diameter pivot disk

Wing nut

$1/2''$

$1/4''$

$10^{3/4}''$

$1^{7/8}''$

1"

$1/2''$

$1/4''$

Drill $3/16''$ hole for bolt

Rear ladder support

Pivot disk

Drill $3/4''$ hole for pivot pin

Drill $3/4''$ hole 2" deep

Pivot block

3"

End View

$1/4 \times 20 \times 1^{1/4}''$ thumb screw

Drill $3/16''$ hole for thumb screw

Pivot pin $3/4'' \times 2^{1/2}''$ diameter

1"

$5/8''$

$1/2''$

$1/4''$

$1/2''$

$2^{1/2}''$

3"

$1^{1/2}''$

1"

$1^{3/16}''$ radius

1"

$5/16''$

$1/2''$

$1^{1/2}''$

Side View

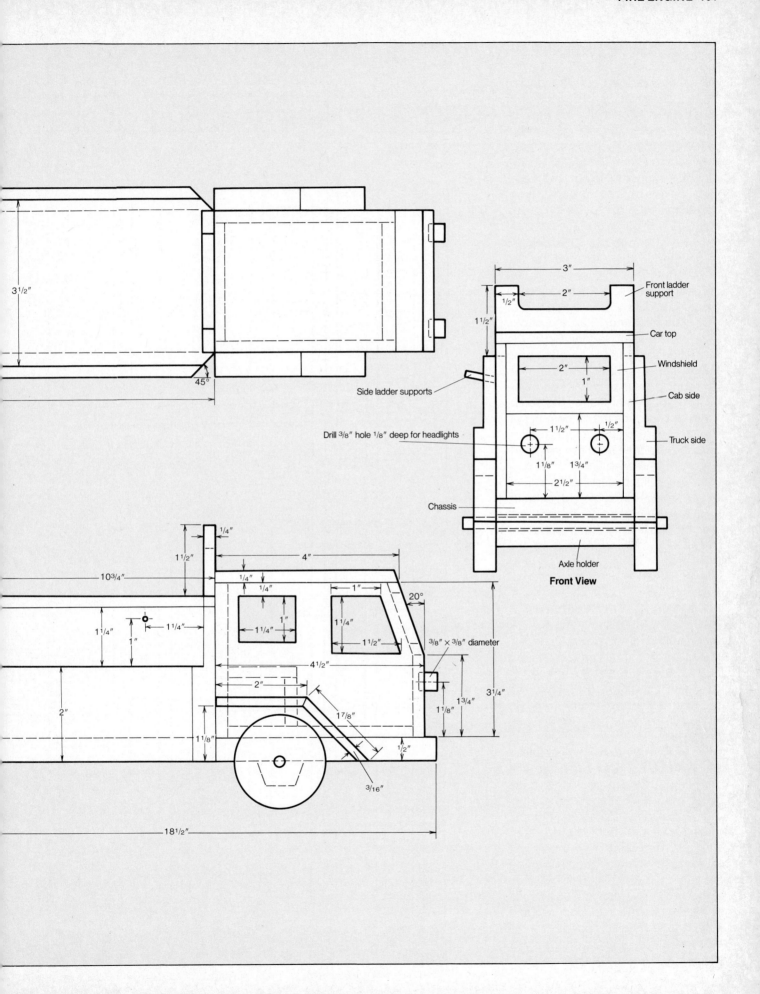

Front View

Front ladder support

Car top

Windshield

Cab side

Truck side

Side ladder supports

Drill ³⁄₈″ hole ¹⁄₈″ deep for headlights

Chassis

Axle holder

3″
2″
1½″
½″
2″
1″
1½″
½″
1⅛″
1¾″
2½″

3½″
45°

¼″
1½″
10¾″
¼″
¼″
1″
4″
20°
1″
1″
1¼″
1½″
1¼″
1¼″
1¼″
1″
4½″
2″
³⁄₈″ × ³⁄₈″ diameter
1¾″
3¼″
1⅛″
1⅛″
17⁄₈″
2″
½″
³⁄₁₆″
18½″

main-body sides to the chassis and the top to the sides. Glue the two main-ladder holders with the spacer block to the pivot disk. Glue the pivot post to the pivot disk. The cab assembly is next. Glue the cab bottom to the cab back. Then the seat brace is glued to the seat, and both are glued to the cab bottom and back. Glue the cab front to the cab bottom, and the windshield to the cab front. The sides are glued in place next, followed by the cab top. Drill two 3/8-inch holes in the cab front for the headlights. Glue the fenders to the cab sides. Assemble the side and extension ladders with a small dot of glue on each rung. Glue the hooks into the extension ladder. Begin the main-ladder assembly by gluing the spacer block and rungs to the main rails. Drill a 3/16-inch hole through the spacer block and rails for the securing bolt. Then glue the extension-ladder stop to the spacer block. Next glue the top braces to the main-ladder top (one at each end).

The six 5/8-inch main-ladder braces are glued to the main-ladder rails, and the four beveled braces are glued to the ends of the main-ladder rails. Glue the ladder top to the braces.

STEP 3
FINISHING AND ASSEMBLING THE FIRE ENGINE

Each subassembly should be finished before final assembly. We painted the pivot assembly and the cab blue, the headlights white, and the main body and chassis red. Do not paint the pivot bolt. We finished the ladders, main-ladder front support, and the wheels with clear finish. When the paint and finish are dry, carefully glue the pivot block and the cab into position. Place the main ladder between the main-ladder holders and insert the 3/16-inch securing bolt, washers, and wing nut. Insert the thumbscrew. Place the extension ladder into the main ladder. The hook will allow it to be stopped in any position. Hang up the side ladders. Glue in the white headlights. The wheels are glued to the axles, with the axles projecting 1/4 inch on each side.

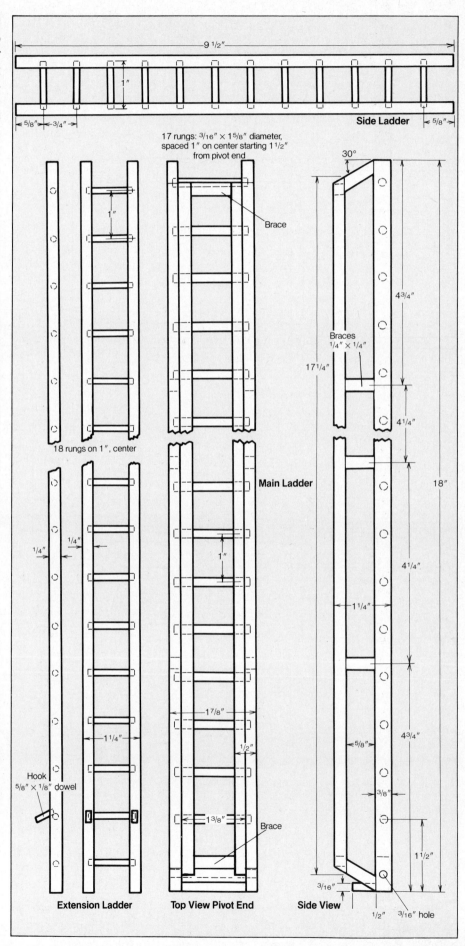

Ferris Wheel

MATERIALS LIST

Wheel-rim pieces (16), 1/2" × 1/2" × 61/4", hardwood

Wheel spokes (16), 1/2" × 1/2" × 59/16", hardwood

Wheel hubs (2), 1/2" × 3" × 3", hardwood

Hub spacers (2), 1/2" × 2" × 2", hardwood

Gondola hangers (8), 5" × 1/4" dowel, hardwood

Gondola-hanger stops (16), 3/16" × 3/4" × 11/8", hardwood

Wheel turners (2), 3/4" × 21/4" diameter, hardwood

Axle (1), 8" × 3/4" dowel, hardwood

Uprights (2), 1/2" × 8" × 14", hardwood or plywood

Base (1), 1/2" × 6" × 12", hardwood or plywood

Passenger platform, top (1), 1/2" × 2" × 6", hardwood

Passenger platform, sides (2), 1/2" × 3/4" × 2", hardwood

Steps, 7/16" × 2" × 31/2", hardwood

Ground platform, bottom (1), 1/2" × 11" × 16", plywood

Ground platform, sides (2), 1/2" × 2" × 16", plywood

Ground platform, ends (4), 1/2" × 2" × 41/2", plywood

Gondola sides (16), 1/4" × 3" × 31/2", hardwood or plywood

Gondola bottoms (8), 1/4" × 3" × 3", hardwood or plywood

Gondola seats (8), 1/4" × 11/4" × 3", hardwood

Seat backs (8), 1/4" × 1" × 3", hardwood

Gondola bars (8), 31/2" × 3/16" dowel, hardwood

Glue dowels (as needed), 3/16" dowel, hardwood

Brads, 1"

Wood putty

Yellow wood glue

Nontoxic paint

Nontoxic clear finish

Tools

Table saw

Saber saw

Band saw

Drill or drill press

Hammer

Nailset

Light wood clamps

Masking tape

Sandpaper, 80, 120, and 220

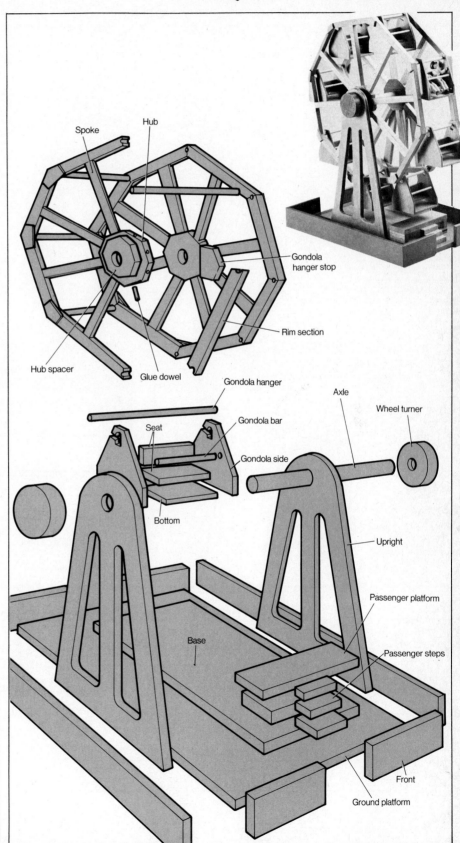

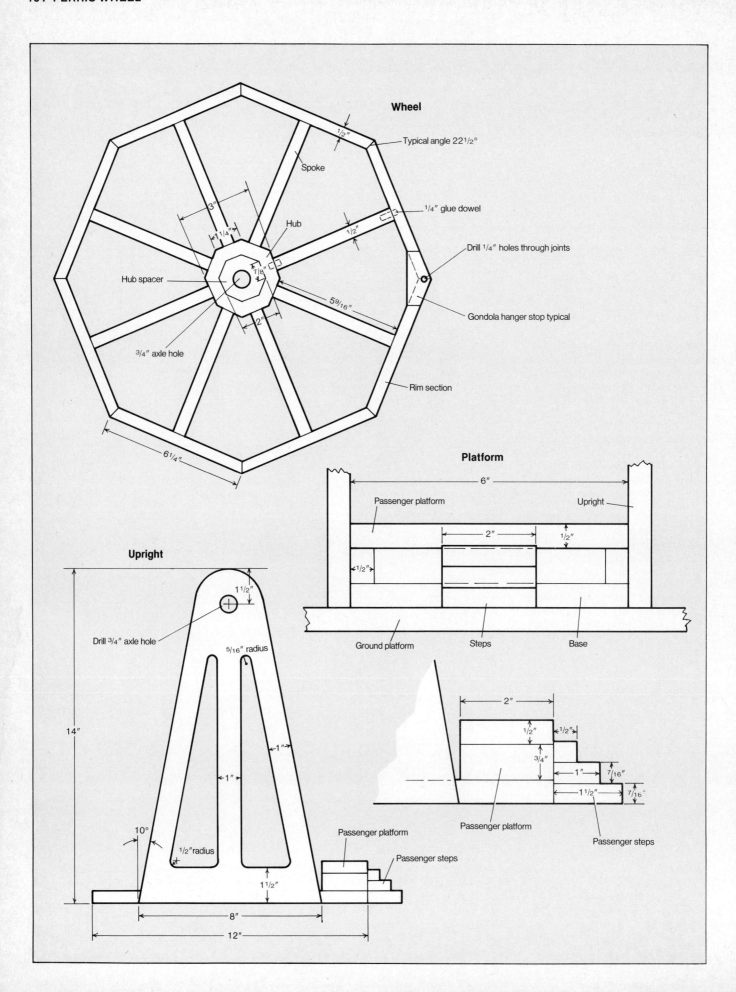

Wheel

1/2"

Typical angle 22 1/2°

Spoke

1/4" glue dowel

Hub

3"

1 1/4"

1/2"

Drill 1/4" holes through joints

Hub spacer

7/8"

Gondola hanger stop typical

5 9/16"

2"

3/4" axle hole

Rim section

6 1/4"

Platform

6"

Passenger platform

Upright

2"

1/2"

1/2"

Ground platform

Steps

Base

Upright

Drill 3/4" axle hole

1 1/2"

5/16" radius

2"

1/2"

1/2"

3/4"

1"

7/16"

14"

1"

1"

Passenger platform

1 1/2"

7/16"

10"

Passenger steps

1/2" radius

Passenger platform

1 1/2"

Passenger platform

8"

Passenger steps

12"

No traveling carnival, state fair, or amusement park is complete without its Ferris wheel, an imitation of the huge revolving wheel designed and built for the 1893 World's Columbian Exposition at Chicago. It was the response of George Ferris, a U.S. engineer, to the Eiffel Tower, which was a highlight of the 1889 Paris Exposition. This model complements the Carousel (see page 137) as a high-ride companion. It is hand-powered, and young operators can enjoy providing small dolls and toy animals with free rides. The gondolas are removable.

STEP 1
CUTTING THE PIECES

Cut out the rim pieces to the sizes indicated, carefully beveling each end at 22½° so that they will form an eight-sided wheel. Cut out the spokes. The hubs are also eight-sided, measuring 1¼ inches on each side. The hub spacers are eight-sided, measuring ⅞ inch on each side. Drill a ¾-inch hole in the center of each hub and hub spacer. The wheel turners are disks, which can be cut on the band saw. Drill a ¾-inch hole ⅜ inch deep in the center of one side of each disk. Cut the gondola hangers to size. The gondola-hanger stops are cut on one side to fit the angle of two sides of the main wheel (see drawing). Lay out the pattern for the uprights on the plywood panel and cut them out on a jigsaw or saber saw. Locate and drill a ¾-inch hole in each upright for the axle. Cut the base panel to size. Cut the pieces of the ground platform to sizes indicated. Cut out the pieces for the gondolas. The sides of the gondolas are tapered and have a ¼-inch hole near the top to fit over the gondola hangers. They also have an opening cut into one side so that they can be slipped on and off the gondola hangers. These can be cut on the band saw or jigsaw. Locate and drill the ³⁄₁₆-inch holes in the gondola sides for the gondola bars. Cut out the pieces for the passenger platform. The three platform steps are ½ inch, 1 inch, and 1½ inches wide. They are

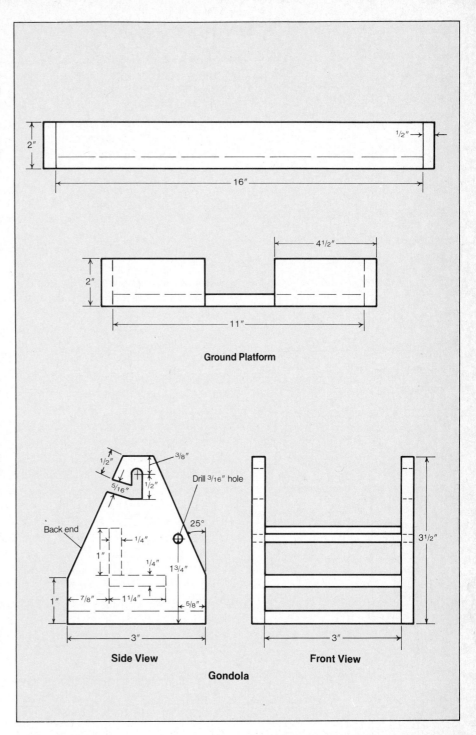

Ground Platform

Side View

Drill ³⁄₁₆" hole

Back end

Front View

Gondola

all ⁷⁄₁₆ inch thick and 2 inches long. Sand all pieces.

STEP 2
ASSEMBLING THE WHEELS

Drill a ³⁄₁₆-inch hole ½ inch deep in the center of each side of the hubs to receive the spokes. Drill a ³⁄₁₆-inch hole ¼ inch deep in the center of each end of the spokes. Drill a ³⁄₁₆-inch hole through the center of each rim piece. Cut thirty-two pieces of ³⁄₁₆-inch dowel ¾ inch long for gluing the wheels together. The spokes are to be glued to the hubs and to the centers of the rim pieces. Try a dry assembly first to make sure everything fits properly with the glue dowels in place. Now you can glue the two halves of the Ferris wheel together. Insert the glue dowels into the hubs with a bit of glue, and then fit the spokes onto the dowels with glue. The spokes should fit snugly against the hubs. Finally, glue the rim pieces to the other ends of the

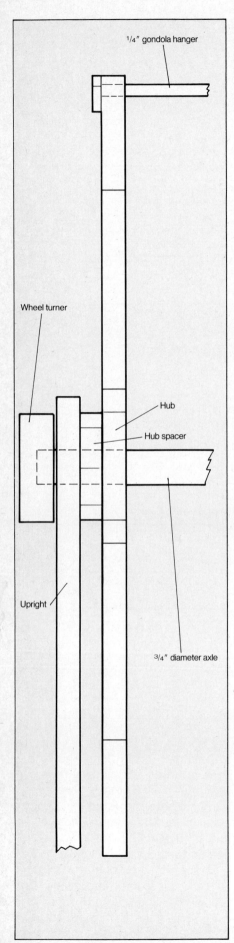

1/4" gondola hanger

Wheel turner

Hub

Hub spacer

Upright

3/4" diameter axle

spokes with glue and dowels, and the rim pieces to each other, forming the eight-sided wheels. Hold the whole assembly together with masking tape until the glue dries. When the glue is dry, drill a 1/4-inch hole through the center of each joint of the rim pieces for the gondola hangers. Glue the gondola-hanger stops across the rim joints on one side of the wheels. These will also give added strength to the rim joints. Glue the hub spacers to the hubs on the same side to which the stops were glued. These are the outsides of the wheels. Now you can assemble both halves of the Ferris wheel. Place one half on a flat surface with the hub-spacer side down. Use scrap wood the same thickness as the hub spacer under the wheel half so it will be steady. Glue one 1/4-inch gondola hanger in each of the holes previously drilled in the rim joints. Insert the axle into the axle hole in the hub as a guide, put the other half of the wheel onto the axle, and glue this half to the gondola hangers glued to the other half. Do not glue the axle at this time. It is merely used as a guide to help keep everything straight. Hold the assembly together with masking tape until the glue dries. Now glue one of the uprights to the center of one side of the base panel, using 3/16-inch glue dowels. Do not glue in the other upright at this time.

STEP 3
ASSEMBLING THE GONDOLAS AND PLATFORMS
Begin the gondola assembly by gluing the seat backs to the seats, securing them with masking tape. Next glue each gondola bottom to one

side only. Now glue the seat units to the sides that are glued to the bottoms. Make sure that the seat back is on the same side as the opening that fits over the hanging bar. The second side of the gondola can now be glued in place. Again, check the hanger opening. Finally, glue in the gondola bars. Assemble the seven parts of the ground platform, using glue and light brads. Set all brads, fill all holes with wood putty, and sand smooth. The passenger platform and steps are assembled with glue only and secured with light clamps or tape.

STEP 4
FINISHING THE FINAL ASSEMBLY
Before the final assembly, the units should be finished separately. Check to make sure all parts are smooth and free of dust. The ground platform is painted a bright green. All other parts are given two coats of clear finish. Do not finish the axle. Begin final assembly by gluing the axle to the hubs and hub spacers. The axle should project 1 inch on each side. Next insert the axle into the axle hole in the upright previously glued to the base. Place the other upright over the axle and glue it to the base, securing it with wood clamps. Glue the wheel turners to the axle ends. Make sure you do not glue the axle to the uprights. Glue the passenger platform to one end of the base, and glue the base to the ground platform. When gluing two finished surfaces together, sand them lightly for better adhesion. Now glue the passenger steps to the ground platform. Finally, hang the gondolas in place.

Carousel

MATERIALS LIST

Base (1), 1/2″ × 15″ diameter, hardwood plywood
Sub-base (1), 1/4″ × 15″ diameter, hardwood plywood
Main platform (1), 1/2″ × 151/4″ × 151/4″, hardwood plywood
Main platform, sides (8), 3/16″ × 1″ × 61/2″, pine
Roof (1), 1/2″ × 151/4″ × 151/4″, hardwood plywood
Roof sides (8), 3/16″ × 1″ × 61/2″, pine
Roof ribs (8), 1/2″ × 2″ × 71/8″, pine
Turning knob (1), 2″ × 2″ × 21/2″, hardwood
Turning rod (1), 7″ × 3/4″ dowel, hardwood
Roof supports (8), 6″ × 3/8″ dowel, hardwood
Center section, sides (8), 1/4″ × 3″ × 53/4″, plywood
Center section, ends (2), 1/2″ × 67/8″ × 67/8″, plywood

Center section, disks (8), 1/4″ × 2″ diameter, plywood
Seat sides (4), 1/4″ × 31/4″ × 31/4″, plywood
Seat backs (2), 1/4″ × 21/2″ × 21/2″, plywood
Seats (2), 1/4″ × 11/4″ × 21/2″, plywood
Seat braces (2), 1/4″ × 3/4″ × 21/2″, plywood
Animals (6), 3/4″ stock, hardwood
Animal poles (6), 61/4″ × 3/16″ dowel, hardwood
Pole knobs (6), 3/4″ wooden balls
Lazy Susan fixture, 6″ diameter
Brass nails, 1/2″
Yellow wood glue
Nontoxic paint
Nontoxic clear finish

Tools

Table saw
Band saw or jigsaw
Drill or drill press
Hammer
Screwdriver
Light wood clamps
Masking tape
Sandpaper, 80, 120, and 220

Every child has enjoyed rides on the carousel or merry-go-round, whether it be the simple spinning platform in the playground or the elaborate machine-operated construction at the amusement park, with its prancing horses and loud music (at one time provided by the steam organ, with its pumping rhythm). For variety, our toy carousel includes a camel and an elephant along with horses, and seats for grandparents and parents to hold the very small. A light flick of the fingers will start it on its merry way.

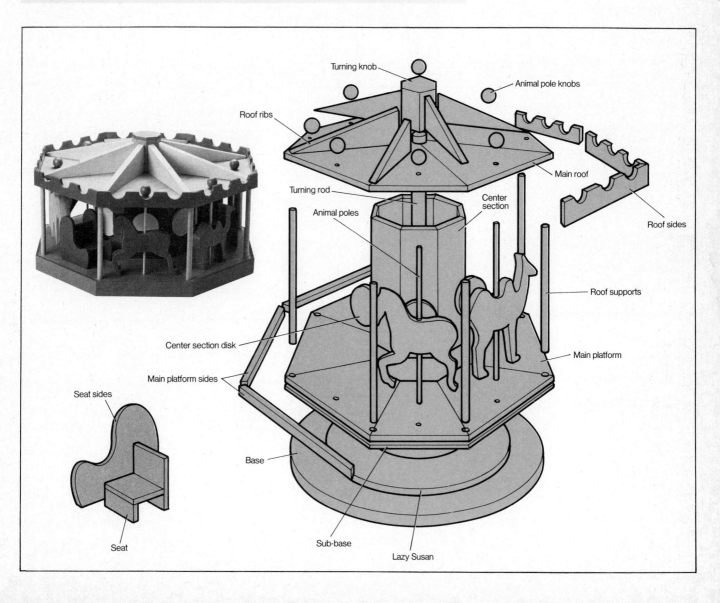

Turning knob
Animal pole knobs
Roof ribs
Main roof
Turning rod
Roof sides
Center section
Animal poles
Roof supports
Center section disk
Main platform
Main platform sides
Seat sides
Base
Seat
Sub-base
Lazy Susan

STEP 1
CUTTING THE PIECES

Cut out the base and sub-base to the sizes indicated. The main platform is made up of eight identical pieces ta-pered at 22½° on each side. The roof is an octagon-shaped solid panel with 6¼-inch sides. Drill a ¾-inch hole in the middle of the roof for the turning rod. Drill the eight ⅜-inch holes for the roof supports and the six ³⁄₁₆-inch holes for the animal poles as indicated.

The center section is an octagon-shaped box with 3-inch sides. The

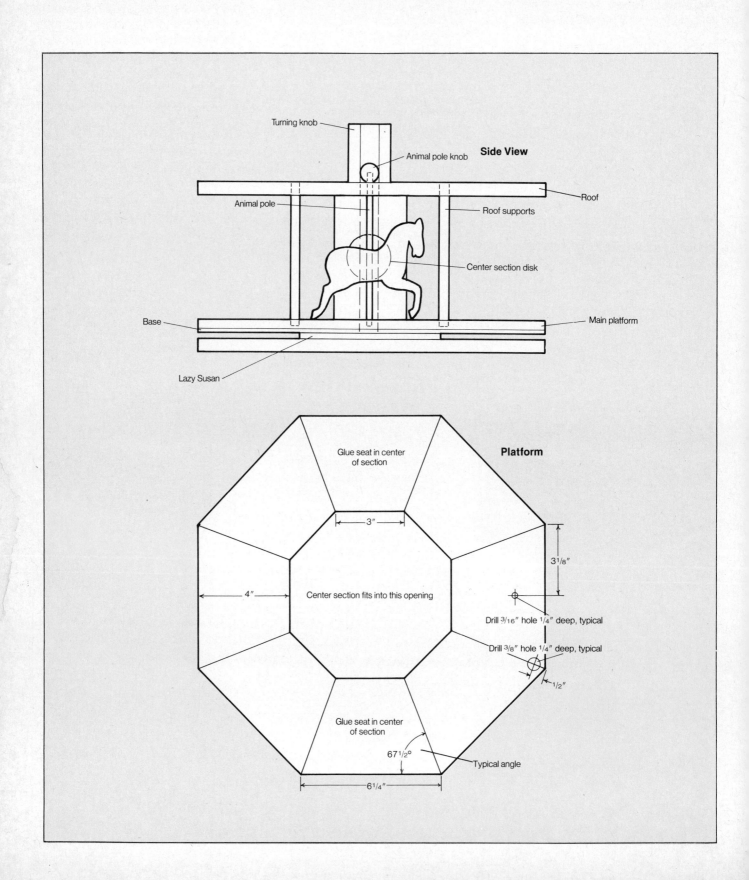

Turning knob

Animal pole knob

Side View

Animal pole

Roof

Roof supports

Center section disk

Base

Main platform

Lazy Susan

Glue seat in center
of section

Platform

3″

Center section fits into this opening

4″

3⅛″

Drill ³⁄₁₆″ hole ¼″ deep, typical

Drill ⅜″ hole ¼″ deep, typical

½″

Glue seat in center
of section

67½°

Typical angle

6¼″

two ends of the box (top and bottom) are octagons that fit inside of the sides. Drill a 3/4-inch hole in the center of each end of the center section for the turning rod. Cut out the center-section disks. Cut out the roof ribs, turning knob, and turning rod. Drill a 3/4-inch hole 1 inch deep in the bottom of the turning knob for the turning rod. Cut the roof-support dowels to size. Cut out the sides for the roof and main platform. The seats are made up of five pieces. The curved sides can be cut on the band saw or jigsaw.

STEP 2
MAKING THE ANIMALS

Lay out the animal patterns on separate square-cut blocks of 3/4-inch hardwood large enough to accommodate the pattern. Make sure the feet of each animal are flush with the bottom of the block. Cut out the upper contour of the animal. Before finishing the animal, and while the block is still square at the bottom, drill the 3/16-inch center hole through the body for the supporting pole. This is best done on a drill press. Then finish cutting out the animal. Cut the supporting poles to size. The pole knobs can be 3/4-inch wood balls or 3/4-inch cubes of hardwood with the edges rounded. Drill a 3/16-inch hole 1/4 inch deep in each knob for the poles.

STEP 3
ASSEMBLING AND FINISHING THE PARTS

Since some parts will be glued together as units and others will be finished before assembly, not all of the steps outlined below need be done in the order given. While you are waiting for the glue to dry on some parts, you can go on and finish other parts. First glue the eight sections of the main platform together, using masking tape as a clamp. When the glue has dried, drill the eight 3/8-inch holes 1/4 inch deep for the roof-support dowels, and drill the six 3/16-inch holes 1/4 inch deep for the animal poles. Glue the 1/4-inch sub-base to the bottom of the main platform. The eight panels of the center are painted

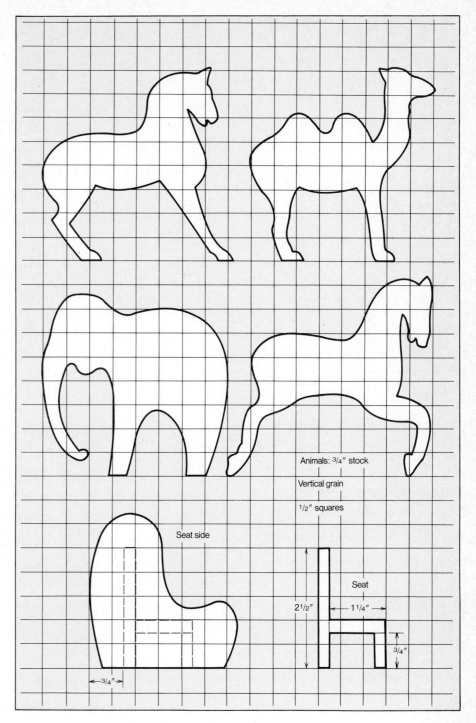

Animals: 3/4" stock

Vertical grain

1/2" squares

Seat side

Seat

2 1/2"   1 1/4"

3/4"

3/4"

before assembly, with bright colors arranged so that no similar colors are side by side. Paint the eight center disks white. Check the fit of the roof and platform side pieces. Paint them in bright colors. We used red for the top and blue for the bottom. Paint the roof ribs yellow. Finish the main platform, roof, turning knob, and the animals with two coats of clear finish. Do not finish the edges of the platform or roof. Also do not finish the

animal poles or support dowels. Paint the pole knobs with a bright color. Make sure the center-section panels (with the bottom end-piece inside) fit the octagonal opening in the main platform. Glue the eight center sections together with the end-pieces inside at the top and bottom, taking care not to mar the painted surfaces. Glue the five parts of the seats together and paint them a bright red.

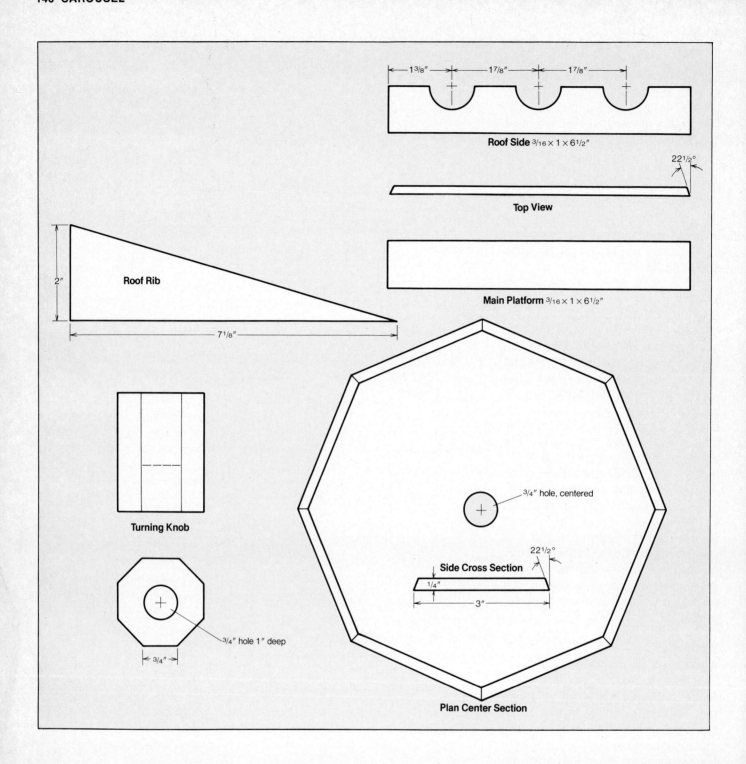

Roof Side $^3/_{16} \times 1 \times 6^1/_2''$

Top View

$22^1/_2°$

Roof Rib

2″

$7^1/_8''$

Main Platform $^3/_{16} \times 1 \times 6^1/_2''$

Turning Knob

$^3/_4''$ hole, centered

$22^1/_2°$

Side Cross Section

$^1/_4''$

3″

$^3/_4''$ hole 1″ deep

$\leftarrow ^3/_4'' \rightarrow$

Plan Center Section

STEP 4
ASSEMBLING THE CAROUSEL

First lay out the position of the lazy Susan fixture on the base and sub-base and drill small holes for the screws. Since the fixture must be attached to the base first, large holes (1 inch in diameter) are drilled through the base opposite the screw holes in the sub-base to give access. Do not attach the lazy Susan at this time.

Glue the sides to the roof and main platform, using brass nails. Glue the center section to the sub-base and the main platform. Place the roof onto the turning rod and on top of the center section (without glue) to check the fit of the roof-support dowels. Then glue in the roof. It is not necessary to glue in the roof-support dowels; the roof ribs will cover them. Glue the turning knob to the roof and

the turning rod. Make sure each face of the knob is toward one of the corners of the roof. Glue in the roof ribs, one on each face of the turning knob and covering the ends of the roof-support dowels. Glue in the seats. Install the lazy Susan in the holes previously drilled. Insert the animal poles through the roof into the animals and into the main platform. Do not glue the poles.

Rocking Horse

MATERIALS LIST
Horse head (1), $3'' \times 13\frac{1}{2}'' \times 14''$
Rocker sides (2), $\frac{3}{4}'' \times 14'' \times 48''$
Saddle seat (1), $\frac{3}{4}'' \times 8\frac{1}{4}'' \times 20''$
Saddle front (1), $\frac{3}{4}'' \times 7\frac{1}{4}'' \times 10''$
Saddle back (1), $\frac{3}{4}'' \times 7\frac{1}{4}'' \times 10''$
Back brace (1), $1\frac{1}{2}'' \times 1\frac{3}{4}'' \times 5\frac{1}{2}''$
Rocker braces (2), $\frac{3}{4}'' \times 9\frac{1}{2}'' \times 10\frac{1}{8}''$
Rocker-brace cleats (4), $\frac{3}{4}'' \times \frac{3}{4}'' \times 9\frac{1}{2}''$
Crossbars (2), $8\frac{1}{2}'' \times 1''$ dowel
Stirrups (2), $\frac{3}{4}'' \times 3'' \times 7''$
Glue dowels (as needed), $\frac{3}{16}''$, $\frac{1}{4}''$, $\frac{3}{8}''$

Brads, $1\frac{1}{4}''$
Yellow wood glue
Nontoxic paint or clear finish

Tools
Table saw
Saber saw
Band saw
Drill or drill press
Drum sander
Belt sander
Wood rasp

Hammer
C-clamps
Bar clamps
Masking tape
Sandpaper, 80, 120, and 220

What house with small children is complete without a rocking horse, that familiar figure of childhood lore? The horse presented here is based on an Early American design and is a particularly sturdy example of the breed. Small riders can hang on to the saddle horns and gallop to their hearts' content, with no need to slow the pace or worry about wearing out their hardy mount. The construction of the rocking horse is fairly straightforward, but there are some tricky angle and bevel cuts and some angle drilling to be done. Follow the text and plans carefully for this work. All the parts for the Rocking Horse should be hardwood.

STEP 1
CUTTING THE ROCKER SIDES
Begin construction with the rocker sides. This is a two-stage operation because the center portion of the sides (where the seat fits) is 12 inches from the floor and beveled at 10° while the rocker ends are 14 inches from the floor. This means you cannot put the whole piece through the saw to cut the bevel in the center section. To get around this, first cut the blanks for the two rocker sides measuring $\frac{3}{4} \times 14 \times 48$ inches. If you cannot obtain wood 14 inches wide, it will have to be glued up. Next enlarge the drawing of the rocker side to full size and transfer it to the wood. Cut out on a band saw or saber saw that part of the rocker curve which runs from the edge of the center sec-

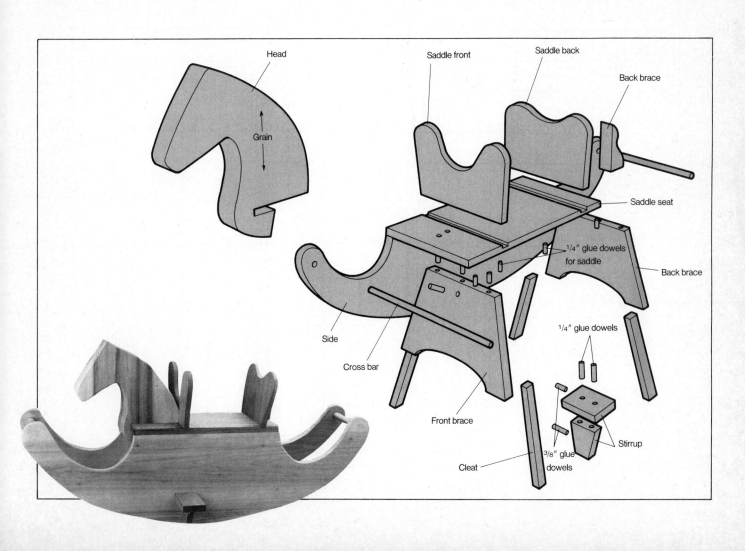

Head

Grain

Saddle front

Saddle back

Back brace

Saddle seat

¼" glue dowels for saddle

Back brace

Side

Cross bar

Front brace

¼" glue dowels

Stirrup

Cleat

⅜" glue dowels

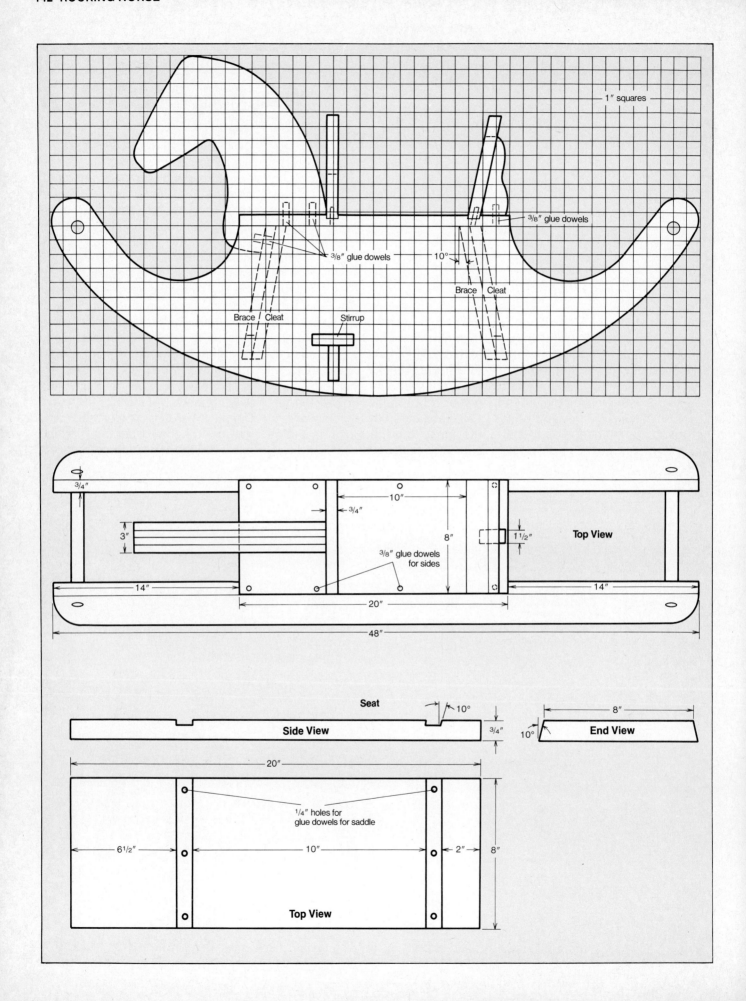

1" squares

³/₈" glue dowels

³/₈" glue dowels

10°

Brace   Cleat

Brace   Cleat

Stirrup

³/₄"

³/₄"

10"

3"

8"

1¹/₂"

Top View

³/₈" glue dowels
for sides

14"

20"

14"

48"

Seat

10°

Side View

³/₄"

10°

8"

End View

20"

¹/₄" holes for
glue dowels for saddle

6¹/₂"

10"

2"

8"

Top View

tion to the rocker top at each end of the rocker panels. Now the rocker side still has two straight sides, but there is space for the table saw blade to make the bevel cut. So, set the rip fence to 12 inches, tilt the blade 10°, place the bottom edge of the side against the fence, and drop the side to the saw table, with the blade in the space you previously cut out. You can now make the bevel cut. After cutting the bevel on both sides, cut out the rest of the rocker curves. Repeat the above for the second side. Round and smooth the edges of the rocker sides (do not round the beveled edges, which fit the saddle seat) with a drum sander and belt sander, or with a wood rasp and sandpaper. Drill the four 1-inch holes ¼ inch deep in the inside tops of both rocker sides for the crossbars. Note that these holes are drilled at an angle of 10° to conform with the sides.

STEP 2
CUTTING THE OTHER PIECES
Enlarge the patterns for the saddle front and back, transfer to the wood, and cut out on the band saw. Round the edges (except the bottom) with a rasp and sand smooth. The saddle seat has a 10° bevel on each long side to match the bevel on the rocker sides. The saddle seat has two ¼- × ¾-inch grooves, one 6½ inches from the front for the saddle front, and one 2 inches from the back cut at 10° for the saddle back to be cut on the table saw. Drill three ¼-inch holes along the center of each groove for glue dowels. Place the saddle front in its groove, and then drill three ¼-inch holes into the front, through the holes previously drilled in the groove. Repeat for the saddle back. Transfer the pattern of the back brace to the wood and cut out. Then cut out the rocker braces, cleats, and stirrups, noting the bevels and angle cuts necessary. Cut two 8½-inch lengths of 1-inch dowel for the cross braces, with a 10° cut at the ends. To do this, cut one 10° angle on the table saw and then reverse the dowel. Use a block of scrap wood cut at 10° as a jig, to hold the first 10° cut steady while making the second cut. The horse

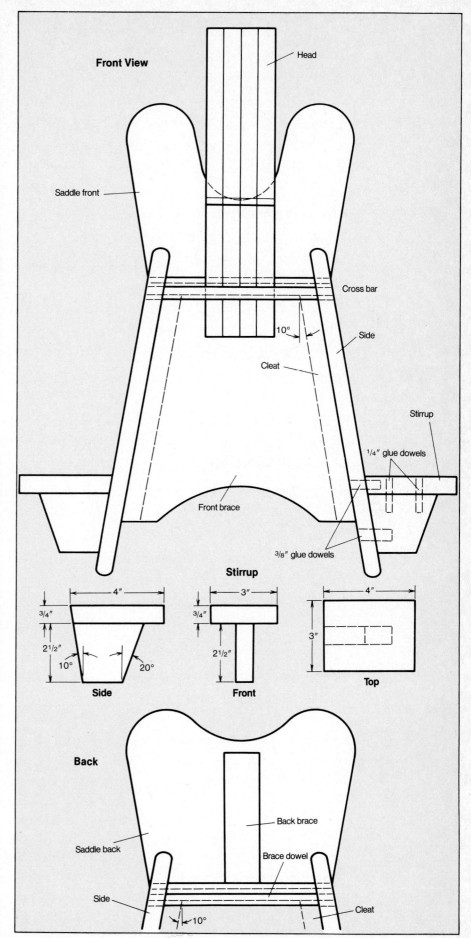

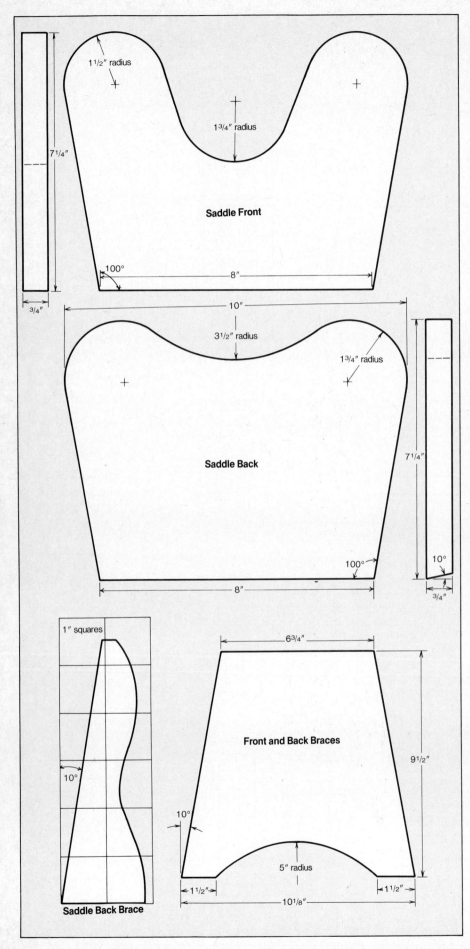

Saddle Front

1 1/2" radius

1 3/4" radius

7 1/4"

100°

8"

3/4"

10"

3 1/2" radius

1 3/4" radius

Saddle Back

7 1/4"

100°

8"

10°

3/4"

1" squares

Saddle Back Brace

10°

6 3/4"

Front and Back Braces

9 1/2"

10°

5" radius

1 1/2"

10 1/8"

1 1/2"

head is made from a block of 3/4-inch stock glued up to a thickness of 3 inches. Make sure the grain runs vertically when you transfer the pattern of the head to the wood. Cut out the head on the band saw carefully, making sure the bottom is flat—so that it will rest properly on the seat—and that the lower part is cut at 10° to fit against the front rocker brace. Round the edges of the head (except the bottom) with a wood rasp and drum sander. Sand all pieces.

STEP 3
ASSEMBLY

Begin the assembly by gluing the two parts of the stirrups together, using 1/4-inch dowels to secure the joint. While the stirrups are drying, attach the rocker brace cleats to the insides of the rocker sides at the proper angle, using glue and brads or dowels. Next attach the stirrups to the rocker sides with glue and dowels from the inside of the rocker sides. The saddle seat is next. Glue one side of the seat to one of the rocker sides, making sure the bevel cuts match and run in the right direction. Use bar clamps and 3/8-inch dowels. Before gluing the second side, try a dry assembly to make sure the rocker braces fit properly. Insert the crossbars into the holes at each end of the rocker sides and clamp the side to the saddle seat. Now try the braces in position between the sides. If they fit, you can proceed. Put a little glue in the holes at the top of the rocker sides, insert the crossbars, and glue the second side to the seat with clamps and 3/8-inch dowels. Glue in the saddle front and back, using 1/4-inch dowels. Glue in the back brace, clamping it to the saddle back and securing it with a 3/8-inch dowel up through the seat. Finally, glue the head into place, securing it with 3/8-inch dowels through the front rocker brace and up through the seat. Give the horse a final sanding, finishing up with 220 sandpaper, and then finish with two coats of a clear nontoxic finish. If you prefer to paint, we suggest brown for the rocker sides and saddle, and red for the horse's head.

Three-Wheel Horse Cart

MATERIALS LIST

Hardwood stock throughout
Seat (1), $3/4'' \times 10'' \times 20''$
Sides (2), $3/4'' \times 6'' \times 7^1/4''$
Side cleats (2), $3/4'' \times 3/4'' \times 5''$
Back (1), $3/4'' \times 5'' \times 7^3/8''$
Rear axle blocks (2), $3/4'' \times 2^1/2'' \times 3''$
Yoke (2), $3/4'' \times 3'' \times 7^1/4''$
Yoke spacer (1), $1'' \times 2^1/4'' \times 3''$
Head (2), $3/4'' \times 8^1/2'' \times 8^1/2''$
Wheels (3), $3/4'' \times 7''$ diameter
Front axle (1), $3'' \times 3/4''$ dowel
Rear axle (1), $11^1/2'' \times 3/4''$ dowel
Front hubcaps (2), $1/2'' \times 1^1/2''$ diameter
Rear hubcaps (2), $3/4'' \times 2''$ diameter
Steering post (1), $3^1/2'' \times 1''$ dowel
Steering arm (1), $12'' \times 1''$ dowel
Gluing pegs (as needed), $3/16''$, $1/4''$, and $3/8''$
   dowels
Yellow wood glue
Nontoxic clear finish or paint

Tools

Table saw	Wood rasp
Band saw	Compass
Drill or drill press	C-clamps
Sandpaper, 80, 120, and 220	

Small children can pretend they're letting the horse have its head on an open stretch, as they ride this three-wheeled cart with the horse's head pointing the way. With hands on the front bar, the horse's head can be moved from side to side, and with feet "walking" on the floor, the child provides mobility.

In this version, the cart has been given a natural finish to enhance the color and texture of the wood and the grace of the horse's head. In cutting out the pieces for the project, therefore, pay particular attention to the grain of the wood, especially in the head, yoke, and side pieces as shown in the plans. The cart is for indoor use only; bumpy surfaces outdoors might crack it.

STEP 1
CUTTING THE PIECES

Lay out the pattern for the seat on a 10- × 20-inch piece of $3/4$-inch hardwood stock and cut out the curves on the band saw. Cut out the sides, side cleats, and rear axle blocks. Note that these pieces are all cut at 20° on one side and 15° on the other. The sides and axle blocks are rounded at the bottom with a radius of $7/8$ inch. Cut out the back, which is beveled at 15° on the top and bottom (the long sides). Cut out the 7-inch-diameter wheels. Round the edges of the wheels with a wood rasp and sandpaper. Lay out the front and rear hubcaps with a compass, and drill the $3/4$-inch holes to the proper depth before cutting them out .

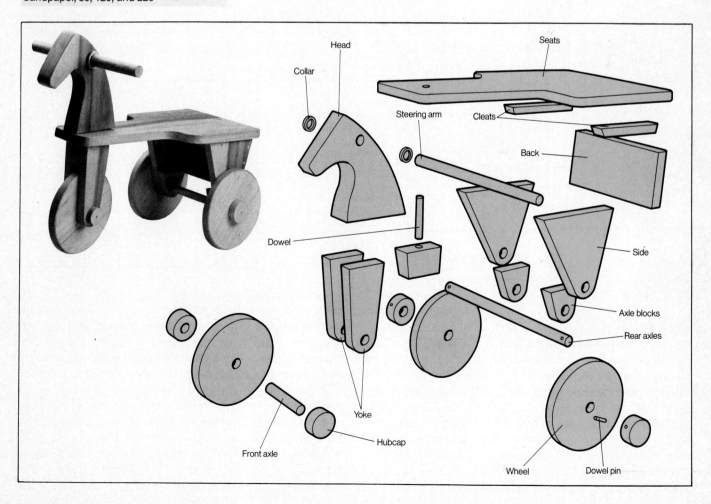

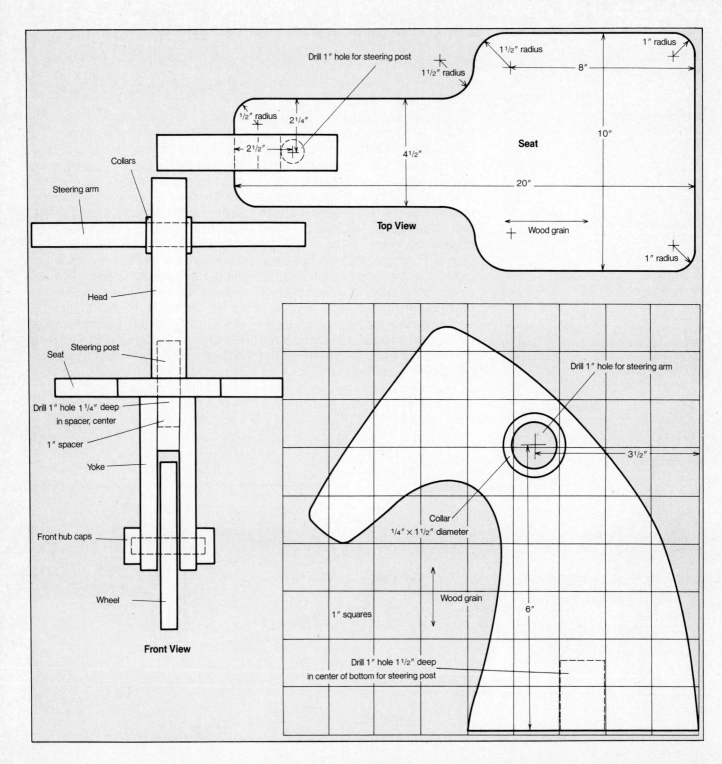

Collars

Steering arm

Head

Seat

Steering post

Drill 1″ hole 1 1/4″ deep in spacer, center

1″ spacer

Yoke

Front hub caps

Wheel

Front View

Drill 1″ hole for steering post

1 1/2″ radius

1 1/2″ radius

1″ radius

1/2″ radius

2 1/4″

2 1/2″

4 1/2″

8″

10″

20″

Seat

1″ radius

Wood grain

Top View

Drill 1″ hole for steering arm

Collar
1/4″ × 1 1/2″ diameter

3 1/2″

Wood grain

6″

1″ squares

Drill 1″ hole 1 1/2″ deep in center of bottom for steering post

STEP 2
THE HEAD AND STEERING YOKE

The 1-inch hole that must be drilled in the head and front wheel yoke for the steering post must be perpendicular to the surface. To assure this, it is advisable to drill the holes before shaping the parts. The head is 1 1/2 inches thick, made up of two 3/4-inch blocks 8 1/2 inches square. First, glue these blocks together with C-clamps, mak-

ing sure the grain of the wood runs in the same (vertical) direction on both pieces. Then, when the glue is dry, drill the 1-inch hole 1 1/2 inches deep in the center, 2 1/2 inches from one edge. This hole should be parallel with the grain. The 1-inch hole for the steering arm can also be drilled at this time. Now enlarge the pattern for the head with 1-inch squares, transfer it to the block, and cut out the head on the band saw. Round the

edges of the head with a wood rasp and sandpaper. Next glue together the three parts of the yoke assembly (two yoke sides and yoke spacer) and drill a 1-inch hole 1 1/4 inches deep in the center of the top of the spacer. The 3/4-inch axle hole can also be drilled through the two sides of the yoke. The center of this hole is 1 inch from the bottom of the yoke. Use a scrap of 1-inch stock between the sides while drilling. The yoke can now be cut to shape on the band saw, as shown.

STEP 3
THE REAR ASSEMBLY
Glue a rear axle block to each of the two sides, and drill the 3/4-inch axle hole 7/8 inch from the bottom of each. Glue the cleats to the top edges of the sides, with the 20° bevel matching the 20° slant of the front edge of the sides. Secure the cleats with 1/4-inch dowels as gluing pegs. Glue the back in place between the two sides. The bottom of the back piece rests on the rear axle blocks and up against the cleats. Secure the back with 1/4-inch glue dowels. The rear assembly is now complete and can be glued to the bottom of the seat. It is centered between the sides of the seat, 7/8 inch from the back edge of the seat. Secure the rear assembly to the seat with 3/8-inch glue dowels.

STEP 4
FINISHING AND ASSEMBLY
Glue the steering arm to the head, using the 1/4-inch collars. Glue the steering post (1-inch dowel) into the hole in the bottom of the head. Pass the post through the hole in the seat to make sure it turns freely; if it doesn't, enlarge the hole slightly with sandpaper. Try the axles in the wheels to make sure the wheels turn freely. In this project, it is the wheels that turn, not the axles. It is also a good idea to make a trial assembly of the wheels, axles, and hubcaps, as well as the head, steering post, and yoke, to make sure there is not too much play between the parts. Since hardwoods sometimes vary in thickness, you may have to make some adjustments. For instance, you may have to put metal washers between the front wheel and the yoke. Before the final assembly, the parts should be finished. Sand all parts carefully, rounding all edges with 80 and 120 sandpaper, and finishing with 220 sandpaper. Remove all dust. Finish with nontoxic clear finish. When the finish is dry, insert the steering post attached to the head through the hole in the seat and glue it into the hole in the top of the yoke. Make sure you do not glue it to the seat. Next

put the front wheel between the sides of the yoke, insert the axle, and glue the hubcaps to the axle. For extra security, you can pin the cap to the axle with a piece of 3/16-inch dowel. And, of course, you can paint the cart instead of using a natural finish, if you prefer.

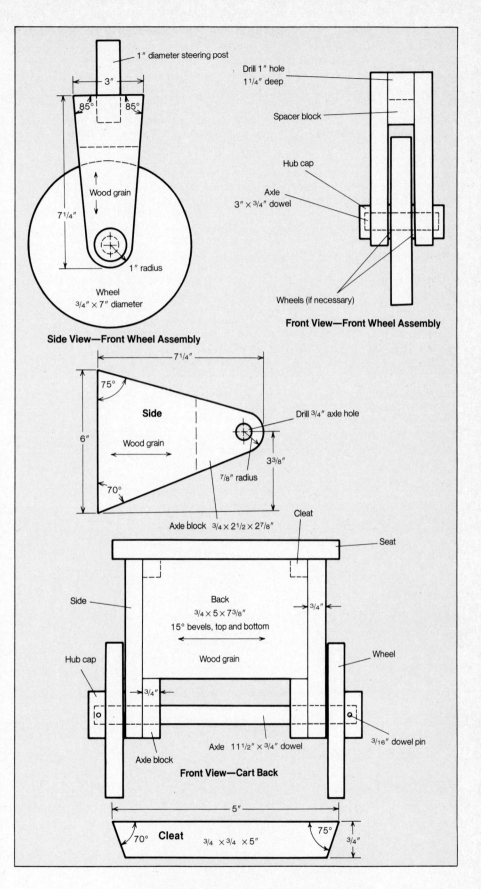

Side View—Front Wheel Assembly

1" diameter steering post
3"
85° 85°
Wood grain
7 1/4"
1" radius
Wheel
3/4" × 7" diameter

Front View—Front Wheel Assembly

Drill 1" hole 1 1/4" deep
Spacer block
Hub cap
Axle 3" × 3/4" dowel
Wheels (if necessary)

Side
7 1/4"
75°
6"
Wood grain
70°
Drill 3/4" axle hole
3 3/8"
7/8" radius
Axle block 3/4 × 2 1/2 × 2 7/8"

Cleat
Seat
Side
Back 3/4 × 5 × 7 3/8"
15° bevels, top and bottom
Wood grain
3/4"
3/4"
Wheel
Hub cap
3/4"
Axle 11 1/2" × 3/4" dowel
Axle block
3/16" dowel pin

Front View—Cart Back

70° Cleat 3/4 × 3/4 × 5"
75°
5"
3/4"

Soap Box Racer

MATERIALS LIST

Chassis (1), 1/2" × 14" × 48", plywood
Chassis bracing, 3/4" × 1" × 16", pine
Cleats (2), 1/2" × 1/2" × 7", pine
Front axle block (1), 1" × 5 1/2" × 12 1/4", pine
Rear axle block (1), 1" × 4 1/2" × 12 1/4", pine
Backrest, front panel (1), 1/2" × 11" × 15", plywood
Backrest, top panel (1), 1/2" × 7" × 15", plywood
Backrest, back panel (1), 1/2" × 12" × 15", plywood
Backrest, side panels (2), 1/2" × 9" × 12", plywood
Hood top (1), 1/2" × 15" × 21 1/2", plywood
Hood front (1), 1/2" × 12" × 15", plywood
Hood sides (2), 1/2" × 12" × 25 1/2", plywood
Dashboard (1), 1/2" × 2" × 15", plywood

Rear Axle Assembly:
Axle holders (2), 1 1/2" × 4" × 6", pine
Crossbar (1), 1 1/2" × 4" × 12", pine
Braces (2), 1 1/2" × 2 3/4" × 2 3/4", pine
Lower brace (1), 3/4" × 2 1/4" × 15", pine

Front Axle Assembly:
Axle holders (2), 1 1/2" × 4" × 6", pine
Crossbar (1), 2" × 4" × 12", pine
Inner brace (1), 1 1/2" × 2" × 12", pine
Lower brace (1), 3/4" × 2 1/4" × 15", pine
Swivel disk (1), 3/4" × 5" diameter, pine
Steering bar (1), 1 1/2" × 2 1/2" × 12", pine
Steering post (1), 5 1/2" × 1" dowel, hardwood
Glue dowels (as needed), 3/8" dowels, hardwood
Steering rope, 1/4" × 8'
Axles (2), 21" × 1/2" threaded rod
Metal washers (4), 1/2"
Hex nuts (8), 1/2"
Wheels (4), 8" lawn-mower wheels
Brads, 1 1/4"
No. 8 × 1 1/4" panhead sheet metal screws
Wood putty
Yellow wood glue
Nontoxic paint

Tools
Table saw
Drill or drill press
Hammer
Nailset
Screwdriver
Clamps
Sandpaper, 80, 120, and 220

In the not-too-distant past, kids who could get hold of a wooden box and a board, hammer and nails, and a little help with the wheels could put together their own racers and scoot down the neighborhood sidewalks and alleys. Nowadays wooden boxes are hard to come by, and the contemporary soapbox racer has been transformed into an elaborate and expensive machine. But there is still something appealing about the original style of racer, perhaps because of its simplicity and availability—it is easy to make and requires few materials and tools.

STEP 1
CUTTING THE PIECES

Cut out the chassis and bevel the front edge at 10° and the back edge

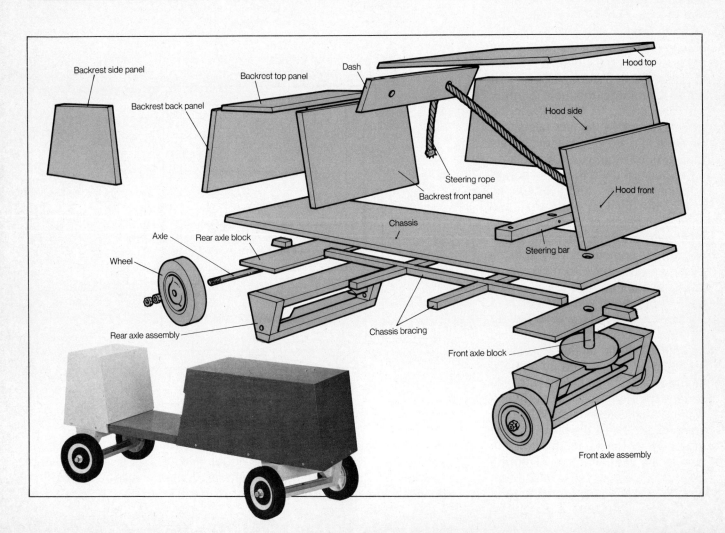

Backrest side panel
Backrest top panel
Backrest back panel
Dash
Hood top
Hood side
Steering rope
Hood front
Backrest front panel
Chassis
Axle
Rear axle block
Wheel
Steering bar
Rear axle assembly
Chassis bracing
Front axle block
Front axle assembly

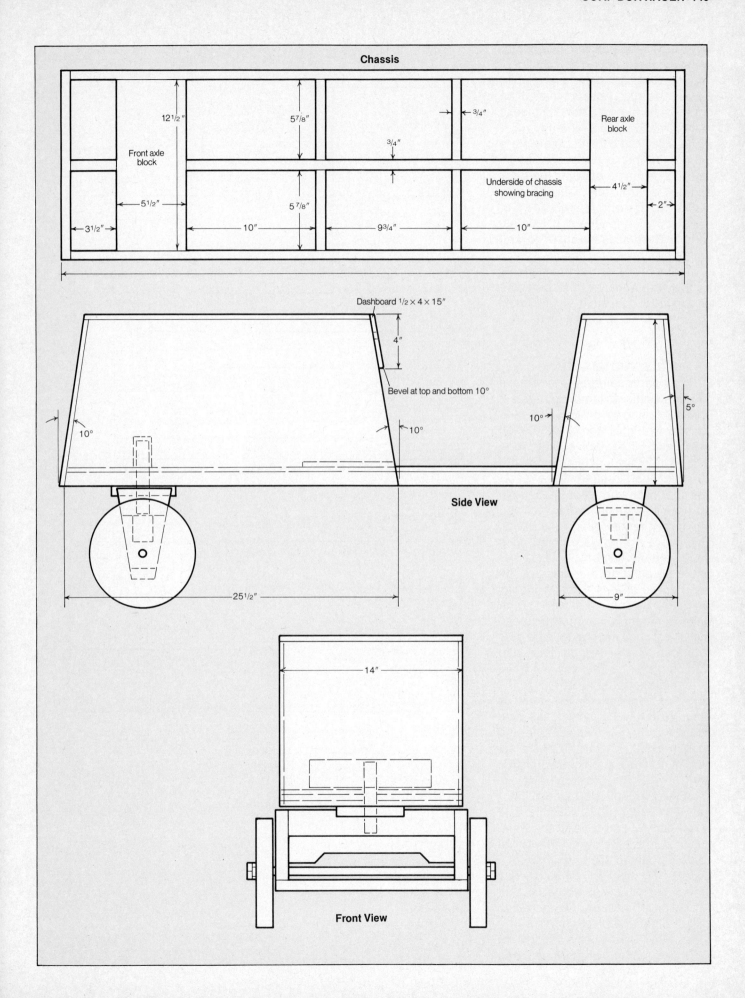

Chassis

12½"

5⅞"

3/4"

Front axle block

Rear axle block

3/4"

Underside of chassis showing bracing

4½"

5½"

5⅞"

3½"

10"

9¾"

10"

2"

Dashboard ½ × 4 × 15"

4"

Bevel at top and bottom 10°

10°

10°

10°

5°

Side View

25½"

9"

14"

Front View

at 5°. Cut out the chassis bracing to sizes indicated, noting that the bracing at the front and back is beveled to conform to the chassis bevels. Cut out the axle blocks. The axle blocks can be made up of several 3/4- × 1-inch strips. The backrest panels are cut from 1/2-inch plywood. The backrest has an angle of 5° at the back and 10° at the front. The hood is sloped 10° at the front and back. Cut out the pieces for the rear axle assembly. The braces are cut at 45°. All other parts have a 10° angle. The inner brace of the front axle assembly is cut at 45°, while the other parts are angled at 10°. Cut out the swivel disk, steering bar, and steering post.

STEP 2
ASSEMBLE THE RACER

Sand all parts carefully and remove all dust. Begin assembly by fastening and bracing the axle blocks to the chassis with glue and brads. Set all brads and fill the holes with wood putty. Drill the 1-inch hole for the steering post through the chassis and the front axle block. Assemble the backrest as a unit, using glue and brads, setting and filling the brads. The hood is also assembled as a unit. Note the two small cleats that are to be glued to the inside of the hood at the driver's end, 1 1/2 inches from the bottom. Drill two 1-inch holes in the dashboard for the steering ropes. Glue the rear axle holders to the crossbar, securing them with 3/8-inch glue dowels. Glue the triangular braces to the holders and the crossbar. Complete the assembly by gluing the lower brace to the axle holders. Drill the axle holders for the 1/2-inch axles. Attach the entire assembly to the axle block with glue and dowels. Put the front axle assembly together in the same manner as the rear assembly. Drill the axle holes. Drill a 1-inch hole for the steering post in the center of the swivel disk through to the crossbar to a depth of 2 inches. Drill a 1-inch hole 2 inches deep in the steering bar. Drill two 3/8-inch holes, one at each end, through the steering bar for the ropes. The steering bar is attached to the steering post with two panhead sheet metal screws.

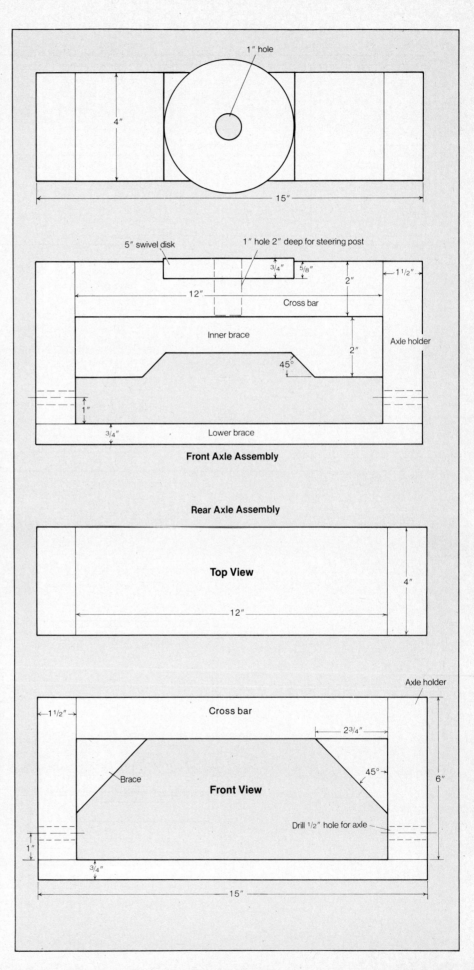

Front Axle Assembly

Rear Axle Assembly

Top View

Front View

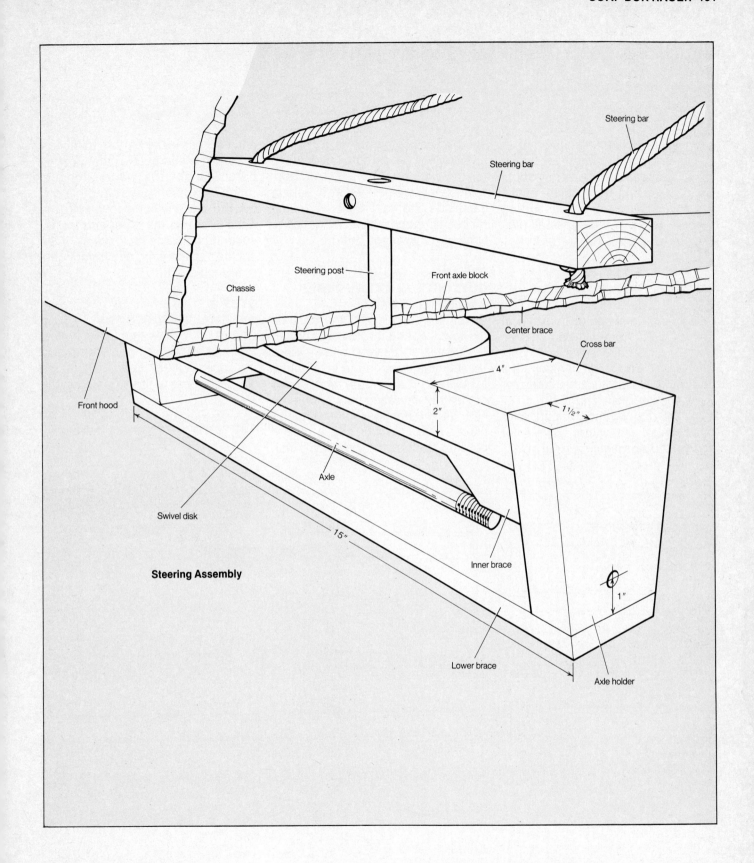

Steering bar

Steering bar

Steering post

Front axle block

Chassis

Center brace

Cross bar

4"

2"

1½"

Front hood

Axle

15"

Inner brace

Swivel disk

1"

Steering Assembly

Lower brace

Axle holder

STEP 3
FINISHING THE RACER

Check all parts to make sure all holes are filled and all parts are sanded smooth. Finish the parts separately so that you can use different colors for some parts if you prefer. Use two or three coats of nontoxic enamel. In assembling the racer, the hood and backrest are not glued to the chassis. Fasten them with panhead sheet metal screws. They hold well in plywood and have an attractive appearance. Insert the steering post through the chassis, secure it to the steering bar, thread the rope through the holes in the dash, and you are ready to roll.

Red Rack Wagon

Amid all the changing fashions in toys, the old red wagon still exercises its appeal. The rack gives this wagon an added dimension, allowing kids more leeway in transporting their cargo or, with care, small passengers and pets.

STEP 1
CUTTING THE BODY PIECES

Cut out the wagon bottom to the size indicated. The shape of the front of the wagon bottom will be cut later. Cut out the wagon sides and back. Cut a $3/8$- × $3/8$-inch rabbet along the bottom inside edge of the sides for the wagon bottom and a $3/8$- × $3/4$-inch rabbet along the back edge for the back of the wagon. The front ends of the side pieces are cut at 20°.

The back piece has a $3/8$- × $3/8$-inch rabbet along the bottom inside edge for the wagon bottom. The wagon-front panels are beveled at 10° along each side and have a $3/8$- × $3/8$-inch rabbet along the inside bottom edge to receive the wagon bottom.

STEP 2
CUTTING THE AXLE HOLDER AND TONGUE PARTS

Cut out the ten pieces of the rear axle assembly, noting the 45° cuts on the crossbar and holder braces. Drill a $1/2$-inch hole through the axle holder for the axle. Cut out the nine pieces of the front axle assembly, noting the 45° cuts on the crossbar and holder braces. The crossbar has a recess cut into the top for the swivel disk

and a recess in the bottom to receive the washer and nuts of the steering bolt. Cut out the wagon tongue, tongue holders, spacer, and handlebar. Drill one end of the tongue for the handlebar and the other end for the securing bolt. The rack stakes, holders, and spacers are all straight cuts of $3/8$-inch stock.

STEP 3
ASSEMBLING THE BODY

Glue the seven wagon-front panels together, securing them with masking tape. Cut the front end of the wagon bottom to fit the rabbet in the

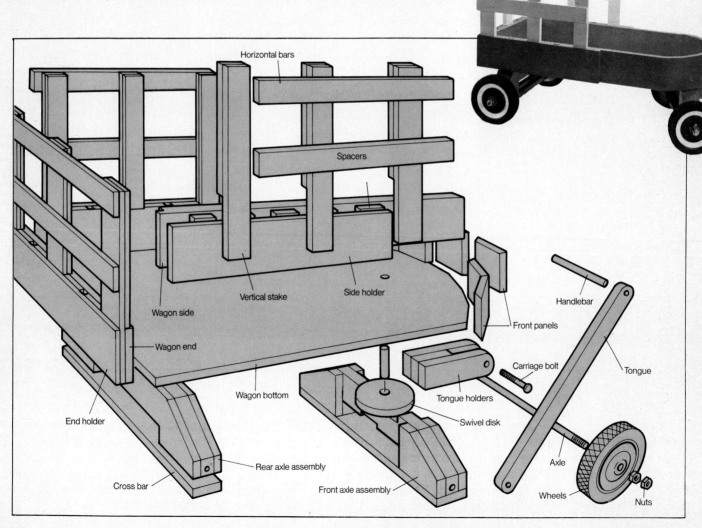

bottom of the front panels. Use the inside edge of the rabbet as a guide. Glue the five parts of the wagon bed together, using C-clamps to hold the

MATERIALS LIST

Wagon bottom (1), $3/4'' \times 14\,1/4'' \times 31\,1/2''$, plywood
Wagon sides (2), $3/4'' \times 4\,1/2'' \times 27''$, pine
Wagon end (1), $3/4'' \times 4\,1/2'' \times 14\,1/4''$, pine
Wagon front panels (7), $3/4'' \times 2\,3/4'' \times 4\,1/2''$, pine
Tongue (1), $3/4'' \times 1\,1/2'' \times 24''$, pine
Handlebar (1), $8\,3/4'' \times 3/4''$ dowel, hardwood
Tongue holders (2), $3/4'' \times 2'' \times 6''$, pine
Spacer (1), $3/4'' \times 2'' \times 3''$, pine

Rear Axle Assembly:
Wagon-bed braces (2), $3/4'' \times 1\,1/2'' \times 11\,3/4''$, pine
Lower brace (1), $3/4'' \times 2\,1/2'' \times 16\,1/2''$, pine
Axle holders (2), $1\,1/2'' \times 1\,1/2'' \times 4''$, pine
Crossbar (1), $1\,1/2'' \times 3'' \times 16\,1/2''$, pine
Holder braces (4), $1/2'' \times 3\,3/4'' \times 4''$, pine

Front Axle Assembly:
Swivel disk (1), $3/4'' \times 5''$ diameter, pine
Axle holders (2), $1\,1/2'' \times 1\,1/2'' \times 4''$, pine
Crossbar (1), $1\,1/2'' \times 3'' \times 15''$, pine
Lower brace (1), $3/4'' \times 2\,1/2'' \times 15''$, pine
Holder braces (4), $1/2'' \times 4'' \times 4\,1/2''$, pine

Rack:
Side holders (2), $3/8'' \times 4\,1/2'' \times 18\,3/4''$, pine or plywood
Rear holder (1), $3/8'' \times 4\,1/2'' \times 15\,7/8''$, pine or plywood
Spacers (14), $3/8'' \times 2'' \times 4\,1/2''$, pine or plywood
Vertical stakes (9), $3/8'' \times 2'' \times 15\,1/2''$, pine or plywood
Vertical-stake stiffeners (9), $3/8'' \times 2'' \times 11''$, pine or plywood
Side horizontal bars (4), $3/8'' \times 2'' \times 16\,3/4''$, pine or plywood
Rear horizontal bars (2), $3/8'' \times 2'' \times 15\,3/4''$, pine or plywood
Axles (2), $20\,1/2'' \times 1/2''$, threaded rod
Steering bolt (1), $1/2 - 13 \times 5''$, carriage bolt
Tongue-securing bolt (1), $1/4 - 20 \times 3''$ carriage bolt
Hex nuts (10), $1/2''$
Metal washers (5), $1/2''$
Wheels (4), $7''$ lawn-mower wheels
Glue dowels (as needed), $3/8''$ dowel, hardwood
No. $10 \times 1\,1/4''$ flat head wood screws
Brads, $1''$
Yellow wood glue
Nontoxic paint

Tools
Table saw
Band saw
Drill or drill press
Block plane
Wood rasp
Screwdriver
C-clamps
Masking tape
Sandpaper, 80, 120, and 220

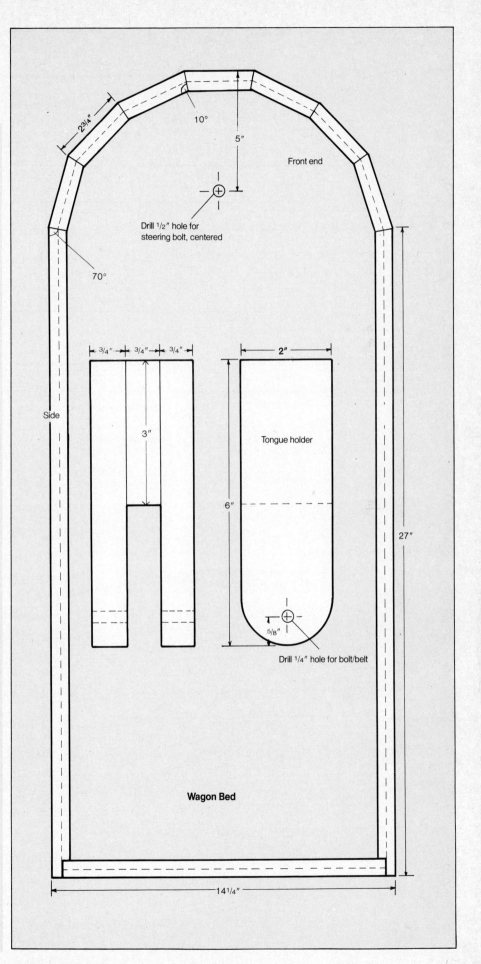

10°

2 3/4"

5"

Front end

Drill 1/2" hole for steering bolt, centered

70°

Side

3/4" 3/4" 3/4"

2"

3"

Tongue holder

6"

27"

5/8"

Drill 1/4" hole for bolt/belt

Wagon Bed

14 1/4"

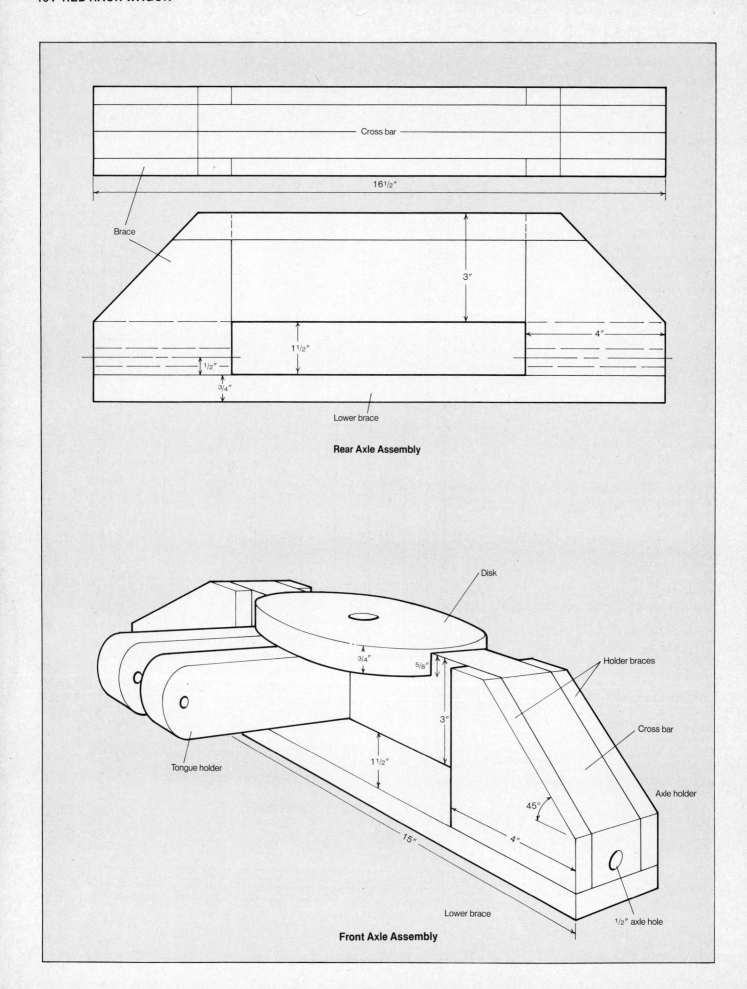

Cross bar

16 1/2"

Brace

3"

4"

1 1/2"

1/2"

3/4"

Lower brace

Rear Axle Assembly

Disk

3/4"

5/8"

Holder braces

3"

Cross bar

Tongue holder

1 1/2"

45°

Axle holder

15"

4"

Lower brace

1/2" axle hole

Front Axle Assembly

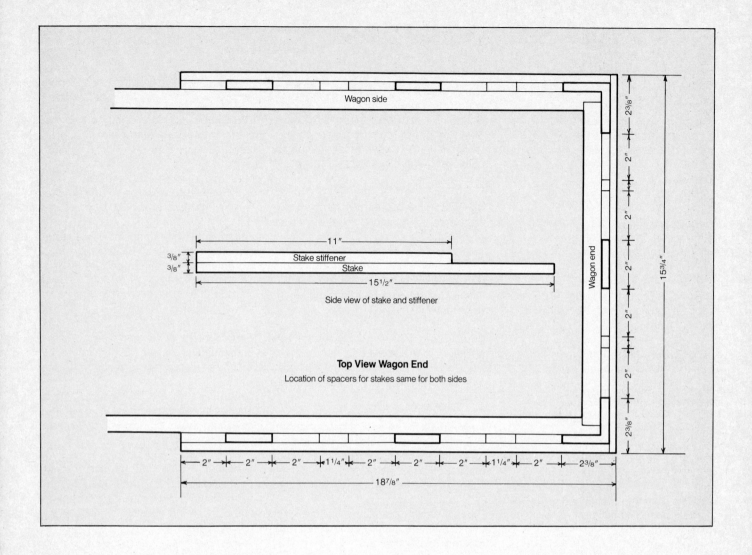

Wagon side

11"

3/8"
3/8"

Stake stiffener

Stake

15 1/2"

Side view of stake and stiffener

Top View Wagon End

Location of spacers for stakes same for both sides

Wagon end

2 3/8"

2"

2"

2"

2"

2"

2 3/8"

15 3/4"

2" — 2" — 2" — 1 1/4" — 2" — 2" — 2" — 1 1/4" — 2" — 2 3/8"

18 7/8"

assembly. Secure the stake spacers to the wagon sides with glue and brads. Next glue the stake holders to the spacer blocks, using brads. Glue the vertical-stake stiffeners to the upper part of the stakes. The lower part of the stakes, which fits into the slots between the spacers, will have to be made slightly smaller so that the stakes can be moved in and out easily. This can be done with a wood rasp and sandpaper. Glue the horizontal bars to the stakes, using brads. Note that the four corner stakes are glued together.

STEP 4
ASSEMBLING THE REAR AXLE SYSTEM
Begin with the rear assembly by gluing the axle holders to the crossbar. Next glue the holder braces to the axle holders and crossbar. Then glue

the lower brace to the holder braces and the axle holders. This assembly is glued to the wagon bottom and secured with 3/8-inch glue dowels. Glue in the wagon-bed braces to the wagon bed and the holder braces, securing them with 1 1/4-inch wood screws.

STEP 5
ASSEMBLING THE FRONT AXLE SYSTEM
For the front axle assembly, glue the axle holders to the crossbar, and then glue the holder braces to both of them. Glue the lower brace to the axle holders. The swivel disk is glued into the recess in the top of the crossbar. Drill a 1/2-inch hole in the center of the disk through the crossbar for the steering bolt. Drill a 1/2-inch hole in the front end of the wagon bed for the bolt. Glue the wagon-tongue holders to the spacer block. Glue this

assembly to the crossbar, using 3/8-inch glue dowels.

STEP 6
FINISHING AND FINAL ASSEMBLY
Before the final assembly, the various parts of the wagon should be finished. Make sure all nail and screw holes are filled and sanded, and that all parts are sanded smooth and clean. Paint the wagon with two or three coats of nontoxic enamel. We used red for the wagon bed, blue for the axle assemblies, and yellow for the rack. When the paint is thoroughly dry, insert the tongue in the holder and secure it with a 1/4-inch carriage bolt. Insert the steering bolt through the wagon bed into the front crossbar, using a washer and two hex nuts. Put the axles in place and secure the wheels with washers and two hex nuts on each wheel.

Glossary

Abrasive Any material used to wear away, smooth, or polish a surface, such as sandpaper used to smooth wood.

Backsaw Short saw having a reinforced back.

Band saw Power saw consisting of continuous flexible steel band passing over two pulleys, used for cutting external curves.

Bevel The inclination that one line or surface makes with another when not at right angles.

Bevel joint Miter joint in which two pieces meet at other than a right angle.

Blind hole A hole that does not go all the way through a piece of material; also called a stopped hole.

Braces Structural supports that give a piece of furniture or a toy strength.

Brads Slender wire nails having either a small, deep head or a projection to one side of the head end.

Butt joint Joint formed by two pieces of wood united end to end without overlapping.

Carriage bolt A flatheaded bolt that cannot be turned from the head.

Chamfer A flat surface made by cutting the corners or edges of the end of a piece of stock.

Chisel Wedgelike tool with a cutting edge at the end of the blade, used for cutting or shaping wood.

Circular saw Power saw consisting of circular disk, usually with a toothed edge.

Clear finish Any of a number of wood finishes that allow the wood grain to be seen.

Cleats Structural members that serve to hold other parts in place.

Combination square Adjustable square for carpentry work, used as a try square, miter square, etc.

Compass Instrument for drawing or describing circles or measuring distances, consisting generally of two movable, rigid legs hinged to each other at one end.

Compass saw Small handsaw with a narrow, tapering blade for cutting curves of small radii.

Coping saw Saw consisting of a light, ribbonlike blade held in a three-sided, U-shaped frame with a handle; used for cutting small curves.

Counterbore The use of a counterbore drill bit to bore a hole at the end of a pilot hole in order to accommodate a wood plug or other covering to hide a screw head.

Countersink The use of a countersink drill bit to bore a beveled hole at the end of a pilot hole in order to accommodate the head of a flathead screw so that it sits slightly below the surface when driven in.

Crosscut saw Handsaw used for cutting across the grain on the wood, ranging from 8 to 12 points.

Dado head Rotary cutter composed of several sawlike blades side by side, for cutting dadoes.

Dovetail saw Backsaw for fine woodworking, as dovetailing.

Dowel A wood pin frequently used to join two pieces of wood. The dowel fits into holes drilled in each piece; this creates a dowel joint. In longer lengths, and different diameters, the dowel serves many functions.

Dressing Planing down of rough wood to various sizes.

Drill press Drilling machine with a single vertical spindle. Best drill for precision drilling, angled holes, or repetitive drilling of holes to a specified depth.

End grain The end of a board showing the grain of the wood in cross section.

Fasteners Nails, screws, brads, and other items that are used to join two items or to secure hardware to furniture or millwork.

Filter mask A device to cover the nose and mouth and prevent inhalation of dust or other material in the air.

Finishing nails Nails having a small globular head, more slender than common nails of the same length; used for finish work, being driven slightly beneath the surface and covered with putty or wood filler.

French curve Flat drafting instrument consisting of several scroll-like curves for drawing curves of varying radii.

Grain The growth pattern in the tree. The grain will look different in different trees and as a result of different sawing techniques.

Hardwood Wood that is cut from deciduous (leaf-bearing) trees. Although all such wood is designated as hardwood, some types are actually physically soft and easy to dent.

Herringbone pattern Pattern consisting of adjoining vertical rows of slanting lines, any two continuous lines forming either a V or an inverted V.

Jigsaw Vertically mounted power saw for cutting curves and other difficult lines.

Kerf The space created by a saw blade as it cuts through wood. All cuts should be made on the outside, or waste side, of lines marked for cutting so that the inside edge of the kerf just touches the mark.

Keyhole saw Compass saw for cutting very small radii such as keyholes, etc.

Miter To cut a beveled edge on a piece of lumber for the purpose of making a miter joint. A miter joint is usually the mating of two 45° angled-ends to make a 90° corner.

Molding Various types of wood used for decorative or practical trim. Molding styles range from flat lath to ornately grooved, carved, or stamped picture frame moldings. It is usually applied to cover joints of dissimilar surfaces.

Nailset Short rod of steel used to drive a nail below or flush with the surface.

On-center A phrase designating the distance between the centers of regularly-spaced holes.

Panhead screw Screw head having the form of a truncated cone.

Particle board Inexpensive sheet material composed of wood chips, or particles, and adhesives pressed into sheets. Fairly brittle and not as easy to nail through as wood.

Pattern The outline, usually on a scaled grid, of a piece composed of curves and angles that cannot be given as dimensions. Some patterns are full-sized and can be used as templates; others must be enlarged.

Pilot holes Holes drilled in stock to make it easier to drive a screw through the stock. Pilot holes are slightly narrower than the diameter of the screw to be used.

Plywood Manufactured wood made up of piles, or layers, for strength and uniformity.

Point size Number of teeth per inch on a saw blade. Lower point sizes cut faster, higher point sizes finer and smoother.

Rabbet A steplike corner cut into the edge of a board so that another board can be seated in the cut to make a rabbet joint.

Radial arm saw Power saw whose blade can be rotated for angle cuts.

Rasp Coarse file having separate conical teeth.

Ripsaw Handsaw used for cutting with the grain of the wood, usually 5½ or 6 points.

Router Power tool used for hollowing out and furrowing.

Saber saw Portable electric jigsaw; varied blades capable of making quite intricate cuts.

Sanding block A padded wood block around which a piece of sandpaper is wrapped for hand sanding of a surface.

Sandpaper A coated abrasive—usually flint, garnet, or aluminum oxide glued to a paper, cloth, or plastic backing. It is used for smoothing or polishing woods.

S curve Curve shaped like an S.

Setscrew Screw passing through a threaded hole in a part to tighten the contact of that part with another.

Softwood Wood that comes from logs of cone-bearing (coniferous) trees.

Solid stock Milled lumber, as opposed to composition woods like plywood or particle board.

Spiral dowels Standard lengths of dowel used in dowelled joints, grooved to allow easy gluing.

Spline A thin piece of wood used as a wedge to strengthen joints. Splines can be cut from such scrap material as leftover paneling.

Stain Any of various forms of water, latex, or oil-based transparent or opaque coloring agents designed to penetrate the surface of the wood to color (stain) the material.

Starter holes Holes drilled inside the outline of a shape to be cut out of a larger shape for the purpose of inserting a cop-ing-saw or saber-saw blade to start the cut.

Straightedge Strip of wood or metal for use in drawing or testing straight lines, plane surfaces, etc.

Table saw Power saw in which table remains horizontal while blade can be tilted for angle cuts.

Tack cloth A piece of cheesecloth or other lint-free fabric treated with turpentine and a small amount of varnish to create a sticky or tacky quality so the rag will pick up and hold all dirt, dust, and lint that it touches.

Thumbscrew Screw, the head of which is so constructed that it may be turned easily with the thumb and a finger.

Tongue and groove Milling treatment of the edges of a board resulting in a protruding tongue on one side and groove the same size on the other. For the purpose of joining several boards.

Try square Device for testing the squareness of carpentry work, consisting of a pair of straightedges fixed at right angles to one another.

Veneer tape A length of narrow veneer wood that can be glued to an edge of a table or chair to hide plywood layers.

Warp A distortion of lumber from its milled shape caused by uneven shrinkage. Warped boards should be avoided when purchasing lumber, and precautions should be taken to prevent stored lumber from warping.

Wood filler Liquid, paste, putty, or plaster materials designed to fill in holes or grain lines so that final finishes may be applied to a smooth surface.

Wood rasp A handtool used for rough shaping of edges or curves.

Index

Metric Chart

LUMBER

Sizes: Metric cross-sections are so close to their nearest Imperial sizes, as noted below, that for most purposes they may be considered equivalents.

Lengths: Metric lengths are based on a 300mm module which is slightly shorter in length than an Imperial foot. It will therefore be important to check your requirements accurately to the nearest inch and consult the table below to find the metric length required.

Areas: The metric area is a square metre. Use the following conversion factors when converting from Imperial data: 100 sq. feet = 9.290 sq. metres.

METRIC SIZES SHOWN BESIDE NEAREST IMPERIAL EQUIVALENT

mm	Inches	mm	Inches
16 × 75	⅝ × 3	44 × 150	1¾ × 6
16 × 100	⅝ × 4	44 × 175	1¾ × 7
16 × 125	⅝ × 5	44 × 200	1¾ × 8
16 × 150	⅝ × 6	44 × 225	1¾ × 9
19 × 75	¾ × 3	44 × 250	1¾ × 10
19 × 100	¾ × 4	44 × 300	1¾ × 12
19 × 125	¾ × 5	50 × 75	2 × 3
19 × 150	¾ × 6	50 × 100	2 × 4
22 × 75	⅞ × 3	50 × 125	2 × 5
22 × 100	⅞ × 4	50 × 150	2 × 6
22 × 125	⅞ × 5	50 × 175	2 × 7
22 × 150	⅞ × 6	50 × 200	2 × 8
25 × 75	1 × 3	50 × 225	2 × 9
25 × 100	1 × 4	50 × 250	2 × 10
25 × 125	1 × 5	50 × 300	2 × 12
25 × 150	1 × 6	63 × 100	2½ × 4
25 × 175	1 × 7	63 × 125	2½ × 5
25 × 200	1 × 8	63 × 150	2½ × 6
25 × 225	1 × 9	63 × 175	2½ × 7
25 × 250	1 × 10	63 × 200	2½ × 8
25 × 300	1 × 12	63 × 225	2½ × 9
32 × 75	1¼ × 3	75 × 100	3 × 4
32 × 100	1¼ × 4	75 × 125	3 × 5
32 × 125	1¼ × 5	75 × 150	3 × 6
32 × 150	1¼ × 6	75 × 175	3 × 7
32 × 175	1¼ × 7	75 × 200	3 × 8
32 × 200	1¼ × 8	75 × 225	3 × 9
32 × 225	1¼ × 9	75 × 250	3 × 10
32 × 250	1¼ × 10	75 × 300	3 × 12
32 × 300	1¼ × 12	100 × 100	4 × 4
38 × 75	1½ × 3	100 × 150	4 × 6
38 × 100	1½ × 4	100 × 200	4 × 8
38 × 125	1½ × 5	100 × 250	4 × 10
38 × 150	1½ × 6	100 × 300	4 × 12
38 × 175	1½ × 7	150 × 150	6 × 6
38 × 200	1½ × 8	150 × 200	6 × 8
38 × 225	1½ × 9	150 × 300	6 × 12
44 × 75	1¾ × 3	200 × 200	8 × 8
44 × 100	1¾ × 4	250 × 250	10 × 10
44 × 125	1¾ × 5	300 × 300	12 × 12

NOMINAL SIZE (This is what you order) Inches	ACTUAL SIZE (This is what you get) Inches
1 × 1	¾ × ¾
1 × 2	¾ × 1½
1 × 3	¾ × 2½
1 × 4	¾ × 3½
1 × 6	¾ × 5½
1 × 8	¾ × 7¼
1 × 10	¾ × 9¼
1 × 12	¾ × 11¼
2 × 2	1¾ × 1¾
2 × 3	1½ × 2½
2 × 4	1½ × 3½
2 × 6	1½ × 5½
2 × 8	1½ × 7¼
2 × 10	1½ × 9¼
2 × 12	1½ × 11¼

METRIC LENGTHS

Lengths Metres	Equiv. Ft. & Inches
1.8m	5′ 10⅞″
2.1m	6′ 10⅝″
2.4m	7′ 10½″
2.7m	8′ 10¼″
3.0m	9′ 10⅛″
3.3m	10′ 9⅞″
3.6m	11′ 9¾″
3.9m	12′ 9½″
4.2m	13′ 9⅜″
4.5m	14′ 9⅓″
4.8m	15′ 9″
5.1m	16′ 8¾″
5.4m	17′ 8⅝″
5.7m	18′ 8⅜″
6.0m	19′ 8¼″
6.3m	20′ 8″
6.6m	21′ 7⅞″
6.9m	22′ 7⅝″
7.2m	23′ 7½″
7.5m	24′ 7¼″
7.8m	25′ 7⅛″

All the dimensions are based on 1 inch = 25 mm.